Astræa's Return; or, the Halcyon Days of France in the Year 2440

ASTRÆA'S RETURN;

OR, THE

HALCYON DAYS OF FRANCE

IN

THE YEAR 2440:

A DREAM.

TRANSLATED FROM THE FRENCH,

BY

HARRIOT AUGUSTA FREEMAN.

O divina virtù! Se mi ti presti
Tanto, che l' ombra del beato regno
Segnata nel mio capo io manifesto
          Del PARADISO di DANTE, Canto primo.

LONDON:

PRINTED FOR THE TRANSLATOR;
And sold by her at No 13, Moore place, Vauxhall road, Lambeth
Also by
T CHAPMAN, Fleet street, and HOOKHAM and CARPENTER,
Old Bond-street.

1797.

TO

Sir JOHN COXE HIPPISLEY, Bart

SIR,

PERMIT me, under the favouring auspices of your patronage, divested of every claim to literary excellence, to present this my first essay in the career of literature, and to entreat you to throw the veil of indulgence over every error or imperfection, which your quick discernment will not fail to discover, in the translation of a Work, performed while labouring under every disadvantage of time and place, being, from the nature of my situation in life, deprived of the enjoyment of solitude, so necessary for literary pursuits, and so ardently and incessantly the object of my most fervent wishes.

(iv)

To you, Sir, whose mind is enriched with extensive literature, it is unneceffary to say any thing in commendation of the Work itself. Long acquainted with the original, you have teftified your tafte for genius and philofophy by placing it in your library the prefent tranflation, however, is enriched with fome additional chapters, taken from a new edition recently publifhed, which I fortunately met with ere the whole manufcript was ready for the prefs, and if I have the happinefs to merit your applaufe, it will be the moft gratifying reward for my labours Yes, Sir, the claims you have already upon my gratitude, which the lapfe of years can never obliterate from my memory, my tongue will ever be as proud to acknowledge as my heart to feel. and the fame of your revered virtues, and of thofe of your amiable Lady, will ever be the theme on which my mind will dwell with peculiar delight. I am therefore particularly happy in the prefent opportunity of paying this public tribute to your worth, of expreffing how highly I am indebted to your philanthropy, and to your generous benevolence, of which I have experienced the moft uncommon inftances. In the ardent hope that your life, fo

valuable

valuable to many, may long be spared, to diffuse the like liberal sentiments and every happiness to your surrounding relations and friends, and depending on the continuation of your favourable opinion, I wish ever to be esteemed, with profound veneration, and grateful regard,

SIR,

Your most obliged,

And devoted

Humble servant.

Stanhope-street,
June 16, 1797.

HARRIOT AUGUSTA FREEMAN.

LIST

OF

SUBSCRIBERS.

A

THE Right Hon. the Earl of Abingdon, Upper Brook-street
Major Ackland, Pembroke, 2 copies
J. T. Appach, Esq. Hackney
Mrs Appach
Mr. Addison, Temple bar
William Atkinson, Esq
Mr Agar, Finsbury-square
Mr Anley

B

The Right Hon. the Countess of Besborough, Cavendish-square
Robert Balfour, Esq. near Edinburgh
George Brown, Esq
Miss Bonwick
———— Blewart, Esq. Temple-bar
Miss Buddle

C

Lady Coghill, Princes-street
Abel Chapman, Esq
Mr Chapman, Fleet-street
Mrs Chapman
Mrs Christie, Finsbury-square
Captain Chivers, Mile end
Mrs Chivers
Mr Chafe, Strand
Mr Clarke
Mr Coleson, Croydon
Mr. Richard Coleson
Frederick Commerell, Esq. Stanwell-heath
C. J. Crome, Esq
Oliver Colt, Esq. Manchester-square
J. N. Couffmaker, Esq
Mr. Curtis

D

Her Grace the Duchess of Devonshire, Piccadilly
Viscount Lord Dudley and Ward, Park-lane
Sir Thomas Durant, Bart. Scottoe, Norfolk
Lady Durant
Sir Francis D'Ivernois, St. James's-place
—— Danvers, Esq
Richard Dowden, Esq.
Mr Dixon
Mr Drury

E

Robert Eaden, Esq.
E Ellis, Esq

F

The Right Hon Earl Fitzwilliam, Grosvenor square
Edward Forster, Esq Walthamstow
—— Fuller, Esq

G

The Right Hon Earl Grosvenor, Grosvenor-square, 4 copies
The Hon Col Grosvenor, Grosvenor street, 3 copies
The Hon Mrs Grosvenor, 3 copies
Jos Greaves, Jun Esq

H.

Lady Anne Hatton, Baker-street
Sir John Coxe Hippisley, Bart.
Lady Hippisley, Warfield Grove, Berks
Miss Hippisley
Miss Windham Hippisley
Miss Louisa Hippisley
Mr Stuart Hippisley
John Harkness, Esq.
—— Harrop, Esq India House
Edward Harrop, Esq
John Harrop, Esq.
Mr. Harison
Mr Hemman, Charing cross
Mrs. Hemman

Mr Horn, Newcastle upon Tyne
Miss Horn
—— Hudson, Esq
Miss Hudson

J

M N Jackson, Esq
Charles Johnstone, Esq 4 copies

K

The Right Hon Lady Kinnaird, Grosvenor-street
Mr King, Great Portland-street

L

William Leighton, Esq Charlton
Mrs Leighton
Miss Leighton
Philip Landen, Esq India House
Mrs Leech, Pall-mall
John Lubbock, Esq M. P Stratford Place
Mrs Lubbock
Miss Lubbock
John William Lubbock, Esq

M

Miss Margrave
Miss Georgiana Meadows, 2 copies
Mrs Mitchell
Miss Mitchell
Mrs Morton, Castle-street
Miss Julia Mountford, Gower-street

O

Owen Ormsby, Esq Stanhope-street
Mrs Ormsby
Miss Ormsby
Mrs Owen, St James's Place

P

Lord Viscount Palmerston, Hanover square
L Pakshe, Esq
Charles Pilgrim, Esq
Mr. Phipps

R.

Her Grace the Duchess of Rutland, Hanover-square
Mrs Rayby
Rowland Richardson, Esq
Captain Rising
Captain Ross
Edmund Rodd, Esq
William Rowley, M. D. Saville Row, 2 copies

S

Sir John Stuart, Bart
Mrs Selby, Great Cumberland Place
Walter Sharp, Esq
Captain Shelly, Mile End
John Spalding, Esq M P Hill-street
R. Solly, Esq
Mr. Stringer, Strand

T.

Miss Tharratt
Lieutenant Tidy
Richard Tuckwell, Esq
Mrs. Tuckwell

V

P Voight, Esq

W.

Lady Wilson, Charlton
Lady Willoughby, Berner's-street
Miss Willoughby
John Walters, Esq Teddington Grove
William Ward, Esq
Thomas Welladvice, Esq
William Wilkinson, Esq
Mr. Wells, Mount street
——— Wood, Esq
Miss Wood
——— Wormald, Esq

EPISTLE

TO THE

YEAR TWO THOUSAND FOUR HUNDRED AND FORTY.

Existence saw him spurn her bounded reign,
And panting Time toil'd after him in vain. JOHNSON

RESPECTABLE and venerable year, deſtined to bring felicity to the inhabitants of this world; thou, alas! whom I have only ſeen in a dream, when thou ſhalt ſpring forth, from the boſom of eternity, thoſe who ſhall ſee thy radiant glory, will trample my aſhes, and thoſe of thirty generations, ſucceſſively extinguiſhed, and buried in the profound abyſs of Death. Kings, who are this day ſeated on thrones, will then be no more, neither will any of their poſterity remain; and thou wilt be the judge both of thoſe deceaſed monarchs, and of thoſe writers, who lived under and were forced to ſubmit their writings to their deſpotic deciſions. The names of thoſe who have been the friends and defenders of humanity, will ſhine with honour; their glory will be pure and radiant; but that vile crowd of kings, who in every ſenſe have tormented the human ſpecies, buried deeper even in oblivion than they will be in the regions of death, ſhall only eſcape ſhame by annihilation.

'Tis the moſt glorious prerogative of human nature, that while the writer's thoughts ennoble his page, they at the ſame time raiſe him from the grave, and render his memory immortal: and while the thunderings of deſpotiſm fall, and are extinguiſhed, the pen of an

author

author overleaps the interval of time, and either punishes or acquits the pretended masters of the universe.

I have availed myself of the natural power with which we are all born, I have, in my solitary hours, cited before the tribunal of my reason the laws, the abuses, the customs of the country, where I lived obscure and unknown I have felt that virtuous indignation, which all feeling beings owe to their oppressors I have detested tyranny, I have censured and combated it with all the weapons in my power, but the representation of thee, O most desirable year! although in contemplation capable of raising and inflaming my ideas, will, I fear, be deemed by thee no better than a more refined degree of slavery. Ah! pardon my errors, the genius of the times oppresses imagination, and prevents it soaring to the more exalted spheres of Liberty The universal stupor actuates me, even the voice of philosophy, discouraged and despised, has lost its power, it calls out from amidst the dwellings of men, but is heard no more than if it proceeded from the bosom of a desert.

Oh! if I could divide the time of my allotted existence into two parts, how gladly would I descend to the grave, and exchange the sad dismal aspect of my present contemporaries, to awaken in those pure and happy days which thou wilt bring forth when man will have recovered his courage, with his liberty, his independence, and his innate virtues. Ah! why cannot I see thee realized? Blissful year! hasten thy coming, fated to enlighten and create the happiness of the world but, alas! my imagination, now freed from all remains of so favourable and delightful a dream, gives me rather to fear that the revolving luminary of the world will then only cast a melancholy light upon a confused mass of ashes and of ruins.

ASTRÆA S

ASTRÆA'S RETURN,

&c.

CHAP. I.

But, ah! what hand the sorrowing prospect brings?
What to us recalls the expiring day?

OFFICIOUS friend! why hast thou disturbed me? Ah! why not let me sleep on? The dream which thou hast interrupted, though but an illusion, was far preferable to the inauspicious truth of day. O! how delightful was the error, and why did I not remain buried in it? But, alas! I am, on the contrary, recalled to witness the frightful and alarming chaos, from which I thought myself happily released. Sit down and listen to me, while my mind is still filled with the striking circumstances of my dream.

I was last evening several hours in conversation with that elderly Englishman, whose soul is so truly honest and sincere. You know how much I esteem and love a real English character; none are better friends, nor do we meet among other nations men whose minds are so generous and so firm. That spirit of liberty which animates them, creates a degree of firmness and of consistency fifiency very rarely to be found among the people of other countries.

"Your nation," said he, "is filled with a multiplicity of strange abuses the mind loses itself in endeavouring to number them, and still more in aiming at comprehending them but, above all, I am astonished at the apparent calm which seems to have taken possession of the minds of people of every order, and of every rank. This seeming tranquillity is certainly the forerunner and breeder of the most alarming intestine commotions. Your metropolis is the most irregular compound, and receptacle of extreme opulence and excessive misery, which are perpetually jarring. How astonishing! that any thing so disproportioned and unequal, consuming itself as it does in all its parts, should continue to exist under so great an inequality.

"In your vast country the metropolis is the grand mover and spring of every action, how many towns, nay whole provinces, are sacrificed to it, and yet this great capital itself may be compared to a diamond in a dunghill. What an unaccountable mixture of wit and folly, of genius and extravagance, of greatness and of meanness! I leave my native island and hasten to Paris, where I hope to find myself in the centre of knowledge, where men, by the mutual union of their talents, assemble together all the pleasures of life, and enjoy that ease which constitutes its greatest charm but, good heavens! how are my hopes disappointed! In this very spot, where there is an abundance of every thing, I find innumerable wretches, who suffer hunger, cold, and every kind of misery, under a variety of wise laws I see a thousand crimes daily committed, every thing is in disorder, in spite of the many regulations of the police, and in every quarter I meet with embarrassments, fetters, and customs, which are contrary to the public good.

"Here you see a crowd of persons, pressing upon each other, to save themselves from being run over by an innumerable train of carriages, which contain persons, who, upon an average, are far from being preferable to those whom they molest. I shudder when I hear the quick step of a pair of horses in streets filled with old men, pregnant women, and children, without a path wherein they may walk in safety: indeed there is nothing so insulting to human nature as that continued indifference about dangers, which are renewed every instant.

"You have one particular quarter of your city which exhales a fœtid odour, and to many it is a deadly blast; and yet thousands, both men and women, are under the necessity of inhabiting that air, impregnated with poison and with death.

"Your temples," continued he, "are more calculated to disgust the people than to edify them: they are made use of as a thoroughfare, and frequently for something worse: one cannot sit down in them without paying; which is a shocking and indecent monopoly in a holy place, where all men, in the presence of the Supreme Being, ought to be equal.

"You have some master-pieces among your dramatic works; but if, after having been pleased with the perusal, I am inclined to go to the representation of them, they are so mutilated and reversed, that I no longer recognise them for the same. You copy from the Greeks and Romans, but you cannot adhere to their manner, which is noble and simple; so great is your attachment to puerilities. In short, all your places of public resort are attended with more inconvenience than entertainment.

"As for all your great and boasted monuments of architecture, what are they but an heap of ruins? Does not the Palais du Louvre, which you shew with so much admiration, reflect more disgrace than honour upon your nation, particularly while there are so many gaudy baubles of edifices, which cost more money to repair than would be expended in compleating your public buildings?

"But all this is nothing, compared with the enormous disproportion of fortunes, and the secret causes which have given rise to it. Were I to descant upon the morals of the great, which are hard-hearted, haughty, and overbearing, under an exterior of politeness and complaisance were I to trace the indigence of the poor, and the impossibility of amending his situation, without hazarding the loss of his integrity; were I to enumerate the sums which a dishonest man acquires, and express the degree of credit and respect he enjoys by every additional proof of roguery, it would lead me in a labyrinth, from whence I should not extricate myself without some difficulty therefore good night. I set out to-morrow, and shall leave Paris for ever I cannot remain any longer in this city, which is so truly unhappy, with every possible means of being otherwise

"I am disgusted with Paris as much as with London. All great cities are alike The opinion of Rousseau we continually find verified, that 'men become more and more depraved and corrupted, notwithstanding the laws they make for their common happiness,' the very reverse of this might reasonably have been expected, but it is the interest of all evil-disposed individuals to oppose the general good.

"I shall

" I shall retire into some village, where pure air, and tranquil pleasures, may be enjoyed, and where I shall lament the fate of those unhappy individuals, who are doomed to inhabit those superb prisons called cities."

In vain I repeated the old adage to him, that Paris was not built in a day, that every thing was now in a state of perfection, if compared with former ages. " In a few years more," said I, " all things will be so changed that you will find all your complaints redressed, and not a wish ungratified, provided it be possible to act according to the vast projects which are now forming. ..."

" Ah!" said he, " that is truly the characteristic of your nation, always making projects! And do you really believe they will ever be realised? You are a true Frenchman, my dear friend, and, with all your good sense, you possess the foible of all your countrymen, but so let it be. I will return and see you when all these fine projects are put in execution, until then I will go and live elsewhere. I cannot live among so many unhappy persons, whose looks, expressive of the sufferings they endure, create continual pangs of grief in my heart.

" I see that it would not be difficult to remedy the most pressing of these evils, but, believe me, it will never be undertaken the method would be simple, and therefore would not be attended to. There are many among you who, with much affectation, are constantly repeating the claims and rights of humanity, but it is merely in order to exempt themselves from the duties annexed thereto. Alas! you have long ceased to err through ignorance, therefore nothing now can operate your cure. Adieu."

CHAP II

Warm fancy, kindling with delight,
Anticipates the lapse of age,
And thus she throws her eagle sight
O'er time's yet undiscover'd page

IT was midnight ere my old English friend left me, I was rather fatigued, I therefore instantly closed my door and went to bed. Soon as Morpheus had shed his influence o'er my eye-lids I fell into an extraordinary dream. Methought I had been sleeping for a succession of ages, and that I at last awoke. I arose, and found an oppressive weight all over me, to which I had never been accustomed, my hands trembled, my legs tottered, and on looking at myself in a glass, I could scarce recollect my own features. I had retired to bed with brown hair, a good complexion, and the appearance of a man in health; but when I rose I felt my forehead furrowed with innumerable wrinkles, my hair was like silver, two great cheek bones, without flesh to cover them, a long nose, a pale and wan complexion o'erspread my countenance. Soon as I began to walk, I mechanically, as it were, leaned upon a cane, to support my tottering limbs, but though I had acquired old age, I had not acquired with it the sullen ill humour which characterises most old men.

On quitting my own house to take my morning walk, I found myself in a large square, which had not been built above three years, a beautiful pyramidal column had just been erected, which seemed to attract the public notice. I approached, and found engraven on the marble, in letters of gold, " The year of our Lord M MIV CXL " At first I imagined it must be an error in my own eye-sight, or rather a mistake of the artists, and was going to obferve it to the bye-ftanders, when my furprife was greatly augmented on raifing my eyes towards the walls, and feeing feveral royal edicts, I read the fame date, M.MIV.CXL, printed upon all the public papers. How! faid I to myfelf, am I grown fo old without perceiving it? I muft have flept feven hundred years. This is moft ftrange indeed.

I found every thing totally changed. Every quarter of the town, with which I formerly was fo well acquainted, I found embellifhed and entirely new. I was loft in admiration, while I contemplated the broad ftreets and fpacious fquares, where every fort of bufinefs was tranfacted without any buftle, or entanglement of carriages. My ears were not now, as formerly, ftunned with confufed cries of men and women carrying provifions to fell; neither was I overtaken or met in the middle of a ftreet by carriages ready to run over me. Any gouty, lame, or otherwife infirm man, might have walked on without danger. The whole city appeared animated and cheerful, but without any buftle or confufion.

I was fo ftruck with every thing I faw around me, that I was fome time ere I difcovered that I was myfelf an object of admiration and furprife to every one: they examined me from head to foot, and fhrugged up their fhoulders, fmiling at each other, as if they faw a perfon in a mafquerade habit; in fhort, the clothes I wore appeared to them as fuch, fo totally different they were to their own.

A citizen (whom I afterwards found was one of the learned men) approached me, and politely, though very gravely, faid, " Good old man, to what purpofe do you put on this difguife? Is it that you wifh to retrace to our minds the ridiculous cuftoms of former extravagant ages?

We have no wish to imitate them, therefore let me advise you to throw off this joke, which is unbecoming your years, and let us see you in your own character."

To this I replied "Do you call difguife the clothes I wore yefterday, and all my life before? It is your marble pillars, and all your public advertifements, which tend to deceive. You feem no longer to acknowledge Louis XVI for your fovereign. I know not what is your motive, but I think it a very dangerous one. Such impofitions are truly ridiculous, for you muft know that nothing can prevail againft the evidence of our own exiftence."

Whether the man was perfuaded that I was either raving, or in my dotage, or whether he had fome other fufpicion, I know not. however, he quietly afked me in what year I was born? I anfwered in 1740. "Well then," faid he, "you are exactly feven hundred years old. We muft not be furprifed at any thing," faid he to the crowd which furrounded me, "Methufalem, and fome other men, have lived to the age of eight or nine hundred years, therefore this man may alfo be privileged, or, perhaps, he has found out an elixir which confers im--mortality."

He fmiled as he fpoke thus, and every perfon came nearer to me with peculiar complacency and refpect. They wifhed to interrogate me, but they were withheld by difcretion; they only whifpered to each other, "This is a man born in the age of Louis the Sixteenth. look at him, how ftrange he looks!"

CHAP.

CHAP. III

To see each joy the sons of pleasure know
Extorted from his fellow creature's woe
Here whilst the courtier glitters in brocade—

I WAS very much at a loss what I should do, when the philosopher, who had spoken to me before, kindly said, "Wonderful old man! you will find some difficulty in recognising the streets and walks, which are all so greatly altered; come with me, I am willing to be your guide; but pray let us go first to some ready made clothes-shop, where you may be decently clad, or I could not accompany you through the streets; for you must acknowledge, that your dress is very ridiculous in these days, that it is inconvenient, and not calculated to promote health; your arms and shoulders are confined, and your whole body very ill at ease; and why let your legs and thighs be exposed to the inclemencies of the weather? that weapon of death, which, in your century, was so necessary an appendage, is, in my opinion, a very useless part of dress; to what purpose should you entangle your legs with arms offensive or defensive in a city where a good police, and a well-regulated government, must be answerable for the life of each individual, and where every kind of combat is prohibited?"

Each century has its particular fashion, and, if I am not mistaken, our's is both agreeable and convenient: in effect his dress, though quite new to me, was not unpleasant; his hat was not of that gloomy colour, nor ridiculous shape, which distinguished those of our times, the crown alone remained the same, which was sufficiently large to admit the whole head, the rim was calculated for conveniency, either to be worn down, as a
shelter

(10)

shelter against the rays of the sun, or against the rain, or to be rolled up round the crown of the hat, which altogether had a very graceful appearance.

His hair was neatly braided, and tied altogether at the crown of his head, with a very small appearance of powder, which did not conceal its natural colour. This was a simple head-dress, very unlike our plastering of powder and pomatum, which made the head appear like a pyramid, neither were there any remains of those formal curls or ridiculous bag-wigs of our former days.

His neck was not strangled with a stuffing of wadding and muslin, but he wore a cravat more or less warm according to the season, his arms were unconfined in sleeves that were comfortably large, and his body at ease in a loose vest, over which he wore a long mantle or cloak, calculated to preserve him from cold or rain, or to hang gracefully loose about him, he had a long scarf round his waist, which was becoming, and of great utility in cold weather, and his legs, instead of being cut in two by those garters which impede circulation, were covered with a long stocking, or pantaloon, and his foot was inclosed in a commodious shoe made in form like a sandal.

We went together into a shop, where I clothed myself from head to foot, and I could scarcely believe myself in a shop, there being so much candour and honest sincerity in the manners and discourse of the master, and so much daylight in his warehouse.

CHAP.

CHAP. IV.

Sure, scenes like these no troubles e'er annoy!
Sure, these denote one universal joy!

MY expenses at the clothes shop amounted to a louis of our money, I took one from my pocket and laid it down, which the master promised to keep as a curious antique coin. It was become the custom to pay ready money in every shop, and the people, who made a point of the most scrupulous integrity, were not acquainted even with the meaning of the word credit, which either on one side or the other served only as an ingenious disguise for roguery. The custom of being in debt was no longer a distinguishing appendage to rank or nobility.

When I came out of the shop the crowd continued to surround me, but their looks were not insulting, they seemed, on the contrary, to eye me with a respectful compassion, saying to each other, " that is the man who is seven hundred years old, how extremely unhappy he must have been during the first years of his life!"

I was surprised to find the streets so clean, and so free from bustle and confusion, and yet the city appeared well populated, but it was likewise well regulated, and in every street I saw a man, whose business was to direct the order of carriages and of foot-passengers, particularly those who were loaded, for whom he took every possible care to open a free passage, and I was pleased to see that their load was always proportioned to their strength, but not, as heretofore, when a number of unhappy wretches were seen bending under a weight which was more calculated for a beast of burden than for a human being. The rich man no longer degraded humanity by the help of a few

pieces

(12)

pieces of money; neither were the women, whose delicate constitutions, and more feeble frames, plainly indicate the intentions of Providence in sending them among us to have been for our domestic comforts, neither were they seen sitting in the public markets, and exciting the compassion of all men of feeling, as well as their disgust, by metamorphosing themselves in various ways from the situation allotted them by nature. Restored to the duties of their state, the women now led a domestic, comfortable life, they attended to their children, comforted their husbands in the various calamities incident to human life, and were never seen out of their proper sphere.

CHAP. V

No loud-tongued drivers with clamorous call,
No rattling carriage drives me to the wall.

I OBSERVED, that those carriages going upwards kept to the right, and those coming downwards to the left, the same regularity was observed by foot-passengers, this simple method of not being molested in the streets had but just been discovered, by this means every passage was secure and easy, and when any public ceremony took place, where great multitudes were assembled, they all equally enjoyed the spectacle without danger of being trampled upon or squeezed to death. neither was there any impediment of carriages, half a hundred might come on, in the same street, without being mutually in each other's way, as they formerly were, and remained sometimes entangled for an hour, while the gilded fool, who suffered himself to be carried, forgetting that he had legs to carry him, called out to his coachman to go on with redoubled vociferation.

But in these days it was quite the reverse, I met a hundred carts and waggons, loaded with different provisions, to one coach, and those I did meet never carried any but men unable to walk, either through infirmity or old age. Where are all those brilliant carriages, so finely gilt, and highly varnished and decorated, which formerly filled the streets of Paris? What! have you no coxcombs? no mistresses? no farmer of the king's revenues? Neither of these three despicable species of beings, who formerly infested the public with so much haughty pride, and seemed to vie with each other in the pleasure of terrifying the honest tradesman, who, with hasty steps, was forced to run for his life, or be crushed to atoms under their splendid wheels? Our young lords drove on the pavement of Paris as if they were engaging in Olympic games, and all their pride consisted in killing their horses, in these cases, those who valued their lives remained in their houses. "These races are no longer allowed," said my guide, "we have proper sumptuary laws, which have repressed that barbarous luxury, which only served to pamper a set of idle lacqueys, and to pervert the use of that noble animal, which is destined to help our industry, and not our pride. The eye of the poor is no longer insulted with the profusions of the favourites of fortune, our lords make use of their legs, by which they enjoy more money and fewer fits of the gout.

"However, we are not totally without carriages, we have a few, which belong to some of the elder magistrates, or to men who are distinguished by their services to their country, or to others who are bending under the weight of years. To such as these, and these only it is permitted to drive slowly through the streets, where the meaneſt citizen is reſpected, if they ever had the misfortune to injure any one, they would inſtantly alight from their carriage and place him there, but ſuch accidents never happen, the titled rich are eſtimable men, who never think themſelves degraded by making way in the ſtreets for thoſe who are obliged to go on foot. Our gracious ſovereign himſelf is often ſeen to walk on foot among us, and he ſometimes honours our houſes with his preſence, and whenever he is fatigued with walking, he makes choice of a ſhop to go in and reſt he loves to recall the natural equality which ſhould reign among men, and therefore he always finds, both in our looks and in our hearts, the real effuſions of love and gratitude, our acclamations ſpring from our hearts, and find acceſs to his, wherein they are received with complacency and love He is another Henry IV. he has all his greatneſs of ſoul, his compaſſionate diſpoſition, and his ſimple manners; but he is more fortunate His very footſteps are revered, and the walks which he frequents are held ſacred; they are ſo far venerated, that the bittereſt enemies would not profane them with quarrelling in or near them, they would bluſh to commit the leaſt diſorder near thoſe places, and ſay, *if the king were to paſs*, which reflection would be ſufficient to keep them at peace How powerful the influence of example! when given by the firſt perſons in the kingdom, how ſtriking! and how it becomes an inviolable law with all other men!"

CHAP. VI.

*Titles are marks of honest men, and wise;
The fool or knave that wears a title, lies.*

I Observed to my guide, that things were very much changed "I see, said I, that every person is dressed with simplicity, and I have not met one man with a gold trimmed coat or laced ruffles. In my time a costly and childish extravagance of dress prevailed among all orders of men, you would have seen a man, who might have passed rather for an automaton, loaded with gold and embroidery, and arrogate great consequence to himself from this glittering apparel" To this my guide rejoined, "and this is what has given us a just contempt for that livery of pride Our eyes are not attracted by outward appearances, if any man among us has made himself known by having excelled in his art, or in his profession, he does not need a magnificent dress to be noticed, he neither wants admirers to sound his praise, nor protectors to introduce him his actions are sufficiently loud, and every citizen is eager to interest himself in his favour, among whom those of his own profession are always the first, and every one is allowed to publish a memorial, wherein may be retraced all the services he has rendered the state. The monarch always invites a man, thus dear to his people, to his court, and converses with him, in order to gain information, for he is not so ridiculous as to believe that wisdom is inherent in him, and he derives some profit from every lesson, particularly when it is on any great subject, and on these occasions he presents him a hat on which his name is embroidered, and this distinction is much more valuable than the blue and red ribbons

which

which formerly decorated men who were sometimes totally unknown to their country. You will readily suppose that a man, whose name was rendered infamous by his bad actions, would not dare to shew himself to the scrutinizing looks of the public. But whoever wears one of these honorary hats may go every where, and at all times he has free access to the foot of the throne. This is an invariable law. Thus if either a prince or a duke have not performed some laudable act, to deserve their name to be embroidered, they may enjoy their riches, but they have no badge of honour to distinguish them, and they are seen with the same indifference, and no more noticed than the obscure citizen who mixes with the crowd.

"These distinctions are authorised by reason and policy; and they are not injurious to any but to those who feel themselves incapable of being raised to any dignity. Man is not sufficiently perfect to be virtuous, merely for the love of virtue abstracted from every other consideration, but the dignity of nobility which arises from virtue is personal, and not hereditary or venal. When the son of an illustrious man has attained the age of twenty-one, he is presented to the honorary tribunal, which decides whether he shall enjoy the prerogatives of his father, and the honour of belonging to a citizen who is dear to his country is confirmed to him, either from his past conduct, or from the hopes he may give of the future. But if the son of an Achilles proves to be a cowardly Thersites, we avert our eyes from him, and spare him the confusion of blushing for his degeneracy; and while his father's name ascends with glory to the throne of his sovereign, his name is consigned to oblivion.

"In your time vices were punished, but no reward was ever granted to virtue, it was indeed a very imperfect legislation. With us, any courageous man who has saved

the

the life of a fellow-creature in any danger, or who may have prevented some public misfortune, or performed some great, or useful exploit, wears the embroidered hat, and his refpectable name thus expofed to public view takes the precedency of him who enjoys the higheft fortune, were he Midas, or Plutus himfelf.

This is a very good way indeed, in my time hats were alfo given, but they were red and they were to be acquired by travelling beyond the feas for them, but they had little value either in themfelve, or by the dignity they conferred And yet men were very ambitious to receive them, and I do not well underftand by what title, or what were the qualifications neceffary to poffefs them, I fear they were not very laudable

CHAP. VII.

Philofophy!
'Tis thine all human wrongs to heal,
'Tis thine to love all nature's weal

WHEN we are engaged in interefting difcourfe, we do not foon perceive the lapfe of time, or the length of a walk. I was no longer fenfible of my years, I even felt younger than I did an hour before, fo much was I affected with pleafure by the afpect of fo many new objects. But, oh! heavens! what do I perceive! how beautiful the banks of the Seine! my enchanted fight is gratified with the fineft monuments of art. The Louvre is finifhed, the fpace between the palace of the Thuilleries and the Louvre is an immenfe fquare, appropriated for the celebration of public feftivals, they have built a new gallery fimilar to the former, in which the

C   pencil

pencil of Perrault is still held in veneration. These two united edifices formed the most noble palaces in the whole world. It was decorated by the performances of all the most distinguished artists. These were the most worthy retinue of sovereign majesty, whose pride consisted in an assemblage of all the fine arts, and of every thing which could constitute the happiness of the realm. Here was a most superb square, capable of containing all the inhabitants of the city, opposite to which was a temple of Justice, whose architecture was consistent with the dignity of its object.

"Can this be the new bridge," I exclaimed to my conductor, "how it is ornamented!" "What do you mean by the new bridge? we have given it another name, and we have altered the name of many other places, and have substituted others more significant or more adapted, for this, though of trifling import in itself, has great influence over the minds of the people. Remember then that this is the bridge of Henry the Great. As it forms the communication of the two divisions of the city, it could not have a better name, nor a more respected one. At equal distances we have placed the statues of some of the great men who, like him, have loved and fought for the good of their country exclusively. We have not hesitated to place beside this great monarch the Chancelier de L'Hôpital the revered Sully, Jeannin, and Colbert. Where is the book of morality, or what public exhortation can be so striking, or so eloquent, as this assembly of heroes, whose silent, but expressive looks convey the necessity and the glory of obtaining public esteem. Your century had not the honour of doing these things."

"Oh! no in my century the greatest difficulties attended every enterprise, the most pompous preparations were made, and, after all, they only proved the forerunner of a mis-

miscarriage, the most trivial impediments were sufficient to put a period to the most lofty springs of pride and ambition. In speculation they performed the finest deeds, and the tongue or the pen seemed the universal and sole instrument of all their performances. However, there is a time for every thing, our's was the age of projects innumerable, your's is that of execution. I heartily congratulate you on the felicity you enjoy, and myself for having lived till now."

CHAP. VIII

' *Fons of bliss! eternal powers!*
' *What force has shook those hated walls?*
' *What arm has rent those threat'ning tow'rs?*
" *It falls—the guilty fabric falls!*"

AS I turned upwards to go over that bridge which was formerly called Pont au Change, I felt great pleasure in discovering that it was no longer crowded with a set of ill-built houses, as it formerly was, as far as my eye could extend, it was gratified with the sight of the gentle current of the Seine, which was a truly delightful prospect, and the only one of its kind.

"These are admirable changes," said I to my companion, "I am charmed with the sight of them."—"Very true, they are so," rejoined he, "only that it is pity they recall a very fatal event to our memory, which was caused by your extreme negligence."—"Our's! how pray? explain yourself."—"It is recorded in history, that you were continually projecting the downfall of those houses, and yet that you never performed your promises. One day

(20)

day when your sheriffs were introducing a sumptuous entertainment by a volley of slender fire-works, which was given to celebrate the anniversary of some saint, to whom doubtless the French owed very great obligations, the noise of the cannon and squibs was sufficient to throw down these old houses, built upon such old bridges, they shook, and fell in upon their inhabitants, the overthrow of the former brought on the ruin of the latter, a thousand persons were lost, and the sheriffs, to whom the houses chiefly belonged, cursed both the fire-works and the entertainment

" The following years were more productive of good. The money which was either expended upon trifles, or hoarded up to become useless, was now employed in rebuilding and repairing the bridges they lamented that they had not followed this plan during the preceding years, but it was the fate of your ages never to discover, or to acknowledge your enormous follies till after they were irremediable. Come and walk this way, you will see some other buildings we have demolished, which I think you will approve of, you see that one of the finest quays in Paris is no longer spoiled by the two wings of that edifice, formerly called the College of the Four Nations, which was only subsisting as a memento of the vindictive temper of a cardinal, and we have erected our town-house, or guildhall, opposite the Louvre. And when we give any entertainment or public rejoicing, we recollect that they are for the enjoyment of the people as well as for our own. The square is spacious, and we never see a man injured by the fire-works, or by blows from the soldiery, who in your time (a thing incredible) would often lame the spectators of such scenes with impunity.

" You

"You see, we have erected the equestrian statues of all the sovereigns, who have succeeded to those of your time, in the centre of each bridge. This assemblage of kings, erected without pomp in the centre of the town, presents a very interesting spectacle, and seem like the tutelary gods of the city, and of the river, of which they command an an entire view.—They are all placed in an open space, like the good Henry IV. and look more popular than if they were confined in narrow recesses. These statues have been raised without much cost, for our kings love their people too well to exhaust their resources, as they did in your days." I saw with much pleasure that they had withdrawn from the statues of some of our kings those chained slaves which were formerly seen at the feet of Louis XIV. and of Louis XV. and that they had erased every fastidious inscription from them, for though this gross flattery was the least dangerous of any, it had been entirely banished from among them, as well as every appearance of falschood and pride.

I inquired for the Bastille, and was told, that it had been rased to its foundation by a prince, who, far from supposing himself the sovereign ruler of men, retained a just fear for the Judge of Kings, and that on the ruins of that dreadful castle (which might be well stiled the palace of revenge, and of royal revenge), a temple dedicated to Clemency had been erected. I was also told, that no citizen ever was confined for any offence without being publicly tried, and as for "lettres de cachet," their very name was unknown to the people, that it now only served to exercise the indefatigable erudition of philosophers who wished to pierce through the cloud of barbarous times, and to discover what could be their use. They had written a book on this subject, entitled, *Parallel of the lettres de cachet, and of the Asiatic cord.*

We traverſed the Thuilleries, where I ſaw every perſon enter without difficulty, which embelliſhed them in my eyes; and I was pleaſed to find I could ſit in this royal garden without being obliged to pay for my ſeat. We were now come to the ſquare of Louis XV my guide taking me by the hand, ſaid, " You muſt have been preſent at the inauguration of this equeſtrian ſtatue?"— " Yes I was very young, but not more curious than I am at preſent."—" Indeed," rejoined my friend, " this is a maſter-piece worthy of our days, we ſtill admire it every day, its perſpective from the oppoſite palace, when the ſetting ſun encompaſſes it with its beautiful laſt rays, is truly auguſt and magnificent, and thoſe delightful avenues from the palace through the gardens altogether prove the plan of this edifice to have been after the exacteſt rules of art The architect has the merit of having foreſeen the effect it would have in future ages. However, I have read that in your time this ſtatue, and the ſquare in which it is placed, was highly cenſured by men, who were as jealous as they were ignorant, if in theſe latter ages, any man was capable of that abſurdity, he would ſoon find himſelf forſaken by all his hearers"

Thus I continued my walk, but it would be tedious to give a long detail of it, and beſides it is impoſſible to recollect every part of a dream however, to proceed with what I chiefly remember, at the corner of every ſtreet I ſaw a beautiful fountain, from whence there iſſued the moſt tranſparent water, as pure as chryſtal, which invited the taſte, ſo ſalutary and healthy it appeared, always limpid and running with abundance

" Behold," ſaid my guide, " the project of your academician Deſparcieux accompliſhed and perfect! See how all thoſe houſes are well ſupplied with the moſt neceſſary and moſt uſeful article of life, which ſo greatly

promotes

promotes cleanliness and coolness. See all these buildings, how commodious! how elegant! There are no more of those fatal high chimneys, or of those sloping Gothic roofs, which menaced destruction to every person who ventured near them in windy weather."

We went into a house and ascended the stairs, which were light and spacious. I cannot say how much I was delighted with the flowers on every landing place, which shed a delightful perfume. But what shall I say of the flat roofs filled with flower-pots, and of all the houses of the same height, which formed a spacious garden. The whole city appeared, from an eminence above, to be crowned with flowers, with fruit, and with verdure.

I observed with pleasure that the hospital for the sick was removed from the centre of the city, and, therefore, if any stranger, or if a citizen falls sick, far from his native country, or removed from his family, he is not imprisoned, as formerly, in a disgusting bed, between a dead corpse and a man expiring there, to inhale the infected breath of death, thus converting a slight indisposition into a dangerous illness. "No," said my guide, "we have divided this into twenty different houses situated at the different extremities of the city. By this means the bad air, which this gulf of infection exhaled, was dispersed, and no longer a nuisance to the capital. Besides, it is no indigence which obliges our sick to go into these hospitals, nor do they enter them, already struck with the idea of death, well knowing the neglect they will experience in them, or in order to secure for themselves a decent burial, which they might be deprived of if they died poor in their own houses; but they go into them, because the most careful and ready assistance is to be procured. O! how changed every thing is in this place from what it was in your time, you will not see any confusion now, nor that horrible mixture of persons and diseases, which made it appear as the abode of revenge rather than that of charity. Every invalid has a bed to himself, and can expire without having to upbraid human nature. The account of the governors and directors have been revised, and O shame! O grief! O most unnatural offence! Men! inhuman and savage men! were convicted of defrauding the poor of those revenues set apart for them, and rejoiced in the sufferings of their fellow-creatures, they had concluded an advantageous bargain with death. But stop . . . the period of these iniquities is elapsed. The asylum of the wretched is now respected as the temple in which the Divinity is pleased to dwell with complacency, the enormous abuses are corrected, and the poor sick have now no other calamities to endure but those imposed on them by nature. When our sufferings come from her hand we support them in silence.

They have the attendance of physicians, eminent for their charity as for their skill, who do not pronounce so many sentences of death, by giving general prescriptions at random to every patient; but they give themselves the trouble of examining every patient, and of giving particular prescriptions to all. By this means health is restored under their humane services, and these men deserve to be among the first order of citizens. And what can be more beautiful, more noble, and more worthy of a virtuous and sensible being than the task of renovating the delicate thread of man's precarious life; that life which is frail and temporary, but which may, by the preserving art of medicine, be strengthened and prolonged? "And where," said I, "is the general hospital situated?"—"We have no such thing among us now," said my friend, "no mad houses, no bedlam; a healthy body has no need of an issue. It was luxury, which, like a burning caustic,

had

had thrown a canker throughout all the healthy members of the state, and your political body was covered with ulcerated sores. Instead of closing these shameful wounds by gentle means, you rendered them more venomous by violence. You thought it possible to crush vice under the weight of cruelty. You were inhuman, because you had not enacted good and wholesome laws.

"You found it easier to torment the unhappy guilty than to prevent disorder and misery by proper means. Your barbarous violence only served to harden their criminal hearts, and to fix them in mad despair. And what was the result? tears, bitter lamentations, raving, and every malediction, poured forth from the lips of those most injured wretches. You seemed to have modelled your mad-houses from the plan of that terrible abode which you called hell, where ministers of pain and suffering accumulated every torture, that they might have the pleasure of inflicting a long series of torments upon these unfortunate beings. In short, you knew not even how to give employment to the indigent to keep them from begging in the streets. All your skill consisted in confining and suffering them to starve. These unhappy wretches, expiring by slow degrees in a corner of the kingdom, have made their complaints ascend, though at the distance of so many centuries, to our ears, and we have erected poor houses, as a tribute to these unfortunate victims of inhumanity, where the poor are effectually, and in the strictest sense of the word, provided for life. That inhuman tyranny over so many unhappy beings, is sufficient to bring many others to light no less criminal."

I remained silent and confused, with my eyes fixed to the ground, for what, in fact, could I answer? for I was but too well convinced of the truth of all that my guide had said. I had lamented and bewailed all these public cala-

(26)

mities in my youth, but now I was confounded with his reproaches, and, after a short silence, I spoke to him thus "Ah! do not open anew all the former wounds of my heart on this melancholy occasion. The God of Nature has repaired, ere now, all the calamities which these poor victims have endured from their fellow-creatures their hard hearts have been well punished, you know . . . . . But let us go forward. I think you have suffered the continuance of one of our political errors. Paris appears in the same degree of population as it was in my time, it was observed that the head was three times larger than the body."—"I am happy to assure you," said my guide, "that the number of inhabitants throughout the whole kingdom amounts to twice the number, that every piece of land is cultivated, and, consequently, the head is now in due proportion with the body. This beautiful city still produces as many illustrious personages, as many learned men, as many men usefully industrious, and as many great geniuses, as all the other cities of France united."—"But allow me to ask one more question, Is your powder magazine still in the centre of the city?"—"No we are not so mad, so imprudent Are there not a sufficient number of volcanos sent us by the hand of nature? We need not prepare any artificial ones, much more dangerous"

CHAP.

(27)

CHAP. IX.

*Age shall the glowing tale relate,
And youth shall drop the scalding tear.*

I Observed several officers, clothed with every ensign of dignity, who publicly received all the complaints of the people, and afterwards reported them to the chief magistrate. Every circumstance relative to the administration of the police was transacted with the utmost celerity. Justice was administered to the poor and to the feeble, whose hearts were expanded in grateful effusions and blessings on the constitution. I bestowed many praises upon these wise and salutary institutions, but said to my guide, " You must not take all the glory of these discoveries to yourselves. Even in my time the city began to be under a good and vigilant police, and he who established good order, and maintained it, ought to be revered even in these days. Among many other wise regulations, he prohibited the custom of having those heavy signs at every door, which were a great blemish to the town, and threatened destruction to the inhabitants whenever they walked under them; of having established proper luminaries for the streets, upon the best and most useful plan, and of having secured the speedy assistance of engines, and by that means promoted the preservation of the citizens in case of fire, which were formerly so frequent."

" Yes," replied my guide, " this magistrate was indefatigable, he was attentive to fulfil his duties, extensive though they were, but police had not then received all the perfection which it might be capable of, and the chief resource of your unquiet and feeble government consisted

sisted in sending a great number of spies about the city, whose motives were rather the gratification of a sort of malicious curiosity than the public utility.

"The secrets of the public being thus artfully unveiled only served to mislead the magistrate with false appearances, and this band of informers, who were seduced by dint of bribes, formed a corrupted mass, which infested the whole society, and deprived it of its sweetest enjoyments. The heart could never communicate with its friend, the delightful intercourse of congenial minds was interrupted, and you were under the cruel alternative of being either hypocrites, or of being imprudent. It were in vain for the minds of men to soar up, with patriotic sentiments, towards a reform, which would secure their liberties: they were unable to indulge those delightful sensations; they soon perceived they were only snares which might lead them into danger, and therefore fell back into their usual state of apathy and inaction, sad and solitary. In short, they were continually obliged to disguise their words and sentiments. O! how painful for a generous man to remain silent! and see the monsters of avarice and oppression smile, while they cut the throats of their fellow-creatures, who knew them, and yet dared not to name them."

CHAP. X.

Be niggards of advice on no pretence,
For the worst avarice is that of sense;
With mean complacence ne'er betray your trust,
Nor be so civil as to prove unjust.
Fear not the anger of the wise to raise,
Those best can bear reproof who merit praise.

"I Entreat you to tell me who that man is, who wears a mask, whose step is so precipitate that he seems to be flying from the pursuit of some enemy? Who can he be?"—"He is an author who has published a bad work. Not that I mean to imply that the imperfections of this work consisted in the want of stile or of good sense, for it is possible to write an excellent work, replete with understanding, which may be incorrect in composition; but this man has published principles which are eminently dangerous, and contrary to sound moral, to that universal moral which influences every heart. To repair his fault he wears a mask, that he may conceal his shame, until he has obliterated it by a composition which may do him more credit. He is visited every day by two virtuous men, who take pains to oppose his erroneous opinions with gentleness and eloquence, who listen to and answer his objections, and who engage him to retract his errors from conviction. When he has done this he will then be restored to the community, and will derive a greater glory from the acknowledgment of his faults for, indeed, what can be greater than to abjure errors, and to embrace, with sincerity, the light which pervades every unprejudiced understanding?"—"But if his work had been approved of by . . . . . ."—"And who pray shall

dare

dare to judge of a work before the public? Who can possibly guess at the sort of influence of such and such sentiments under such and such circumstances? Every writer among us is personally answerable for what he writes, and never disguises his name. It is the public who disgraces him, whenever he swerves from those sacred principles which are the basis of the conduct and probity of man, but it is the same public who supports and protects him, whenever he discovers any new idea which may prove useful in repressing certain abuses. In short, the public voice is the only judge in these cases, and that alone is attended to. Every author, who is a public man, is judged by the public voice, and not by the caprice of a man, whose understanding cannot be so just or so extensive as to enable him to discover, or rather discriminate, what may be worthy of praise or of blame from the nation.

"It has often been proved, that the degree of civil liberty enjoyed may be ascertained from the liberty of the press. The one cannot be injured without the other and the power of thinking should be unrestrained it is a crime against humanity to stifle it in its sanctuary, and ever to prescribe the most distant limits to its rapid flight. Ah! what shall I call my own, if I am not master of my own thoughts?"

I replied thus to my friend, "In my time men in office felt the greatest dread of the pen of a good author. Their haughty and guilty soul shuddered in its darkest recesses, if the pen of equity dared to unveil that which they had not blushed to commit Instead of protecting this public censure, which, had it been properly administered, would have proved the most powerful curb to crime and vice, all works of this nature were condemned to undergo an examination, which always proved more or less fatal to the work, inasmuch as it contained

tained the moſt important truths, which theſe judges never failed to curtail. The ſoarings of genius were under the ſubordination of a cruel and envious enemy, its ſublime and lofty wing was therefore always deprived of thoſe brighteſt plumes, which enabled it to ſoar above the common prejudices in which the world was immerſed."

I ſaw every perſon laugh who was near me, and one of them obſerved, that it muſt have been very ridiculous to ſee grave men employed in curtailing a thought in two, and in weighing ſyllables. " It is very ſurpriſing," continued he, " that you ever produced any good work, having all theſe fetters to encounter. Is it poſſible to dance lightly and gracefully under the weight of chains? O! as to that, our beſt authors at laſt determined to ſhake off theſe abſurd ſhocks. Fear makes the ſoul degenerate, and that man who is animated with the love of humanity ought to be proud and courageous."

" Well," ſaid my elder companion, " you may write your ſentiments freely, we ſhall never oppreſs your genius with fetters, and there are no uſeleſs books publiſhed now, for they ſoon fall in the mire, which is their proper element. Our government is far above any thing that can be ſaid or written. It fears not the moſt enlightened pen, becauſe all its proceedings are upright and ſincere. We can never be too loud in its praiſe, and when the intereſt of our country is concerned, every man can become an author, though without aſſuming the title.

(32)

CHAP. XI.

*Fly swift, ye years, ye minutes, haste,
And in the future lose the past*

WHAT do I hear! you are all authors, say you? I wonder the whole city is not blown up in the air, since it contains so much saltpetre Heavens! what a whole nation of authors! yes, but they are without gall, without pride or presumption. Every man writes down his reflections, and at a certain age he collects the best of them, out of which he composes a work, more or less voluminous, according to his extent or knowledge, or manner of expressing himself, and this book is the soul of the defunct. On the day of his funeral this book is read aloud, and this is the best panegyric which can be given of him. Children respect and venerate these works of their ancestors, and meditate upon them all their lives Such are our funeral obsequies, and I think they are more suitable to the occasion, and convey a more durable impression upon the heart than all your sumptuous mausoleums, and your tomb stones, abounding in silly inscriptions, which were dictated by pride and arrogance, and very frequently to silence the loud tongue of fame on the real characters of those they represent.

Thus we think it our duty to engrave a true image of our lives for the benefit of our progeny This honourable memento is the only monument existing upon earth to recall us to the minds of our offspring, and, to make our memory dear to them, we do not neglect this duty, they are immortal lessons which we leave to our posterity, for which their affection will be the greater. Portraits and
statues

Statues only transmit the corporeal features; how much more valuable to possess their very soul, and all the virtuous sentiments with which it has abounded, which receive double force when animated by the warm enthusiasm of the heart. The history of our thoughts and of our actions serves as an instruction for our families, and teaches us, by drawing right comparisons, to form a proper judgment of things, and to perfect our understandings. It is to be observed, however, that all the leading authors, and the men of genius of the age, are like so many suns which attract the whole mass of ideas, and cause them to circulate: it is they who engrave the first impressions, and is their generous souls burn with the love of humanity, they have the united voice of the whole nation asserting the sublime and victorious power which has subdued corruption and superstition. "Permit me, however, gentlemen," said I, "to defend my own century, inasmuch, at least, as it may be commended. We have had virtuous men, and men of genius!"—"Yes, but you were so barbarous as to misunderstand and persecute them. We have been obliged to make an expiatory reparation to their injured memory; we have erected their busts in the public square, where they receive the well-merited homage of foreigners as well as our own. They trample under their feet the effigy of their tyrants, as, for instance, the bust of Richelieu is under the buskin of Corneille. It must be confessed that you have had some very astonishing men, and we cannot understand what could be the motive which could urge their rash persecutors to so much rage and virulence; they seemed to proportion their mean persecutions to the degree of elevation to which these lofty eagles soared, but they are now abandoned to that disgraceful oblivion which they so well deserve."

(34)

Saying these words, my friend led me towards a spot where I saw the busts of all the illustrious men of my own times. Here I saw Corneille, Moliere, La Fontaine, Montesquieu, Rousseau, Buffon, Voltaire, Mirabeau, &c &c. "What!" said I "are all these great writers known to you?"—' Yes, their names are the alphabet we teach our children; and, as soon as they have attained a mature age, we give them your celebrated Encyclopedia, which we have carefully revised.'—" You greatly surprise me, I must own—what, the Encyclopedia an elementary book! Oh! how sublime the flight you have taken towards the high sciences, and how I ardently long to be instructed by you! Open all your treasures to me, and let me enjoy all the precious fruits accumulated by the glorious labours of six hundred years!"

CHAP. XII.

Philosophy! oh, share the meed
Of freedom's noblest deed!
'Tis thine each truth to scan,
Guardian of bliss, and friend of man!

" PRAY, do you teach Greek and Latin to the children, who, in my time, were ready to die with the wearisome construction of Latin nouns and the Greek lexicon? Do you waste away ten of the most precious years of their lives in giving them a superficial tincture of two dead languages, which they will never make use of?"— " Oh! no, we know better how to employ their time. The Greek tongue is undoubtedly venerable, from its antiquity, but we have the most perfect translations of Homer, Plato, and Sophocles, although it has been

maintained

maintained by some of your pedants that it was impossible to do justice to their beauty. As for the Latin language, which was more modern, and therefore not so valuable, it is entirely dead for us."—" What! has the French language at length prevailed over every other?"—" Yes, for the translations were so perfect, that it has been unnecessary to refer to the original copies, and, in addition to that, we have produced works which have been thought worthy to efface the memory of the ancients. These new poems are incomparably more useful, more interesting to us, and have a much nearer affinity to our morals, to our constitution, to our progress in our physical and political discoveries, and, in short, to our moral views, of which we ought never to lose sight. The two ancient tongues of which we have just been speaking are only known to a few learned persons. Titus Livius is read in the same manner as we would read the Alcoran."—" But, I perceive that this college still bears engraven upon its frontispiece its former title, SCHOOL OF THE FOUR NATIONS."—" It is true, we have preserved this edifice under its former name, but we have changed it to a better use. There are four different classes, wherein are taught the four most useful languages, the English, the Italian, the German, and Spanish. While we are enriched by the treasures of these living languages, we have nothing to envy from the ancient. The last-mentioned tongue, whose nation bore within her bosom those seeds of greatness which no reverse could ever completely destroy, finally became enlightened in the most extraordinary manner by one of those powerful strokes of fate which can neither be expected nor foreseen. This revolution was a happy one, because it was produced by an enlightened understanding, whereas among many other nations, great events arise chiefly from national prejudices, while the mind is

left

left in the obscure shade which these prejudices unavoidably create

"Folly and pedantry are banished from this college, wherein foreigners are invited, in order to facilitate the pronunciation of those languages which are taught, the best authors are here translated, and from such a fund of knowledge and mutual correspondence the most brilliant discoveries are made There are likewise other advantages to be derived. From the extending intercourse of thought, national enmities are extinguished, people have discovered that a few private customs do not destroy that universal intelligence which agrees from one end of the world to the other, and that they all were nearly agreed in those very opinions which have kindled such long and violent dissentions."—"But what is become of the university, the eldest daughter of kings?"—" She is a forsaken princess. This old maiden, after having received the very last sighs of a fastidious and degenerated tongue, thought she might again new-clothe and new-model it, so as to receive new applause, she proposed periods, hemisticks, and thought to revive the language of Augustus with a barbarous and unintelligible jargon, which no one understood but herself At length it was discovered that her voice was exhausted, that her abilities were degenerated, that she was equally tedious to the court, the city, and her disciples. This being the case, she was cited to the tribunal of the French academy, to give an account of the services she had rendered to the nation who had maintained, honoured, and pensioned her during four centuries. She attempted to plead her cause in her own strange idiom, which even the Latinists themselves would never have understood as for the real French language, she knew not a word of it, and therefore she would not attempt to speak it before her judges.

"The

"The academy felt for her embarrassment, and they charitably desired her to keep silence; she was then taught to speak the language of the country, and since that time, being divested of her ancient head-dress, of her stateliness, and of her ferula, she applies herself to the teaching of this beautiful tongue, which the French academy renders more perfect every day. The latter being less bashful, and less scrupulous, knows how to call her to account without enervating her, and she is always docile and tractable."—"And pray," resumed I, "what is become of the military school?"—"It has experienced the fate of all the other colleges," rejoined my friend. "In this school were re-united every abuse which prevailed in other colleges, besides those privileged abuses peculiar to its institution, of which there were many. Men are not so easily formed as soldiers."—"Pardon me for intruding on your goodness, but this is a very important point, which I cannot relinquish, as I wish to be particularly informed on this subject. In my time, nothing was spoken of but education, every pedantic fellow thought himself capable of writing on this subject. Happy for the author while he was only tedious; the best of them, even the most simple, or the most profound, and the most rational, were often condemned to be burned by the hand of the executioner, and were contemptuously spoken of by persons who were incapable of understanding them. Inform me then, I entreat you, what method you have taken to form men worthy of society?"

"Men, such as you mention, are formed and educated by the wise laws and fatherly tenderness of our constitution rather than by any other institution. But as to what relates to the sole cultivation of the understanding, our method is to familiarise children to the operations of algebra while we teach them their letters. This method is simple, but of general utility. Nothing more is necessary but to know how to read, even the very shadow of difficulties has disappeared. The algebraical characters are no longer mistaken among the vulgar for magical conjurations. We have observed that this science was well calculated to accustom the mind to see every thing strictly as it is, and that this precision is most valuable when applied to the arts. Formerly children were taught a multiplicity of things, which were useless to the happiness of life. We have, on the contrary, selected those objects only which could give them ideas founded upon truth and reason, they were all indiscriminately taught the dead languages, which seemed to contain universal knowledge and yet these languages were not adapted to give them the least idea of those men they had to live with. We, on the contrary, are satisfied to teach them the national tongue, and we even permit them to modify it according to their own taste, as we do not wish to have grammarians, but men of eloquence and genius. The stile bespeaks the man, and the man whose soul is great, and aspiring to lofty subjects, ought to be permitted to use an idiom peculiar to his feelings, very different to the cold nomenclature, the only resource of weak minds, who have nothing to boast of but a memory.

" Our children are not taught much of history, for most histories are a disgrace to humanity, every page of which is a tissue of crime and folly. God forbid we should place such terrible examples of robberies, murders, and ambition before their eyes! The pedantry of history has represented kings like so many gods. We teach our children another sort of moral, much more safe, we give them more salutary ideas. These cold chronologers, these nomenclators of every age, all these writers, either corrupted by their superiors, or filled with romantic ideas, who

who have themselves shewn the first symptoms of disgust for their idols, are now extinct, with all the panegyrists of those princes of the earth of whom they sang. What! shall we employ that time which is so short, which flows so rapidly, in arranging in the minds of our children a set of useless names, dates, innumerable facts, genealogical branches, &c? What wretched futilities, when it is possible to contemplate the whole field of the moral and physical world! It is in vain to alledge that history furnishes examples which may instruct future ages, these examples are more pernicious, and only serve to teach the most complete depravity, and to render it more terrible and haughty, by displaying the abject slavery of man towards his fellow, and demonstrating cries of liberty expiring under the blows of a few men, who founded their right of establishing a certain place of tyranny, on that which had been founded by their ancestors. If ever there has existed a virtuous and estimable man, he was cotemporary with monsters, and was overpowered by their successful machinations, and this picture, wherein virtue is trampled under foot and oppressed, though too faithfully copied from facts, is no less dangerous to present. None but men of mature age can contemplate this melancholy copy without shuddering, for his understanding conceives a secret joy at the transitory triumph of vice, and at the eternal triumph destined for virtue. But from children this picture must be concealed, they ought to contract habits of friendship and familiarity with all notions of order and equity, and let them be the foundation and basis of all their sentiments. We do not teach them that idle morality which consists in frivolous questions, ours is a practical morality, which applies to all their actions, and speaks in beautiful metaphors, and which forms their hearts to gentieness, to courage, to the sacrifice of their own self-love, and, in a word, to generosity.

"We hold all metaphysical subjects in great contempt, it is only an obscure space, wherein every man erected a chimerical and useless system, in which he sought for some imperfect image of the Divinity, and while with subtle arguments upon his divine attributes he totally disfigured his divine essence, and bewildered human reason by presenting some ill-founded point whereon to establish belief, he always found himself farther from the truth. but by the aid of physical researches, that grand key of nature, that palpable and living science, we make them traverse the whole labyrinth of the marvellous assemblage, and teach them to feel the intelligence and wisdom of the Creator This science, in which we have dived to the profoundest depth, has preserved our youth from a multiplicity of errors, and the unformed mass of prejudice has ceded to the pure light which this heavenly science sheds over every object.

"When our young men are arrived at a certain age, we permit them to read the poets, our's have known how to unite wisdom to enthusiasm they are not men who impose upon reason by the cadence and harmony of words, and who feel themselves as it were bewitched into a labyrinth of false and chimerical ideas, for the sake of displaying the flowery productions of the brain; or who amuse themselves in adorning a set of dwarfs, in clothing their childish ideas in that garb most agreeable to children, diverting them with some toy or bauble worthy of little minds, such as those who are too frequently the subjects of their poetical praise. Our poets are the singers of the great actions which render men illustrious· their heroes are chosen wherever courage and virtue are to be found, that venal and false trumpet, which proudly flattered the

colossusses

coloffuses of the earth, is for ever deftroyed. Our poetry has only preferved the trumpet of truth, which will and ought to refound throughout all ages, becaufe her voice will be that of pofterity. Such are the models upon which our children are formed, and thus they receive juft ideas of true greatnefs, while the rake, the fhuttle, and the hammer, are more dazzling objects to us than a fceptre, a diadem, a royal mantle, &c."

CHAP XIII.

To give each generous purpofe birth,
And renovate the gladden'd earth

"ALLOW me to afk you in what language the doctors of divinity hold their arguments are they ftill famed for their ridiculous pride? do they continue to wear their long robes and fur caps?"—"There are now no difputes among our divines, for the language we ufe here, as well as every where, is the French, and therefore we have no more fophiftical cavillers amongft us thank God, thefe halls no longer echo to their barbarous phrafes, more fenfelefs, if poffible, than the extravagant meanings they wifhed to give them. We have difcovered that the benches on which your Hibernian doctors were feated, were compofed of a certain fort of wood which had the fatal power of overturning the beft organifed brain in the world."—"Oh! that I had lived in your time! the wretched cavillers have been the torment of my youthful years, and for a long time I concluded myfelf an ideot, becaufe I could not underftand them.— But pray tell me what ufe you make of that palace which was erected by a certain Cardinal who wrote bad poetry with enthusiasm, and ordered good heads to be cut off with all possible indifference?"—"Ah!" replied my guide, "that spacious building contains several large halls, wherein a course of study is pursued, much more useful to human nature. Here are dissected all sorts of bodies, and the most skilful anatomists are employed in examining from the spoils of death, into the causes of, and in finding resources against, the physical evils. They do not employ their time in analising a set of stupid propositions, tending to no good, but they endeavour to discover the hidden causes of our cruel diseases, and never does the scalpel lay open her insensible bodies under their hands but for some particular good to their posterity. Such are the doctors who are established, honoured, and pensioned by the state. Surgery is reconciled with physic, and physic is no longer at variance with itself."

"Oh! what a happy prodigy! nothing could equal the bitterness of their dissentions. The animosity between pretty women, the jealous fury of the poets, the bitter gall between painters, all these were gentle passions in comparison to the hatred which in my time inflamed the votaries of Æsculapius. A certain jester was heard to say, that physic has often been on the point of calling in the aid of surgery after these violent quarrels."—"Well, my friend, in these days every thing is changed, our sons of Æsculapius are all friends, and not rivals, they form but one body, and are ever ready to lend each other mutual help; thus their united operations have the most miraculous effects. The physicians are not ashamed to lend a hand themselves to those operations which may be thought suitable. When he prescribes a remedy, he does not leave it to the ineptitude of a subaltern to prepare it, whose negligence or ignorance might prove equally fatal, but he is present while they

they are preparing, and judges of the quality and quantity of the dose himself, for these are very important articles, from whence the cure of a man chiefly depends. The patient is not surrounded by two or three physicians, who are ridiculously subordinate to each other, and yet dispute and watch each others looks, expecting some blunder, at which they may gratify their sarcastic risibility. The draughts given to the sick are not the result of experiments, or the mixture of the most opposite principles. The weakened stomach of the patient is no longer the receptacle of all the poisons of the north and of the south, but the beneficent juices of those vegetables, the produce of our own native soil, are best appropriated to our constitution, and dissipate the humours without violence to the interior system. This art is esteemed one of the first among us, because all systematic and practical observances are banished from it, for these have been as fatal to the study of physic as the avidity of kings and the cruelty of ministers."

"It affords me great pleasure to know that things are such as you represent them. I love your physicians, since they are no more a set of interested cruel quacks, who, without remorse or feeling, murdered their patients by their barbarous experiments. But apropos, to what story do they ascend in their visits to the sick?"—"To every story where a man may be found who needs their succour."— "That is most wonderful, in my time our most celebrated physicians would never visit higher than the first, and, as our pretty women would not receive any visitors but such as wore laced ruffles, they, on the other hand, would not cure any persons but such as kept their carriage."—"I say physician among us was capable of such inhumanity, he would be branded with indelible disgrace. Every man has a right to call in their aid, all their glory consists in recalling the bloom of health, and, if the unfortunate patient cannot produce an adequate falary, which is very rare, government takes the expenfe upon itfelf. A regifter is held of all the fick who have been cured, and of thofe who have died within the month. To the name of the dead perfon is affixed the name of his phyfician, who is obliged to give an account of all his prefcriptions, and to juftify the courfe he has followed with him from the beginning, it is a troublefome detail to enter upon, but the life of one man is precious, and every method of preferving it fhould be adopted, befides, it is very much to the intereft of all phyficians to put this wife law in practice.

" The art of phyfic is now fimplified, and difembarraffed of many foreign branches of fcience, which were fuppofed to appertain to it, fuch as anatomy, chymiftry, botany, and mathematics, while each of thefe would require the whole life of a man to be thoroughly acquainted with them, befides, your phyficians all pretended to be fine wits, ours are fatisfied with the knowledge of every malady, with the power of difcovering all their various fymptoms, and of underftanding every different conftitution. They never employ any of thofe medicinal waters, or of thofe myfterious recipes which take their rife in their own brain, and ferve as experiments upon their patients. A very fmall number of remedies are fufficient. We have found that nature acts with uniformity both in the vegetation of plants and in animal nutrition. Behold a gardener, they fay, how careful he is to promote the equal circulation of the fap, that is, of the univerfal fpirit all over the tree! if it becomes fickly, it is owing to the thickening quality of this marvellous fluid. Thus every difeafe which may attend the human race have no other caufe but the coagulation of the blood and humours, whereas if they are

reftored

restored to their natural state of liquifaction, circulation will recover its course, and health will return florescent on the countenance of him who was of a pale and sallow complexion. This principle being established, it does not require a vast store of knowledge to maintain or to restore the course of nature; for they are obvious to every man of experience. Among the remedies most universal amongst us, we esteem all odoriferous herbs, which abound in volatile salts, as being infinitely serviceable in dissolving the thickness of the blood: it is the most precious gift of nature to preserve health; we extend its use to all diseases, and we have seen the most rapid cures performed by them."

CHAP. XIV.

For pleasure here has never learn'd to cloy,
But days of toil enliven hours of joy.

"I BEG you will inform me what that lonely building is destined for, which I discover at some distance in the country?"—"It is the hospital for inoculation, which you formerly rejected with so much stupid obstinacy, as you did every other useful present. This obstinacy was entirely the effect of self-love, which blinded you to your own interests; had it not been for a few women who were in love with their own beauty, and who would rather have lost their life than their pretty face, or for some princes, who dreaded the kingdom of Pluto, you would never have hazarded to make use of this happy discovery; as it was fully crowned with success, those women who were not ranked among the beauties were forced to be silent; and those who had no diadems to lose were

were not lefs happy to remain a little longer on earth. Soon or late truth muft pierce the cloud of ignorance, and reign over the moft untoward hearts; we now practife inoculation amongft us as much as it was practifed in your time in China, in Turky, and in England. We are very far from banifhing falutary remedies from amongft us becaufe they are novel, nor do we difpute furioufly on their efficacy for no other caufe but to be noticed and captivate the eye of the public.

"Thanks to our activity, and to our inquifitive fpirit, we have difcovered many admirable fecrets, which it is not yet time to expofe to your view; we have dived fo deeply in the ftudy of thofe wonderful fimples, which your ignorance caufed you to trample under your feet, that we perfectly underftand the cure of confumptions, dropfies, and afthmas, and other difeafes, which your improper remedies have always augmented. Even the dreadful malady called hydrophobia is now treated with perfpicuity, and every perfon knows how to watch over his own health and preferve it; we never depend entirely on the phyfician, however fkilful he may be, we have taken the trouble to ftudy our own conftitutions, inftead of expecting a ftranger to guefs at it; but it is temperance, the true elixir, the grand reftorer, and preferver of health, which contributes to form healthy and vigorous men, in whofe pure bodies the greateft and moft noble fouls are lodged."

CHAP.

CHAP XV

But mercy is above the sceptred sway,
It is enthroned in the hearts of kings,
It is an attribute of God himself,
And earthly power doth then shew likest God's
When mercy seasons justice

"HAPPY mortals! what, you have no more theologists among you? I do not see those immense folio volumes, which seemed like the foundation-pillars of our libraries, those heavy masses which none but the printer had ever read; but, however, theology is a very sublime science, and'"——"As we never speak of the Supreme Being but to bless and praise him, without disputing on the subject of his divine attributes, which will ever remain impenetrable, we are all agreed never to write on a subject so sublime, and so far above our intelligence, for it is the soul which feels what God is, and needs no foreign power to enable it to spring forward towards the divine essence

"Every book of theology and jurisprudence are sealed up under immense iron weights, and kept in the subterraneous vaults under the great library, and, if we are ever at war with any neighbouring nation, instead of pointing the great cannons against them, we will send them those dangerous books. We preserve these volumes of inflammable matter to serve us against our enemies, they will soon destroy each other when they possess these subtle poisons which attack both the head and the heart"

"It is extraordinary to be without theology, however, this I can conceive but to have no court of jurisprudence, it is what I cannot understand."—"We have a

court

(48)

court of jurisprudence, but it is very different to yours, which was Gothic and absurd. it wore all the impression of your antique slavery, you had adopted a set of laws, which were neither suitable to your morals, nor to your climate. As the minds of men have been enlightened by degrees, by degrees they have discovered and reform'd the abuses which had rendered the sanctuary of justice a den of thieves, it has been a matter of surprise, that the odious monster, who devoured the substance of the widow and of the orphan, could be suffered to enjoy for so long a time his guilty impunity we cannot conceive how your attornies were ever suffered to walk the streets peaceably without being stoned to death by some desperate hand. The august arm which held the sword of justice has given a deadly stroke to this crowd of bodies without souls, who could only be said to possess the instinct of the wolf, the cunning of the fox, and the croaking of the raven; their own clerks, whom they suffered to starve, and who were weary of their life, were the first to reveal their iniquities, and to arm themselves against them. Their race disappeared before the avenging hand of Themis. Such was the dreadful and tragical end of these robbers, who ruined whole families while they scribbled their destruction upon scrolls of parchment in order to render it the more certain."

" In my time it was thought, that, without the help of their ministry, a great part of the citizens would remain idle at the tribunals, and that the tribunals themselves would become the theatre of licentiousness and madness It is true, it was the manufacturers of stamped paper who spoke thus. However, let me ask you, how your causes are pleaded or judged, if you have neither solicitors nor counsellors ?"—Oh !" said my friend, " our affairs are managed in the best manner possible we have continued

the

the order of judge-advocates, who are well acquainted with the excellence and nobility of the institution, which is the more respectable as it is more disinterested. It is they who take upon themselves the task of exposing, in a clear but laconic style, the cause of the oppressed, with proper emphasis, but not with the view of displaying their powers of declamation. There are no more of those long pleas, filled with invectives, which sometimes cost the pleader his life, by the fermenting heat in which he threw his blood to display his powers. The wicked man, whose cause is unjust, supposes these pleaders to be men of incorruptible integrity, as they become responsible, on their honour, for the causes which they undertake, and make a boast of having abandoned the opposite party, who, they say, is already condemned by their refusal to plead for him, and stand trembling and excusing himself to the judge without a friend to plead his defence, while he who is the supreme judge of all has already acquitted the defenceless man, and condemned the protected oppressor.

"Every person is now restored to the primitive right of pleading his own cause, law-suits are never suffered to have time for becoming intricate, they are elucidated and judged in their infancy, and the longest term that is ever granted, when the affair is obscure, is a whole year. But the judges never receive bribes, they have blushed at that shameful privilege, which, though so trifling in its origin, they afterwards insensibly raised to very exorbitant sums, they found, that by accepting these presents, they gave an example of rapacity, and that, if there exists a time when interest ought not to prevail, it is the awful and honourable moment when he pronounces a sentence of justice."—"I perceive that you have made prodigious alterations in our laws."—"Your laws," rejoined my friend, 'can you possibly apply that name to such a collection of indigested and unconnected stuff, containing nothing but grotesque imitations, ideas without order, and customs in opposition to each other? could you possibly adopt such a barbarous plan, which could neither be said to have order or object, which displayed nothing but a formal compilation, where the palace of genius was sunk in a miry abyss? There appeared some men, at last, who were so much the friends of their fellow-creatures, so intelligent and so courageous, as to meditate an entire reform of this code, and to perform a work, exact in all its proportions, out of this strange jumble of unconnected matter.

"Our kings have bestowed all their attention to this vast project, in which so many millions were concerned, and we have found out, that the most excellent and important study is that of legislation. The names of Lycurgus, of Solon, and of those who have followed their footsteps, are the most respectable of all, and the only names which ought to be recorded in history; the ray of light issued from the north, and as if nature had particularly determined to humble our pride, she has so ordered it, that it was a woman who began this important revolution.

"Then did justice speak in the voice of nature, who is the sovereign law-giver, the mother of all virtues, and of all that is good upon earth; her precepts, having reason and humanity for their support, have been clear, wise, distinct, and not very numerous. All general cases have been foreseen, and established by the law beyond the power of correcting. All particular cases have naturally derived from the code, as the branches which spring from the fertile trunk, and integrity, more wise than jurisprudence itself, applied practical probity to every circumstance.

"These new laws are particularly sparing of human blood; the punishment is always in proportion to the crime.

crime. We have banished all captious interrogatories and tortures, which were only worthy of a tribunal of inquisitors, or for a nation of cannibals. We never put a thief to death, for we think it an injustice most truly inhuman to take the life of a man who has never been guilty of murder, all the gold in the world is not worth the life of one man, we punish him with the loss of liberty. We very rarely shed the blood of our fellow-creatures, but when we find ourselves obliged to it, in order to set a dreadful example to the wicked, we do it in the most striking manner. We have no mercy for a minister who makes an ill use of the confidence of his sovereign to the injury of the people, but we do not suffer the criminal to languish in dungeons; the punishment quickly follows the offence, and, if we have any doubts arise as to his criminality, we rather grant him his pardon than render ourselves responsible for the life of an innocent man. When a criminal is taken, he is publicly chained, and every person may see him, as he is to be a striking example of the vigilance of justice. Over the iron grate which confines him is seen an inscription, which remains there for ever, stating the full cause of his imprisonment. We do not confine living men in the gloomy shades of night; it is an ineffectual punishment, though more horrible than the darkness of the grave. It is in the full glare of day that a man undergoes his chastisement, and every man knows why his fellow-citizen is condemned either to prison or public labour, and he who, after three times chastising, is not reformed, is seared with a hot iron, not between the shoulders, but in the forehead, and for ever banished his country.'—" Tell me,' said I, " what is become of that quick and infallible means of executing an inhuman revenge, and of gratifying pride, by persecution, called lettres de cachet?'—" If you were seriously to ask that question,"

question," replied my guide with severity, " it would be an insult to our monarch, to the nation, and to myself Both lettres de cachet and the rack are abolished from among us, they now pollute the pages of your history, where alone they exist, to brand you with everlasting shame.'

~~~~

CHAP. XVI

Yet think not that the wretch, who finds a flaw
To baffle justice and elude the law,
Unpunish'd lives, he pays atonement due,
Each hour his malefactions rise to view
Vengeance more fierce than engines, racks, and wheels
Unseen, unheard, his mangled bosom feels
What greater curse can earth or heaven devise
Than his, who, self condemn'd, in torture lies?
From agony of mind who knows no rest,
But bears his own accuser in his breast.

MY attention was suddenly called off by certain distant gloomy sounds which assailed my ears, they seemed to murmur in the wind, and conveyed the expressions of disaster and death The muffled drums at length approached, beating the alarm, and marching round the city, while the dismal sounds vibrated in every heart, and inspired terror and dismay I saw every citizen coming forth from his habitation, and with every expression of sadness speak to his neighbour, with uplifted hands to heaven, and with weeping I went up to one of them, and inquired wherefore those funeral bells, and what accident had happened?

He

(53)

He answered with sighs, "that it was one of the most afflicting accidents Justice," pursued he, "is this day under the sad necessity of condemning one of our fellow-citizens to lose his life, of which he is no longer worthy, having imbrued his murderous hand in the blood of his fellow creature. It is now more than thirty years since the light of the sun has been polluted by a deed so atrocious, it must be expiated before the setting of that beneficent luminary. Oh! what tears I have shed at the fatal consequences of a blind and fatal spirit of revenge! Have you been informed of the dreadful crime which was committed the night before the last? Oh, how grievous! it was not sufficient to lose a good citizen, but we must lose another by public execution!"—He sobbed as he pursued his recital —" Listen, listen, to the account of the sad event, which spreads universal terror and mourning

" One of our countrymen, of a sanguine constitution, born with a violent temper, and with a character full of fire, but possessing many virtues and valuable qualities, was excessively in love with a young girl, whom he was on the point of obtaining in marriage, her character was as gentle as that of her lover was impetuous she flattered herself that she might soften his manners, but, at length, having witnessed several traits of unpardonable warmth, which frequently escaped him (notwithstanding the care he took to disguise it), she trembled for the fatal consequences of an union with a man whose disposition was so impetuous

" Every woman is, by our laws, fully at liberty to dispose of herself according to her inclinations She therefore determined, lest she should be unhappy, to accept the offer of another man, whose disposition was more suitable to her own. The torch of his Hymen kindled a violent rage in his enamoured heart, which, from its earliest

youth,

youth, had never known moderation. He sent repeated challenges to his happy rival, who despised them all, for there is more real bravery in treating an insult with contempt, and in conquering a just resentment, than in accepting, like a madman, of a challenge which reason and the laws equally prohibit. This passionate man, attending only to the dictates of his jealousy, attacked his rival the night before last at the corner of a bye-path out of the city, and, upon his repeatedly refusing to engage him in a duel, he seized the thick branch of a tree, having no other weapon (not being allowed to carry any), and extended him dead at his feet. After this dreadful stroke the inhuman wretch dared to come amongst us, but his crime was already engraven on his forehead. Soon as we saw him we discovered the crime he wished to conceal. We adjudged him criminal without yet knowing the full extent of his crime, and in a short time we perceived several persons, whose eyes were bathed in tears, who were moving on with slow steps, carrying the bloody corpse, which cried aloud for vengeance to the throne of justice.

"At the age of fourteen we are always made acquainted with the laws of our country, and we are obliged to transcribe them ourselves, and we take an oath of fulfilling them with the strictest exactitude. These laws enjoin us to declare every infringement of them to justice, and every transaction which tends to the subversion of the order of society; but justice never pursues any delinquent, except in cases of real destruction of civil order. These sacred oaths we renew every ten years, and we all are equally watchful over the sacred trust.

"Yesterday the civil admonition was issued, and whoever dares, after this, to conceal any circumstance against the laws which he may be informed of would draw indelible

delible infamy upon himself. It is by this means that the murder was instantly discovered. None but the wicked monster, who has long been familiarised with crime, could deliberately deny the murder he has committed, and we have no such monsters among us, they exist now only in the history of your times.

"Come with me and hear the voice of justice pronounce her formidable sentence, it is the day of her triumph, and, however fatal it may be, we must applaud You will not see an unhappy man brought from the dark dungeon, after having been six months deprived of the light of the sun, whose hollow eyes and sickly aspect bespeak the preliminary punishment he has endured, more horrible than that he is going to undergo, moving with dying steps towards a scaffold erected in a confined spot. In your time the criminal was judged with secrefy, and often suffered the torments of the wheel in the silence of the night, near the door of his fellow-creature who was awakened by the lamentable and piteous cries of the unhappy sufferer, uncertain whether the poor wretch was falling under the hand of the assassin or of the executioner! We have none of those torments which make nature shudder, we respect human nature even in those who have disgraced its dignity. Those tragic scenes, however horrible, had lost their power, and, far from impressing a character of energetic awe capable of deterring men from crime, they hardened his heart against every sentiment of virtue

"Our criminal, far from being dragged along in a manner disgraceful to the name of justice, will not even be chained Ah! why should his hands be loaded with chains when he voluntarily resigns himself to death? Justice has only the right of condemning him to lose his life, but not to brand him with the mark of slavery, so degrading to man You will see him walking freely in the midst of a few soldiers, who are only placed there to restrain the multitude we do not fear that he will disgrace himself a second time, by endeavouring to escape from the terrible voice by which he is called Ah! whither should he fly? what people will ever receive an homicide among them? and how shall he erase the dreadful mark which the divine hand impresses on the forehead of a murderer? The expression of all the disquietude caused by remorse is there depicted, and the eye, accustomed to view countenances expressive of virtue, will soon distinguish a guilty one, in short, how should the unhappy criminal breathe freely under the immense weight which oppresses his heart."

At length we arrived in an immense square, in the centre of which as the palace of justice, the hall of audience was distinguished by a lofty flight of steps, and upon this sort of amphitheatre the senate assembled, in presence of the people, to treat of public affairs, or of the interests of the nation. The multitude of citizens assembled inspired them with sentiments worthy of the sacred cause entrusted to their charge the death of one man was regarded as a calamity for the nation, and the judges accompanied the judgment with all the solemnity necessary to so important an event; the order of advocates were ready, on the one hand, to speak in favour of the innocent, and to keep silence against the guilty, on the other hand, there stood the prelate, accompanied by the pastors, who were bare headed, and silently imploring the God of Mercies, and edified the multitude by their conduct, full of humanity The criminal appeared walking, and had on a bloody shirt, he struck his breast with every appearance of a sincere repentance, but his countenance did not express that fearful dread which is not becoming a man, who ought to know how to meet death with proper fortitude

titude, particularly when he knows he has deserved it. He was ordered to walk by a sort of iron cage, wherein the dead body of the man he had murdered was exposed to his view, at the sight of which his heart was struck with the keenest remorse, and he was permitted to retire from this sad object. He approached his judges, and fell upon one knee to kiss the sacred book of the laws, which were then laid open, and the article concerning homicide was read aloud, and placed under his eyes that he might read it himself. He fell on his knees a second time, and acknowledged himself guilty; then the chief judge, standing on the throne of justice, read his sentence of condemnation with a voice full of majesty and awful solemnity; all the counsellors and advocates now seated themselves, and gave notice that not one among them could undertake his defence. Then the chief judge held out his hand to the criminal, and deigned to raise him from his knees, saying, "Nothing now remains for you but to die with becoming fortitude, that you may obtain the pardon of God and of men. We do not hate you; we pity you, and your memory shall not be odious to us. Shew a voluntary obedience to the law, and respect her salutary vigour. Behold our tears that flow; they will testify that love will be the sentiment which shall prevail in our hearts when justice shall have accomplished her fatal ministry. Death is less dreadful than infamy; submit, therefore, to the one that you may be freed from the other. The choice is still left to you; if you wish to live, you may, but it will be in infamy, branded with disgrace, and looked with our indignation; you will see the light of that sun who will accuse you each day of having deprived one of your fellow-creatures of his beneficent influence; his light will become odious to you, for the looks of every one of us will continually express

express the horror and the contempt we have for an assassin, you will bear along with you, wherever you go, the weight of your remorse, and the eternal shame of having resisted the just laws which now condemn you. Be equitable towards society, and judge yourself."

The criminal made a sign with his head, by which it was understood that he confessed himself deserving of death. He then prepared himself to endure it with courage, and with that decency which, in these last moments, is the greatest honour to a man. He was no longer treated as a criminal, he was surrounded by several pastors, the prelate, having given him the kiss of peace, and taken off his bloody shirt, gave him a white tunic to put on, as an emblem of his reconciliation with the rest of mankind. His relations and his friends all ran to him and embraced him: he appeared to receive consolation in their caresses, and in seeing himself covered with that garment which was the pledge of the pardon of his country: these testimonies of their regard diminished the horror he felt in his last moments, he even lost sight of death while lost in their embraces. The prelate then addressed himself to the people, made choice of that moment to make a vehement and pathetic speech on the danger of the passions, what he said was so true and so affecting, that every heart was seized with admiration and terror, every one promised to keep a strict watch over himself, to stifle the first seeds of resentment which gain strength insensibly, and soon become unruly and inordinate passions.

In the mean time, a deputy from the senate carried the sentence of death to the monarch, that he might sign it with his own hand. No person could be put to death without the sanction of him in whom the power chiefly resided: this good father would have saved the life of an unfortunate

unfortunate man, but in this moment he sacrificed the strongest feelings of his heart to the necessity of executing an exemplary justice. The deputy returned, then the bells recommenced the funereal peal, the drums repeated their mournful movement, and the lamentations of a numerous people mingling with these melancholy sounds, gave an image of some universal disaster, the friends and relations of the unfortunate man gave him the last embrace, the prelate implored the mercy of the Supreme Being, and all the people, with eyes uplifted towards the vault of heaven, and with an unanimous voice, cried aloud, *Great God! open thy bosom to him! Merciful God! pardon him, as we do ourselves!* It was one universal voice which ascended towards heaven to mitigate the just wrath of God. He was again led with slow steps towards the iron cage, still surrounded by his relations. Six fusileers, who wore a black crape over their forehead, drew near, the criminal kneeled, and the chief of the senate gave the signal by raising up the book of the laws, the fusileers fired, and the soul departed, the body was taken up, as he had expiated his crime by death, he was restored to his rank among his fellow-citizens, his name, which had been erased, was again inscribed on the public registers, with the names of those who died on the same day. This people were not so basely cruel as to persecute the memory of a man even to his very grave, and to reflect his disgrace and his crime upon his innocent family, they were not delighted to dishonour a family of useful citizens and to make them unhappy, for the purpose of humbling them. His corpse was carried to the place where several others lay, who had paid the inevitable tribute of nature. His relations had only the grief of parting with a friend to endure, and on the very same evening, an office of trust becoming vacant, the King conferred the honourable

charge

(60)

charge to the criminal's brother. This choice, evidently dictated by equity and benevolence, was applauded by every one.

I was moved to tears, penetrated with all I saw and heard, and said to the citizen who had been speaking to me all this time, "Oh! how much mankind is respected among you! the death of one man causes an universal mourning for the nation!"—"This," said he, "proceeds from the wisdom and humanity of our laws, they rather incline towards reformation than to punishment, and the method of terrifying crime is not by rendering the punishment common, but formidable. We take precautions to prevent crimes: we have houses of confinement destined to solitude, where the guilty are placed, and have persons who inspire them with repentance, who soften their hardened hearts by degrees, and open them to the pure charms of virtue, whose pure attractions must be felt by the most depraved. Do we see the physician abandon his patient to death upon the very first appearances of a violent fever? Why then should we abandon those hearts who may be susceptible of reform? There are very few hearts so corrupt but what might be corrected by perseverance, and the blood of our fellow-creatures will never cement our tranquility or happiness. Your penal laws were all in favour of the rich, and their whole weight fell on the head of the poor. Gold was become the god of all nations. Gaols and gibbets surrounded every private estate, and tyranny, with sword in hand, bargained for the life, the blood, and the labours of the indigent; there was no just proportion in the chastisement, and therefore the people accustomed themselves not to see any in their crimes. The least offence was punished as an enormous crime. What was the consequence? the multiplicity of penal laws multiplied the crimes, and the infringers became

became as cruel as the judges; thus, while the legislator was endeavouring to unite the members of society, he tightened the bonds so close as to produce convulsive emotions, these bonds, instead of procuring ease, they lacerated the members, and mankind with grief of heart acknowledged, too late, that the tortures of execution will never repair virtue.

CHAP. XVII.

WE thus conversed a long time on this important and serious subject; but as it gained upon us, and that we were falling into that state of effervescence which produces excess of sentiment and the loss of that calm so necessary for sound reasoning, I suddenly interrupted my friend by the following question. "I beg you will inform me which of the two disputants now prevail, the Jansenist or the Molinist?" My friend answered me by a loud burst of laughter; it was some time ere I could produce an answer from him. "but," said I, "pray do answer, do answer me. Here were formerly the Capuchins, there the Cordeliers, yonder were the Carmelites. What are become of all those celibataries, with their sandals, their beards, and their scourges?"—"In our state we no longer fatten a set of automatons, as weary of their condition as they were tedious to others, who made the foolish vow of never being men, and who broke up all connection with them. We have, however,

con-

considered them as more to be pitied than blamed, engaged as they were from their earliest years in a state with which they were not acquainted, it was not themselves, but the laws that were reprehensible in permitting them blindly to dispose of a liberty, the value of which they were not acquainted with. Those whose houses of retreat were pompously erected in the midst of the tumult of cities, felt by degrees the pleasing charms of society, and resigned themselves to them. While they witnessed the happiness of happy fathers and brothers, who were united, of families enjoying peace and tranquillity, they sighed to think they never could share such felicity; they secretly lamented the error of that moment, which had made them renounce a life so desirable, and, cursing each other with desperate violence, they hastened the moment which was to open the gates of their prison. It soon arrived, and they shook off the yoke without a crisis, without a struggle, because the hour was come. They issued forth in crowds, and with every demonstration of the greatest joy, from slaves they became men.

"These robust monks, in whom the bloom of youth and of health seemed to revive, whose complexions were florid with love and joy, were united to those pure virgins, who, under the monastic veil, had often sighed after a more healthful and more happy condition. They fulfilled the duties of Hymen with an edifying fervour of soul, and their chaste wombs brought forth offspring worthy of such delightful unions. Their fortunate husbands were much less eager to solicit the canonization of their worm eaten bones; they were satisfied with being good fathers and good citizens, and I firmly believe they went just as soon to heaven for not having made their hell of this life. It is true that this reform appeared rather extraordinary to the bishop of Rome, but he very soon after became so

seriously

seriously engaged in his own affairs, that... "—" Who do you mean by the bishop of Rome?"—" Well then, to speak more conformably to the ancient system of things, it is the pope, but, as I have already told you, we have altered many Gothic terms, we no longer understand what is meant by canonicals, bulls, benefices, bishoprics, with immense revenues, we do not go to kiss the slipper of the successor of an apostle, whose master gave him every example of humility; and as this apostle preached poverty to his disciples, as much by his example as by his words, we do not send the purest gold, so necessary to the state, for indulgences, the futility of which this wise magician understood full well. All this caused him some displeasure at first, for we never like to lose our right, though never so unlawful; but he soon felt that his real dependance was heaven, and that terrestrial things were not appertaining to his reign, and, that in short, the riches of this life were nothing but vanity, as well as every thing else in this sublunary world.

'Time, who with an invisible and merciless hand undermines the loftiest habitations of pride and ambition, has sapped the foundation of this superb and incredible monument of human credulity; it fell without noise, its only strength was lodged in public opinion, opinion changed, and the whole fabric evaporated like smoke. Thus, after a dreadful conflagration, nothing is seen remaining but a thin vapour in lieu of whole volumes of flames and smoke.

" That part of Italy is now under the dominion of a prince worthy of reigning, and that antique city has again beheld her Cæsars. By this appellation I mean men such as the great Titus, Marcus Aurelius, Julian, but not those monsters who wore a human face, without the least resemblance of human nature. That beautiful

country

country was renovated soon as it was purged from such idle vermin, who vegetated in filth. That kingdom now holds its rank among other civilized nations, and wears an animated and cheerful aspect. After having been, during seventeen centuries, shackled by the most ridiculous chains of superstition, she is now restored to the free use of reason, and triumphs in the purest enjoyments of science and philosophy.'

CHAP XVIII

Unskilful he to fawn or seek for power,
By doctrines fashion'd to the varying hour,
Far other aims his heart had learn'd to prize,
More bent to raise the wretched than to rise.

"YOU tell me this revolution has been effected by the most peaceful and happy means, proceed then, delightful instructor! and give me an account of it."—" Yes this happy revolution was the work of philosophy, whose silent operations, like those of nature, are so much the more sure, as they work insensibly."—" But I have many difficulties to propose, a religion of some sort must be professed . . ."—" Undoubtedly," he replied with transport, " can there exist a being so ungrateful as to remain unmoved in the midst of the continual miracles of the creation, and under the brilliant vault of heaven! We adore the Supreme Being, but our method of paying adoration no longer causes disputes or persecutions. We have but few clergymen, and those we have are wise, enlightened, and tolerating, they are not even acquainted with the spirit of faction, and are consequently

the

the more cherished and respected; their only ambition is, that their hearts and hands may be pure enough to be raised to the Father of Men, and, like him, they love all mankind with equal affection. The spirit of peace and concord animates all their words and actions, and therefore, as I have already said, they are universally beloved, we have a good prelate, who lives with the ministers under his jurisdiction as he would with his brothers or equals. These charges are not given till after the age of forty; for then, and not till then, the turbulence of passion is somewhat abated, and tardy reason at length resumes her peaceable empire over man. They set the example of the highest degree of human virtue by the daily actions of their lives, it is they who comfort the afflicted, who enable the wretched to acquire the knowledge of that good and merciful Being, who from his throne contemplates all their troubles and difficulties, in order to reward them. It is these charitable ministers of religion, who go in search of indigence when concealed under the cloak of shame, and who relieve them without exciting the painful blush of conscious obligation, it is they who seek to reconcile those whom dissentions have divided, by words of gentleness and peace, by their influence the bitterest enemies embrace and are friends, while their hearts, which were before oppressed with tormenting passions, are now alive to generous friendship and gratitude only, in a word, they fulfill all the duties of men who take upon themselves to instruct in the name of the Eternal Ruler of the World."

"I revere those ministers of whom you speak, though yet unknown to them, but have you not among you a set of people, who consecrate their whole lives in repeating every day, at appointed hours, with a monotonous tone, a set of canticles, psalms, and hymns? Does no one

one aspire to canonization? and pray who are your saints?"—" Our saints! no doubt you mean by saints those who aspire to a higher degree of perfection, those who raise themselves above the weaknesses of human nature: yes; we have some such heavenly men, but they do not, as you may naturally suppose, lead an obscure and solitary life, neither do they make a merit of fasting, or of reciting psalms in bad Latin, or of remaining dumb or stupid all their lives it is abroad, in the face of day, that they display the strength and constancy of their virtue They voluntarily take upon themselves all sorts of painful offices, and those which disgust all other men, for they think such charitable actions far more acceptable to God than prayers.

"They never avoid danger in order to secure themselves, but take an active part towards the relief of their countrymen They have been seen to assist in extinguishing a fire, working the engines, and springing through the flames for the public good If any person happens to fall in the water, they will plunge in after them, in order to save the unfortunate wretch from impending death Thus these generous victims of charitable zeal are stimulated by an active courage, inspired by the sublime idea of being useful to their fellow-creatures, they make a point of these duties with as much pleasure and delight as if they were the most agreeable occupations All their actions are directed towards the good of mankind and of their country their own interests they never place in competition with these, some are engaged, night and day, in attending a sick bed, and wait upon the patients, comforting and serving them with their own hands. Others descend into the quarries, there to explore and extract the riches of nature Sometimes they become mechanics, seamen, or pioneers, they are

always

always ready, and, were it not for the cheerful benevolence which animates all their deeds, they might rather be taken for slaves bending beneath the yoke of a tyrant than for members of a free people. But they expect a reward in futurity, they are therefore insensible to present sufferings, and the sacrifice they make of the luxuries of this life is founded on useful motives, and not on bigotry and caprice.

"After this, I need not tell you how much they are respected during life, and after death, and, as our warmest gratitude would be insufficient, we leave the acknowledgement of this immense debt to be acquitted by the Author of all Good, persuaded that he alone knows the proportionate reward for such meritorious labours.

"Such are the saints whom we venerate, without believing any thing of them, but that they are an honour to human nature, in which state they live in the highest degree of perfection. they work no other kinds of miracles but those I have been relating. The martyrs of Christianity had certainly great merit in suffering the cruelest torments and deaths rather than to sacrifice the inward conviction of truths which they had adopted, both in mind and heart, but there is more real greatness of soul in consecrating a whole life to servile occupations in order to become the perpetual benefactors of suffering nature, to dry up the tears of sorrow, and to prevent dissentions and effusion of blood. These extraordinary men make no shew of their heroic virtue. when they stoop to mean offices, it is not with a view of attracting public notice or veneration, nor do they present their mode of life as a model for imitation, they never interfere with the conduct, or censure the faults of others.

When these good men quit this scene, to rejoin the Perfect Being from whom they are emanated, we do not encase

encafe their corpfe, or any part of their garments, in gold or filver, more vile even than the inanimated clay, but we write their hiftory and endeavour to imitate it."—" The more I ftep forward," faid I, " the more great and unexpected changes I find"—" Oh! you will fee many others ftill greater. Indeed, if fo many writers did not teftify the fame things, we fhould certainly call the truth of your hiftories of former ages in queftion for how can it be poffible, that men, who devoted themfelves to the fervice of the altars, were turbulent cabalifts, intolerant perfecutors, hating each other, becaufe they differed in their opinions on incomprehenfibilities or vain fubtleties? Weak mortals! how could they prefume to found the defigns of the Moft High, and judge them from their own fenfelefs paffions!

" I have read in fome of your hiftories, that thofe who had the leaft charity, and confequently the leaft religion, were thofe who preached it to others That the number of thofe who wore this lucrative cloak of religion had multiplied to an incredible degree, and that they lived in luxury, indolence, and a moft fcandalous celibacy, that your churches rather refembled market-places, where both fight and fmell were equally offended, and that your ceremonies were better calculated to entertain or amufe than to raife the foul to God .... but hufh, I hear the facred trumpet, which gives notice that the hour of prayer is at hand .... come and learn what our religion is, come into this neighbouring temple, and render thanks to your Creator for having once more given you to fee the rifing fun.

CHAP

(69)

CHAP. XIX.

Father of light and life ! thou Good Supreme !
O teach me what is good ! teach me thyself !
Save me from folly, vanity, and vice,
From every low pursuit ! and feed my soul
With knowledge, conscious peace, and virtue pure,
Sacred, substantial, never fading bliss !

HE turned the corner of a street, and I perceived, in the centre of a beautiful square, a temple in the form of a rotunda, ornamented with a magnificent dome. This edifice, supported by one single row of columns, had four large porches or gates; upon each of the four pediments was engraved this inscription TEMPLE OF GOD. Already had the hand of time given a venerable and majestic appearance to its walls. When we arrived at the temple-gate, how great was my surprise to find the following lines engraven in large characters over each gate

Hope not, vain man, th' eternal mind to know,
But grateful love and silent praise bestow;
So vast the theme, that finite reason strays,
Lost and confounded, in the endless maze
So wond'rous great ! that man a god must be
To know God's nature, and eternity ——

On reading these lines, I turned towards my guide, and, in a low voice, said, " You cannot say, however, that these lines were produced in your century."—" No certainly," he replied, " but though they were written in your's, that circumstance does not speak in their praise, unless your teachers of theology had confined their belief

F 3

to the sense of those beautiful words, instead of which, though they seem to have been dictated by God himself, they have remained mingled and buried with other works of no value, and yet I believe there never were finer written on the subject, nor can they be better placed."

We followed the people, who, with looks composed, with modest pace, and measured steps, all went and took their seats in the temple, either upon forms or benches, and the men were separated from the women. The altar was in the centre, and totally unadorned. The priest was so stationed as to be plainly seen by every one, and the choir of singers alternately repeated the sacred hymns after the priest had pronounced them. Their sweet manner of singing was expressive of the sentiment of respect for the Divine Majesty with which their hearts were penetrated. There were neither statues nor allegorical images, nor paintings to be seen; the name of God alone, several times repeated and traced upon the walls in different languages, served to ornament them; in short, every unsuitable decoration was carefully avoided. God alone was in his holy temple.

Nor was the dome of this august edifice closed up by a vault of marble or of painted canvas, but, on raising their eyes towards heaven, the clear azure vault was plainly discovered through the transparent glass. Sometimes the firmament was clear and serene, and presented an image of the goodness of the Creator, other times, thick and heavy clouds burst in torrents of rain, which recalled to mind the miseries of this life and its short duration; when the thunder is heard in dreadful peals, it recalls the awful idea of an angry God, and the necessity of ceasing to offend him, in short, the calm which succeeds the storm is an image of the pardon we may expect, if we submit to his decrees. The sweet and pure breath of spring, shedding its balfamic influence over the whole earth, ferves to imprefs this confoling truth on their foul, that the treafures of divine mercy and goodnefs are inexhauftible.

Thus the elements and feafons fpoke to the hearts of this people, whofe fenfibility and gratitude taught them to underftand their eloquent language, and difcovered the great Mafter of the Univerfe in all his works.

In this temple no difcordant founds were heard, the children's voices were trained to a majeftic and fimple modulation; an organ was the only inftrument which accompanied them, and refembled altogether the finging of the immortal fpirits.

During the prayer, I faw no perfon coming in or going out, as they formerly did. No public beggar was feen to interrupt the piety of individuals, but the money-boxes for voluntary charities were placed in corners behind the doors; for this people knew how to beftow charitable donations without wifhing to be obferved; and thus they, without interruption, continued their acts of adoration, penetrated with a profound and religious refpect. The awful filence which prevailed in every part of the temple, and the facred terror with which I was deeply imprefled, gave my mind a very ftrong idea of the prefence of the Divinity.

The paftor of this pious flock made an exhortation, both fimple and eloquent, though not fo much from the ftile as from the matter it contained. He fpoke of the Supreme Being in a manner calculated to infpire the pureft love, and of men, he faid fuch things as filled them with the love of humanity, with meeknefs, and patience; he fought rather to move the heart than to difplay the depth of his learning; his difcourfe was that of a father to his children, advifing them upon thofe things which were proper to be done, and it made fo much more impression on their hearts, as it proceeded from the lips of a perfectly good man a man whose whole life was spent in the practice of all he preached I felt no weariness in hearing him, as I formerly felt at the sermons of our preachers, which were filled with metaphors, declamations, and, what was still worse, detached pieces of poetry, which ought never to be brought into such discourses

"In this manner," said my guide, " the public are accustomed to assemble every morning for prayers, which continue during an hour, never longer, for long forms of worship only cause the mind to become weary and inattentive after which the doors of this noble edifice are constantly shut We have very few religious festivals, but we have some civil, which tend to recreate and relax the people, without encouraging disorder or riot.

"Man ought never to be unemployed, nature has destined him for action; she never interrupts the course of her functions, but she is constant in her effectual and salutary operations for the good of mankind However, rest is necessary, and a time is fixed for cessation of labour, as also for the hour of prayer. You shall hear the form which is always used among us, and which is repeated and meditated by every one

"Oh! thou sole uncreated Being! intelligent Creator of
" this vast universe! which, in thy goodness, thou hast
" given to man, and permitted so weak a creature to receive
" the most valuable gifts from thy almighty hand, and to
" contemplate and reflect upon thy great and glorious
" works for him, not like the brute, survey them unmoved,
" but let him for ever pay the tribute of praise, of grati-
" tude, and of homage, to thy almighty power, and to thy
" wisdom. We admire thy marvellous works, we bless thy
" sovereign hand, which rules all things. We adore thee as
" a master, but we love thee as the Universal Father of all

" created

(73)

" created beings. Yes, thou art good as thou art great,
" all thy works proclaim thy goodness; but, above all,
" our hearts tell us how supremely good thou art.

" If, while in this mortal life, we are afflicted with any
" temporary evil, no doubt, it is that they are inevitable,
" and moreover, it is thy will, we, therefore, submit with
" confidence, and hope in thy infinite mercy, and, far from
" repining, we give thee thanks for having created us to
" know thee.

" Let every creature worship and honour thee according
" to the manner which his heart dictates, we set no limits
" to his zeal. Thou deignest not to enlighten us, thou
" only speakest by the transcendant voice of nature, we
" have no way of shewing our homage, but by worshiping
" and blessing thee, by presenting our supplications to thy
' throne, as weak miserable beings, who are in continual
" need of thy assisting arm.

" Deign, O eternal God! to disperse the clouds of
" darkness which hang before our eyes, and give us to
" know if thou art pleased to accept our feeble endeavours
" to praise thee, and if our manner of worshipping thee
" may prove acceptable, or if any other form, ancient or
" modern, be more agreeable, graciously enlighten us,
" and we will be faithful to thy dictates; but if thou art
" pleased with the faint tribute of praise which we offer to
" thy greatness, and to thy paternal tenderness, give us con-
" stancy to persevere in the sentiments which animate us.
" Oh, thou Great Preserver of all human kind! who, with
" one look, embracest the whole creation, kindle in the
" hearts of all mankind the same love of thee, in the same
" sentiments of thy greatness, that we may all, in bonds of
" unity and love, address to thee the same hymn of praise
" and gratitude.

" We

"We dare not offer any request to thee; we only ask thee to give us virtue and goodness. We are far from wishing to set limits to our lives; we know that whether thou leavest us on earth, or whether thou takest us to thee, we are still under thy all-seeing eye, and that thou knowest that which is best for us, thy inscrutable decrees we adore in silence, and with humility and submission we are resigned to thy will, but we dare to supplicate thee, that whether we are to quit this life by an easy or a painful death, thou wilt draw us to thee, who art the eternal source of all happiness. Our hearts sigh after thy divine presence, let this mortal garb pass away, and let us be received into thy bosom. The faint but glorious images we have here below of thy greatness serve but to increase our desire of seeing the fullness of it. Thy unnumbered benefits, for which thou seemest to have created us, have exalted and emboldened us to approach thy throne with confidence, and after having done so much in favour of thy creatures, the work of thy hands, we trust, thou wilt crown thy work, by conferring eternal happiness on thy children in thine everlasting kingdom."

After hearing this prayer, I could not help observing to my companion the opinion I formed of his religion, which, I told him, was that of the ancient patriarchs who worshipped God upon the summit of mountains in spirit and in truth. "You are very right," he said, "our religion is truly that of Adam, that of Enoch, and that of Elias, it is certainly the most ancient, and I believe the simplest religion to be the best. To worship God, respect our neighbour, attend to the voice of conscience, that inward monitor and judge, who constantly is on the watch within us, and never to stifle this heavenly secret voice, for every thing else is imposture, deceit, and error, this is true religion. Our priests, far from

pretending

pretending to be exclusively inspired of God, call themselves our equals, acknowledge that they are, like ourselves, immersed in darkness, and have no other guide but the inward ray of light which God has deigned to implant within us, they point out, without oftentation, without tyrannic pride, that which ought to be observed, and are indulgent to the faults of their fellow-creatures. Our morals are pure and simple, we have no violent controversies, consequently we have no fanatics, no superstition, and no impiety, we have discovered the happy method of always being at peace, for which we sincerely thank the Great Author of all Good."

—— "You worship God," said I, "but do you admit the immortality of the soul? what is your opinion on this great and impenetrable secret? all the philosophers have endeavoured to discover it. Both the wise men and the fool have given their opinion on this head. It has produced innumerable poetic pieces, and a variety of systems, it seems to have enflamed the imaginations of all legislators. What sentiments are entertained of it in this enlightened century?"

To these questions he answered after the following manner. "We need only employ our sight in order to be filled with adoration towards the Great Author of Creation, and we need only reflect upon ourselves in order to feel that we have something within us that lives, feels, thinks, and determines. We believe that our soul is distinct from matter, that it is by its nature intelligent, we do not reason on this subject, for we love to believe every thing which ennobles human nature. That system which tends to exalt it most becomes the most valuable to us, and we think those ideas which dignify and honour the creatures of God, can never be false, by adopting the most sublime plan, we do not deceive ourselves, and we

enter

enter into the defigns of our Creator. Incredulity is the effect of weakness, but an intelligent being confirms his faith, by entertaining the moſt exalted ideas of his maker, and of all his works. Why ſhould we debaſe ourſelves by ſuppoſing we are to fall into annihilation, while we conſtantly feel that we have wings capable of ſoaring upwards God himſelf, and that nothing can oppoſe this noble ambition. Were it poſſible that we had deceived ourſelves as to the ſyſtem of nature, it might be ſaid that men had invented a more beautiful order of things than that which exiſted; but it is impoſſible that the ſyſtem of annihilation ſhould proceed from God—ſuch a plan would ſet limits, not only to his ſovereign power, but alſo to his ſovereign goodneſs.

"We believe that every ſoul has the ſame eſſence, but that they differ in their qualities. The ſoul of man, and that of an animal, are equally immaterial; but the former is by many degrees nearer to perfection, and therein conſiſts its ſuperiority, which, however, is liable to change.

"We likewiſe believe that the planets and all other celeſtial bodies are inhabited; but that the objects of ſenſe, and the manner of feeling, is different in every one. This unbounded magnificence, this chain of an infinity of worlds, this radiant circle, was deſtined to enter into the vaſt plan of creation, and theſe ſuns, thoſe ſpacious worlds, ſo beautiful and ſo diverſified, appear to us as ſo many habitations all prepared for man; they are all correſpondent and ſubordinate to each other, and will ſerve as ſo many gradations by which the human ſoul will aſcend as upon a glorious ladder, till it ariſes, at laſt, to the higheſt ſummit of perfection. In this journey it never loſes the recollection of what it has ſeen or heard, it preſerves every former idea, which is a treaſure by which it is always accompanied. If, during this mortal exiſtence, the ſoul has been enabled to ſoar towards the diſcovery of any ſublime truth, we are encouraged to believe that it afterwards receives the reward moſt calculated to confer everlaſting happineſs, by overleaping the ſeveral inhabited worlds, which remain beneath, and is the abode of leſs active and leſs energetic ſouls, and by aſcending rapidly, in conſequence of the virtues and ſublime knowledge it has acquired. For inſtance, the ſoul of Newton, by its own activity, flew up towards the heavenly ſpheres, which he had diſcovered and poiſed. It were unjuſt, therefore, to ſuppoſe that the breath of death could have power to deſtroy a genius ſo truly eminent. Such a deſtruction would be more afflicting and more inconceivable than that of the whole material world. It would be equally abſurd to ſay that the ſoul of ſuch a man could ever be upon a level with that of a being who had paſſed his whole mortal life in the enjoyments of ſenſe, and plunged in ſtupid inactivity. Indeed it were uſeleſs for a ſoul to aim at perfection if no reward is to enſue, if it is not exalted above its preſent ſtate in a future exiſtence, after having enjoyed a foretaſte of that felicity which is the reſult of a conſtant contemplation and exerciſe of every virtue. Yes, we feel the powerful influence of an intimate voice, beyond the power of all ſceptical objections, which tells our ſoul ' to extend all its faculties, to deſpiſe death, which can have no power over it, and to improve the life which is given us by intellectual purſuits.'

"As for thoſe degenerate ſouls, which have debaſed themſelves by remaining in vice and inactivity, they will return to the ſame ſtate from which they began to be, and thus fall back into a retrogradation of their firſt courſe. They are deſtined to remain a long time on the ſad banks

(78)

of annihilation, to follow the propensities of sense and matter, and to leave a vile brutal race to fill their place, and while those sublime souls expand their lofty genius, and elevate themselves towards the divine uncreated light, these plunge still deeper in darkness, from whence spring the faintest rays of existence, a mere consciousness of misery, for instance, a monarch, who may have debased his noble origin, will be transformed into a mole, a minister of state will animate the vile body of a venomous serpent, inhabiting pestiferous marshes, while the author, whom he perhaps disdained, or rather whom he would not acknowledge, has gained a glorious seat among those intelligent beings who were the friends of mankind

"Pythagoras has discovered this equality of souls, he had conceived the transmigration from one body to another, but he taught that these souls remained constantly in the same orbit, and that they never left their own planet. Our metempsychosis is much more rational, and far superior to that of the ancients

"Those noble and generous spirits, who have sought for and promoted the happiness of their fellow-creatures, will find in death a glorious and shining path, leading them to everlasting bliss. "Well, what think you of our system?"—"It charms me, for it neither contradicts the power or the goodness of God. That the soul of man should, by a progressive course, ascend up into different worlds, and visit an infinity of other spheres all this appears highly answerable to the dignity of the great Monarch of Creation, who displays all his domains, and the works of his hands, to his creatures, whom he has made to contemplate them."

"Yes, my brother," he replied with enthusiasm, "this is a truly interesting picture, to see all these glorious suns

thus

thus explored, to see these happy souls, enriching and unceasingly perfecting themselves in their course, wherein they make unnumbered discoveries, and becoming more sublime as they approach nearer to the Supreme Being, where they acquire a more perfect knowledge of him, and love him with an enlightened love, immersing in the fullness of his greatness Yes, thou hast cause to rejoice, O man! thou hastenest from one marvellous work to another a prospect ever new, ever miraculous, awaits thee thy hopes are infinitely great and glorious. thou wilt traverse the whole immense expanse of nature, until thou art lost in that infinite Being from whom thou tracest thy lofty origin."—"But the wicked," cried I, "those who have transgressed against all law, natural and divine, who have steeled their hearts against the voice of pity, those who have shed innocent blood, kings, who have reigned for themselves only, what will become of them? Though I am not inclined either to hatred or revenge, I would gladly build a hell with my own hands, and in it I would hurl some cruel souls, who have often filled me with indignation at the sight of the various afflictions they have caused, both to the feeble and to the just."—"It is not given," he answered, ' to weakness like our's, subject as we are to a variety of passions, to pronounce on the manner in which God will punish the wicked, but it is most certain that they will feel the weight of his justice. That those beings who have been perfidious, cruel, or indifferent to the sufferings of others, will be for ever banished his presence Never will the soul of Socrates, or of Marcus Aurelius, meet that of the impious Nero, for they must always remain at infinite distances Thus far we may dare to aver, but it does not belong to us to fix the weight which will fill the eternal

nal balance of divine justice. We believe that those faults which have not totally clouded the human understanding, that the heart, which has not debased itself, that kings, who have not believed themselves gods, may in time be purified, by improving their species, during a long course of years, and that they will descend into other spheres, where physical evil will predominate, and be the useful scourge, which will make them feel their dependance, and how much they themselves stand in need of mercy, and this will rectify every delusion of pride but if they humble themselves beneath the chastising hand of God, if they follow the light of reason, which dictates submission, if they acknowledge how very far they still continue from that perfection which they might acquire, if they use every exertion to attain it, then their pilgrimage will be infinitely abridged, they may die, while they are still in their prime, and be lamented, while they, though rejoicing at their departure from this sad abode of sorrow, will pity the fate of those who are doomed to remain behind upon this terraqueous globe, from which they are delivered. Therefore he who fears death knows not what it is he dreads, his terrors are the offspring of ignorance, and that ignorance is one of his punishments for his faults. Perhaps the most guilty will be punished by the loss of liberty they will not be annihilated, for the very idea of annihilation is repugnant to nature. There can be no annihilation under a God who is Creator, Preserver, and Restorer. Let not the wicked hope to shelter themselves by falling into nought, they will always be pursued by that all-seeing, all penetrating eye. Persecutors of all denominations will stupidly vegetate in the lowest class of existence, they will incessantly be given up to new destruction,

which

which will continually make them fensible of their misfortune and dependence. But God alone knows the term of their punishment, or the time of their release.

~~~~

CHAP. XX.

He asks no lot reach cometh to deck his brow,
No golden mitre has bounded with claim

"BEHOLD," said my guide, "a living faint now walking by, that man in a simple clothing of violet stuff, supporting himself upon a staff, whose gait and look neither proclaim oftentation nor affected modesty! it is our prelate."—"What! your prelate on foot?"— "Yes," said my guide, "after the example of the first apostle. A sedan chair has lately been given him, which he never uses but in cases of the greatest necessity. His revenue is almost all distributed among the poor he does not inquire, ere he deals out his benefits, whether the object of them is attached to *his* private opinions or to those of another; but he divides his succours to the relief of all the unfortunate indiscriminately. they are men, and that is a sufficient motive. He is neither obstinate nor fanatical, nor a persecutor he takes no advantage of the sacred authority, with which he is invested, to usurp more than belongs to his charge, or to place himself upon a level with the throne. His countenance is always serene, the perfect index of a gentle, equal, and peaceable soul, which is never betrayed into any kind of warmth, but the active zeal for doing good. He often says to the persons he meets in his walks from one friendly visit to another, 'Remember, my friends, what St Paul says, charity surpasseth faith. Be compassionate, be benevo-

G   lent,

lent, and you will have accomplished the law. Reprove your neighbour if he errs, but let it be without pride or bitterness. Do not persecute any one on account of their opinions, and beware of preferring yourself to him whom you witness in the commission of a fault, for to-morrow you may be as guilty as he is, perhaps even more so. When you preach, let it be by your own example. Beware of fanaticism, it has already produced too many evils by its obstinacy, therefore we ought to dread and prevent even the smallest appearances of it. It is a monster which seems at first to flatter the human mind, and to elevate the soul which admits it, but very soon it displays cunning, perfidy, and cruelty. It tramples every virtue under foot, and soon becomes the most terrible scourge of all mankind.'"

"But tell me," said I, "who is that magistrate who speaks to him with so much friendship and cordiality?"— "It is one of the fathers of the country, it is the chief of the senate, who is inviting him to dine with him. During their sober and short repast, their conversation will often run upon subjects highly becoming their respective functions in life, such as the best means of relieving the miseries of the poor indigent, of the widow, and of the orphan. These are the interests which bring them together, and which excite all their zeal and benevolence but they never waste time in the frivolous discussion of those antique and puerile prerogatives, which have been the subject of contention among the gravest men of your time."

CHAP XXI.

No mist obstructs thy piercing sight,
Thou bid'st the mind her greatness know,
Soaring thou point'st to realms of light,
And scorn'st to rest below

"BUT who pray is that young man whom I see at a little distance, surrounded by the gazing multitude? How every movement of his limbs bespeaks the joy of his soul His eyes glisten, and his whole countenance is animated. What can have happened to him? Where does he come from?" My guide thus gravely answered "He has just been initiated, I will explain my meaning although we admit very few ceremonies in our religion, we have one which answers to that which you denominated your FIRST COMMUNION. When a young man has attained those years which are commonly called years of maturity, we begin to observe all his actions, we study his propensities, his character we strictly examine in every point of view. If he appears to discover a taste for solitary places, calculated to inspire reflection, if he is observed to fix his eyes with eager emotion towards the vast expanse of the firmament, contemplating with delightful ecstacy that azure curtain, which seems ready to open to his view, then there is no more time to be lost, it proves that his reason has attained a state of maturity, and that he can receive with advantage the demonstration of the marvels which the Creator has operated

"We then fix upon one of those nights, when the firmament is clear and serene, and the whole assemblage of the celestial bodies shine with unrivalled lustre; the young man, accompanied by his relations and his friends,

(84)

is led to the obfervatory here we fuddenly apply a telefcope to his eyes, we bring down to his view the planets Mars, Saturn, Jupiter, with all the other immenfe floating bodies, all in due order in the regions of fpace thus we open to him the infinite abyfs, all thofe blazing funs are brought to his aftonifhed fight, and a paftor, by whom we are always accompanied at this auguft ceremony, fpeaks to him after the following manner, in a voice both awful and commanding 'Young man! behold the God of the Univerfe, who reveals himfelf to you in the midft of his glorious works. Adore the Creator of thofe worlds, that glorious Being, whofe extenfive power is far beyond the reach of our fight, or even of our imagination Adore that Almighty God, whofe refplendent Majefty is difplayed in thofe heavenly bodies, who invariably obey his laws. While you contemplate the prodigies created by his hand, learn to underftand with what munificence he can reward the heart which raifes its wifhes towards him, never forget that, amidft his moft perfect works, man (being endowed with the faculty of feeing and of conceiving them, though only in a fmall degree) holds the firft rank, and that, being the child of God, he ought to prove himfelf worthy of his high origin'"

"Then the fcene changes a microfcope is brought to him, a new world is difplayed, more aftonifhing, and, if poffible, more marvellous than the former. Thefe living atoms, which his eye now perceives for the firft time, which move in their inconceivable diminutivenefs, endowed with the fame organs as thofe which diftinguifh beings of the greateft magnitude, manifeft to his aftonifhed fenfes an undifcovered attribute of the great Creator's intelligence and power.

"The

(85)

"The pastor then continues in the same tone as before ' Feeble mortals as we are, placed between two points of infinitude, oppressed on all sides under the weight of divine greatness, let us adore in reverent silence the same hand which has kindled so many blazing suns, and has imprinted life and motion to so many imperceptible atoms. Undoubtedly that piercing eye, which has formed the delicate structure of the heart, of the nerves and fibres of the hand worm, will read the very inmost recesses of our hearts. What most secret thought can be hidden from his sight, before whom the *Via lactea*, or Milky Way, is no more than the eye of the mite. Let all our thoughts be worthy of that Being who knows and observes them. How often during the day the heart might spring forward toward its Maker, and there imbibe new life and strength! Alas! all the time allotted for our life cannot be better employed than in erecting an altar to him in the deep recesses of our souls, where we may offer continual supplication and praise to him.'

"The young man, moved and astonished, receives a double impression in the same instant, he weeps with joy; his ardent curiosity is inflamed at every step he takes, in these new worlds, and is insatiable, all his words are a hymn of admiration, his heart palpitates with surprize and respect, and in these moments can you conceive with what true energy of soul, with what truth he pays adoration to the omnipotent Being? How he is animated with his presence! How that telescope extends and aggrandises his ideas, and renders them worthy of an inhabitant of this astonishing universe! It excludes all terrestrial ambition, and preserves the mind from all secret enmities and jealousies, he cherishes all men, animated with the breath of life, and feels himself the brother of every living being.

"Hence-

"Henceforward this young man will place all his glory and pleasure in acquiring every day more knowledge respecting this prodigious collection of miracles. He thinks less meanly of himself since he has enjoyed the precious advantage of contemplating such wonders. He says to himself, 'God has now manifested himself to me, I have visited Saturn, Jupiter, the Georgium Sidus, and the vast multitude of stars in the *Via lactea*, I feel my existence ennobled, since God has deigned to establish a relation between my nothingness and his incomprehensible greatness O! how happy I am now, having received an increase of life in the increase of knowledge! I can now feel some faint idea of the destiny which awaits the virtuous man! O most omnipotent God! let me adore thee, let me love thee eternally.'

"He often returns to enjoy the delightful study of these sublime objects from this day he is initiated among thinking beings, but he scrupulously keeps the secret, that he may not deprive others of the same degree of pleasure and surprise which he has himself experienced. On the day which is consecrated to the praises of the Creator, it is a most edifying sight to see these numerous worshippers of the Deity upon the observatory, falling on their knees, their eyes fixed to a telescope, and their hearts lifted up in prayer, soaring up in spirit towards the great disposer of these pompous miracles Then we sing hymns which are composed in the vulgar tongue, by the best composers of the nation, they are sung by every person and understood by all, and they are fully expressive of the wisdom and clemency of the Deity We cannot conceive how so many nations could, in former ages, call upon God in a language they did not understand, these people were either very absurd or enthusiastically zealous

"It frequently happens that a young man is transported with enthusiasm, and expresses aloud to the whole assembly the sentiments with which his heart is inspired; he communicates his ardour to the coldest hearts, and enflames them with the same vehement love of God with which his own is replete. At these times the eternal God seems to descend amongst us and to listen to his children, who mutually exert all their powers of praising and exalting him, and speak of his clemency and his paternal care over us with gratitude and love

"Our philosophers and astronomers reveal all their discoveries to us in these days of festival and rejoicing; they seem like the heralds of the Divinity, and make us feel his presence in every object, even in the most inanimate. Every created thing they tell us is filled with God, and every object is filled with his praise Thus we even doubt the existence of one single atheist in the whole extensive kingdom not that he has any cause to fear making a discovery of his sentiments, for we should pity him too much to inflict any other punishment upon him than the shame he must naturally feel for them. We should simply banish him from among us, if he publicly persisted in being the obstinately declared enemy of truths so palpable, so consoling and salutary, but, ere we dismissed him from the society of rational beings, we should expose to his view a full experimental course of natural philosophy, it would then be impossible for him to deny the demonstrative ground whereon to anchor evidence, which this profound study would present. This science, which has discovered such astonishing and yet such simple affinities, such accumulated wonders, which were lying dormant within its deep recesses, and are now exposed to light. In short, nature is so enlightened, and our knowledge so enlarged, that he who could deny the existence of an intelligent Creator would be regarded, not only as a madman, but as a perverse and wicked being, for whom the whole nation would mourn as for the most miserable of mankind.

"Heaven be praised, as no one among us has the rage of wishing to be distinguished by sentiments and opinions diametrically opposite to the universal judgment of all men, we are all agreed on this important point, which, being once established, I shall have no difficulty in making you understand, that every principle of the purest morality are deduced from this solid basis

"It was thought impossible, in your time, to establish a religion truly spiritual, and founded on truth however, you were greatly mistaken, it was an outrage to human nature, and an opinion highly derogatory to the excellence of the Supreme Being, nor could it be very difficult to conceive a true idea of the divine essence, for *it is the soul which feels the existence of a God*, for why should falsehood be more natural to man than truth? Was it so very difficult to banish those impostors who made a traffic of sacred things? Who pretended they were the mediators between the Divinity and man, and who disseminated prejudices still more vile and despicable than the *gold for which they sold them?*

"In short, Idolatry, that antique monster whom painters, statuaries, and poets, have vied with envious emulation to deify, for the misfortune and blindness of all mankind, she herself is fallen, and is our most glorious triumph Our religion has for its basis the unity of one God, who is a spiritual and uncreated being there is but one sun to enlighten the whole universe, and there need but one illumined source to spread the light of truth in the human understanding. Every other foreign support and fictitious doctrine only served to stifle the true

light,

light, and misled it by a false one, this was the deceitful *ignis fatuus* by which many have been thrown into labyrinths of doubt and perplexity, and which has given to many a false energy, which never went further than the imagination; it was a state of mental intoxication, which was dangerous, as it was erroneous. It was this mistaken spirit of religion which gave rise to fanaticism; different kinds of worship were prescribed, and the liberty of man, deprived of its dearest privilege, justly revolted against its oppressors. We abhor that kind of tyranny, we require no sentiments from the heart but those it can feel; and can there exist any capable of steeling themselves against those piercing and energetic flashes of truth which are presented to us for our real happiness?

"When we misrepresent the light of reason, and suppose her capable of being a doubtful or deceitful guide, we attack the infinitely perfect author and source of it, whose divine law, proclaimed throughout all the works of nature, is preferable to all those fictitious religions invented by priests. The best proof that can be adduced of their truth or falsehood may be derived from their fatal consequences; they may be compared to a tottering edifice, which is perpetually in need of props; but the law of nature is a strong and immoveable tower, which produces no discord but peace and equality. Those wicked knaves, who have represented the eternal God of truth, under the form of their own passions, and have given the appellation of virtue to the most atrocious actions, are guilty of having plunged into the horrors of atheism many thousand souls, whose sensibility found it more consistent to annihilate every idea of a Supreme Being than to believe him to be a formidable and barbarous avenger.

"

"As we, on the contrary, raise our souls to the Great Creator, confiding in his goodness, so strikingly impressed over all his works, the shadows of this life, the transitory evils which afflict us, sorrow or death, do not terrify us; undoubtedly all these things are necessary and useful, and productive of our future felicity, though we know not how or when, but there must be some limits to our knowledge, we must not know the secrets of God therefore, let the whole universe be dissolved, why should we fear? Whatever revolution may happen, we shall fly to the bosom of the eternal God, the author of all nature."

CHAP. XXII

*Now favour'd mortal, no ——
To forthe th' captive state,
I ope the book of fate,
Mark what its reg'sters u fold!*

ON my leaving the temple I was conducted to a place not far distant where a monument had been recently erected, which my guide requested I would attentively observe it was all of marble, and well calculated to excite in me the keenest curiosity I longed to pierce through the veil, and to peruse the tale conveyed under each emblematic figure with which it was environed, and my guide refused to explain it to me, that I might have the pleasure of discovering it myself.

My attention was particularly arrested by the chief figure of the whole group, which, by the sweet majesty of her aspect, by her noble form, and the surrounding attributes of peace and concord I immediately knew to be that of Humanity Around her were several statues of women in the attitude of kneeling, with every expression of grief and remorse. These emblems, alas! were not difficult to penetrate they represented all those unhappy nations who were imploring the pardon of Humanity for all the cruel injuries they had committed against her during twenty centuries.

Among the most conspicuous of these, the figure of France was particularly striking, she was on her knees supplicating forgiveness for the horrible massacre of the night of St Bartholomew, for the cruel revocation of the edict of Nantes, and for the persecution of those worthy men who sprung from that city. Her aspect was so mild that I should not have supposed her capable of such enormities. The next figure of consequence was that of England, who was in the act of abjuring her fanaticism, and the factions of the two roses, she was holding out her hand to Philosophy, and promising never to shed any human blood, save that of tyrants The figure of Holland was expressing her detestation for the factions of Gomar and of Arminius, and her sorrow for the execution of the virtuous Barnevelt. Germany was standing aloof, her haughty looks relaxing into melancholy and horror while she perused the historic page of her intestine divisions, of her enthusiastic furors and theologic rage, which had always been most singularly contrasted by her natural phlegmatic character. Poland viewed with indignation the retrospect of her despicable confederates, which, even in my time, had renewed the atrocities of the crusades The figure of Spain, more guilty than either of her sister kingdoms, was in the attitude of mournful despair lamenting her sordid avarice, which had caused her to imbrue her hands in the blood of thirty millions of the hapless inhabitants of the new world, and to pursue the deplorable remains of a thousand nations into the recesses of the

rocks,

rocks, or through the impervious forests, teaching the wild beasts of the woods (though less ferocious than themselves) to lap the blood of men . . . . . In vain, however, were all her supplications for pardon, all her expressions of despair, it was impossible that Spain should ever obtain forgiveness, who had injured humanity in every point, had she committed no other cruelty but condemning a set of fellow-creatures to work in the mines, this alone would have pronounced sentence against her

The statuary had represented several mutilated slaves, who, raising their eyes to heaven, called down vengeance upon their oppressors, the expression of their countenance excited sentiments of horror and dread, so nearly they resembled nature, being carved in the sanguine veined marble which retraced the memory of atrocities which can never be forgotten

Afar off in the back ground, Italy (the original cause of so many evils, the primitive source of those furors which overspread the whole world) was discovered prostrated, with her head bowed to the earth, smothering in her bosom the ardent torch of excommunication She dared not even approach to solicit her pardon I wished to contemplate her form, and to examine that part of her countenance which could be seen, but on a nearer approach, I found that her whole face had recently been burnt up by a thunderbolt, and that she was wholly disfigured and blackened by the lightning.

Humanity, amidst this groupe of women, seemed to raise her benign and radiant countenance with increased indulgence, and contemplated their penitent humility with complacency I observed that the sculptor had given her the features of that free and courageous nation who had been the first to shake off the galling chains of tyranny. Her head was adorned with the cap of the ever great and justly-celebrated TELL, which was a diadem far more respectable than any ever worn by the greatest monarch. She sweetly smiled upon Philosophy, her sister, whose pure white hands were extended towards heaven, to which she also raised her eyes with the expression of the purest love.

From the contemplation of this piece I was led to another at a short distance. It was the figure of an AMERICAN raised upon a pedestal, his head was bare, his eyes expressed a haughty courage, his attitude was noble and commanding, and his arm was extended and pointing to the shattered remains of twenty sceptres which lay at his feet, over the pedestal this inscription was engraven TO THE AVENGER OF THE NEW WORLD.

I could not refrain an exclamation of joy and surprise that escaped me.—" There, said my guide, with an ardour equal to my own, "you see that Nature has at last created that astonishing man, that immortal being who was to deliver the new world from the most atrocious and insulting tyranny, his lofty genius, his noble audacity, his patience, his fortitude, his virtuous and laudable desire of revenge, have been rewarded. He has disolved the chains of his countrymen. Unnumbered slaves, oppressed under the most odious slavery, seemed only to wait his signal to become so many heroes. It was accomplished, and the effect was more quick and more violent than that of a torrent, when with a sudden burst it subdues every opposing force, or even that of the electric fire issuing from the thundercloud. In the same instant they all shed the blood of their inhuman tyrants, French, Spanish, English, Dutch, and Portuguese, they have all fallen, by fire, sword, or poison, the victims of their own inhumanity. The American soil has been drenched with that blood for which it had long thirsted, and the spirits of those departed heroes who had been basely murdered by

these

these inhuman Europeans appeared satisfied with the just atonement

"The inhabitants have recovered their indisputable rights, the heroic avenger of his country's wrongs, who has also restored freedom to many other nations in the new world, is, by the former, revered as a god, and by the latter is a beneficent being, worthy of all their gratitude and all their love; they have presented crowns and sceptres to him, but he despises them all. He came amongst them like a tempestuous blast, extending itself over the habitations of the guilty to sink them in destruction; he was the exterminating angel to whom God had committed his avenging sword, he has proved, that, soon or late, cruelty will be punished, and that the eternal Being reserves those exalted souls, in whom courage and goodness are blended, for great and awful occasions, when he finds them upon earth to restore that just equilibrium which the iniquity of ferocious ambition has been able to destroy."

CHAP. XXIII

Did ever earth a scene display,
More glorious to the eye of day,
Than millions with according mind,
Who claim the rights of human kind

I WAS so well pleased with my conductor that I was in continual apprehension lest he should leave me. It was now the dinner hour, and being far distant from my own house, and having survived all my acquaintance, I was looking about for some tavern or eating-house, where
I might

I might invite him to dine with me, in return for his politeness and complaisance towards me, but we went through several streets without meeting even one

At length I asked my friend what was become of all the cooks, tavern-keepers, and wine-merchants, who could be, at the same time, united and divided in the same sort of business, always at variance, and yet so numerous as to exceed in number every other business in this great city. " Yes," said my guide, " that was another, among the many errors of your civilization. In these houses a mortal adulteration of wine was tolerated, pernicious to those who were in health as well as to those who were sick. The poor, that is the three-fourths of the inhabitants, who had not the means of sending for the neat wines of the country, driven, by thirst and the necessity of re-invigorating their spirits, to these houses of refreshment, found in them a flow poison, which by degrees undermined the very best constitutions, instead of that wholesome beverage, the moderate use of which was so calculated to restore health to the sick, and strength to the weak "—" Alas !" said I, " what was to be done ? The duties on importation were so oppressive that they even exceeded the price of the commodity It might have been supposed, that the use of wine was forbidden by the law, or that the soil and climate of France was like that of England however, to these people it was of little consequence whether a whole city was poisoned, provided the leases of their farms increased from year to year. Thus, while whole families were ruined by their specious paper money, the health of individuals, on the other hand, was impaired by the pernicious quality of the wine, which, however, w is not experienced by the rich, as they, by the means of bribery and corruption, were in the habit of eluding the duty therefore it was a matter of no mo-

ment

ment to those whether the populace diminished or not, for this was the appellation bestowed on the labouring or trading part of the nation."—"How was it possible that these rich, as you call them, should overlook customs so pernicious and so fatal to society? What! could they allow a dangerous poison to be publickly sold in the city? and where then was the exactitude of the magistrate who ought ever to keep a watchful eye over the public welfare? Ah! barbarous people! With us, the wine-merchant, or retailer, who may be accused of the least adulteration, if he is found guilty, he is put to death. But, on the other hand, we have exterminated all that race of tax-gatherers who corrupted all nature's gifts. All our wines are brought to market in their true natural state, and the citizen of Paris, either rich or poor, may drink a glass of good and salutary wine, to the health of his king, whom he dearly loves, and who is grateful for the esteem and love of all his subjects."—"And pray, is bread dear among you?"—"It seldom varies, but almost always remains at the same price, because we have had the wise precaution to establish public granaries, which are always stored with corn, in case of want, and because we are not so imprudent as to sell it to foreigners, lest we should have occasion to purchase again at a double price, three months after. The interests of the cultivator and of the consumer have been balanced together, and they are both gainers, not that exportation is prohibited, for it is thought advantageous to the nation, but it is restrained within judicious bounds. We have an enlightened an upright man at the head of those affairs, whose duty it is to keep the just equilibrium between our advantage or disadvantage, and besides, the kingdom is divided by canals, calculated to facilitate a free circulation. We have united the river Soane to the Moselle and the Loire, by which we have completed a new junction

of

of two feas, infinitely more effential to commerce than the former by this means the treafures of commerce are carried from Amfterdam to Nantes, and from Rouen to Marfeilles We have alfo finifhed the canal of Provence, the only conveniency in which that beautiful province (favoured by the fun's kindeft rays) was deficient It was in vain that a citizen of genius, and zealous for the public good, offered his ufeful difcoveries and his courage to execute the plans he had formed this generous man was fuffered to dance attendance during twenty years, and to remain in a ftate of inaction, while a fet of frivolous workmen were employed in edifices equally extravagant as they were abfurd and ufelefs In fhort, our lands are fo well cultivated, the condition of the ploughman is become fo honourable, and the fpirit of liberty and good order prevails fo univerfally throughout all our villages and country towns, that if any man in power dared to attempt taking any advantage of his power, to introduce monopoly or innovations of any kind, he would immediately feel the hand of juftice, who would reftrain his temerity Juftice is no longer an empty name as it was in your time, her fword is fufpended over every guilty head, and with more feverity, if poffible, upon the wealthy and great than upon the middling clafs, for we think the former ever more inclined to rapine and oppreffion than the latter."—" I am delighted with all that you tell me upon this important fubject Pray continue to relate every particular. I find you have adopted the wife method of ftoring up your corn in magazines, which is the only fure means of preventing public calamity, in my time many ferious errors were committed on this fubject, much time was paffed in calculations and idle reafoning, but the abufes of power were never remedied Some well-difpofed writers produced theories of good order and rational fyftems, and

H upon

upon thefe fprings every thing was expected to be fet in motion. One fubject in particular produced the moft ferious debates, I mean the famous law of exportation, and during thefe difputes the people were ftarving."--"You ought to thank Providence, who watches over this kingdom, for without that protection you muft have been reduced to the grafs of the fields. But the Supreme Being has had mercy upon you, and forgave you, becaufe you knew not what you were doing. Thus far error is ufeful.

"Among us there is a profeffion which is common to every citizen: it is agriculture. The women, as the weaker veffels, and being by nature deftined to the domeftic concerns, never cultivate the ground, but employ themfelves in fpinning, or other proper occupations; for men would blufh to fet them to any thing unworthy of them.

"There are three things which we particularly honour among us: firft, having children, fecondly, fowing a field, and, thirdly, building a houfe: for this reafon the workmen are well treated, and not expected to work above their ftrength. They are not feen before fun-rife fatiguing themfelves till fun-fet, and with exhaufted ftrength in vain implore for a fmall portion of thofe bleffings their hands have produced. Could there be a more cruel and oppreffive condition than that of the common labourers, who returned from their hard labours to a wretched home, where their children were pining for want, and where they filled the fhort fpace of their exiftence with mourning and lamentation? There was no flavery equal to that continual ftruggle they were obliged to exert againft their petty tyrants, who exacted the heavieft tribute out of their poor poffeffions, and plundered them in cafe of inability to pay. The exceffive contempt with which thefe poor honeft people

were

were treated, hardened their hearts against every sentiment, even that of despair, and the poor ploughman, in his deplorable condition, debased and degraded as he was, scarcely felt any distinction between himself and the oxen with which he furrowed the ground.

"Our fertile fields now echo with songs of joy, every father of a family sets the example, the task is moderate, and when it is completed joy recommences. Intervals of rest render their zeal more active, and their leisure hours are indulged with dances and rural entertainments. Formerly, it was the custom to go to towns in quest of pleasure and mirth, but now it is sought for in the villages, where every face is clothed in smiles. Labour no longer wears its former hideous and disgusting aspect, because it does not appear to be the appendage of slaves, they are invited to their duty by gentle words, and this treatment sweetens and facilitates every difficulty. In short, as we no longer suffer a prodigious number of idle members, who, like stagnated humours, impeded the circulation of specie throughout the political body, idleness is totally banished, and every individual enjoys some moments of calm and repose no class of people find themselves oppressed by supporting the other in superfluities. Besides, we have no monks, we have a limited number of priests, of servants, and of valets, and we allow none of those ornamental workmen, whose labours were only consecrated to the idle gratifications of luxury and grandeur. A few hours of daily labour from each inhabitant of the country, assisted by their servants, is sufficient, and bring forth that plentiful stock of provisions with which you will see our markets loaded, and what we cannot consume, we send abroad, which we barter for other merchandise. You see we have a great abundance of every thing necessary for life. The rich no longer monopolize every thing, while the poor are starving. We exclude every fear of not enjoying a sufficiency we are not acquainted with that insatiable avidity which formerly caused the people to buy up three times as much as they could possibly consume We detest lavishers

" If nature is less favourable to us one year than another, we have taken precautions, therefore we never see any sufferers, the granaries are opened, and the wise forecast of man prudently overcomes the inclemencies of the weather and the wrath of heaven Our labouring men are not fed with unhealthy food, but the poor and the opulent all eat the same bread, and if we ever hear that any are in want of that necessary article, we feel it our duty to relieve him Therefore the poorest are freed from all anxiety as to their wants, they know not what it is to be disturbed from the slumber of a few hours, where they enjoyed a temporary oblivion of all their cares by the horrors of famine they can awake without accusing the sun of adding another day to their misery, and while they satisfy the wants of nature, they are in no apprehension of conveying a slow poison within their veins. Those who possess riches employ them in making new and useful experiments, which may serve to enter into the depths of science, or to carry some art to perfection, they erect some noble edifice, they distinguish themselves by some honourable enterprise Instead of expending all their fortunes in gratifying the extravagancies of a concubine, or of exposing it to the cast of a die, it flows with moderation, and adds respectability to the owner, therefore they never find themselves envied for their possessions the public, on the contrary, implore a blessing on the generous hands who are dispensers of the gifts of Providence, and who fulfil its designs in raising such useful monuments.

" But

"But we are struck with horror when we reflect on the morals of the rich in your time; their souls were more vile than the filth of the streets. With gold in their hands, and the basest meanness in their hearts, they had formed a conspiracy against the poor; they took every advantage which their superiority gave them over these unfortunate beings; they had no regard for their laborious exertions, nor did they ever reward the long services of their youth to place them above the dread of want in their old age. These omissions were overlooked by the laws, which only acted in conjunction with the wealthy, while the poor alone were made to feel their rigour. As when a house is burning, the flames spread and destroy its neighbouring house, so did these wealthy owners of estates and farms devour the limits of their poor powerless neighbour; but if these ever dared to pluck an apple from off their grounds, oh! it was a crime which merited death, or the total ruin of their families. . . ." Alas! what answer could I make to such accusations? I was ashamed and confounded, and, with my eyes fixed to the ground, I fell into a profound reverie, and walked on, buried in my own thoughts. "You shall have other causes for reflection," said my guide, "you may now take notice, since your eyes are fixed to the ground, that the blood of animals no longer flows in rivulets through the streets, which was a barbarous custom of your times, well calculated to inspire ideas of slaughter and massacre. The air of our city is preserved from those cadaverous odours which engendered so many distempers. Cleanliness is one of the least equivocal marks of good order and public harmony; you see how it reigns in every place. We have had the salubrious, and no less moral precaution, to establish the slaughter-houses out of the city. If nature has condemned us to feed on the flesh of animals, we ought at least to spare ourselves

(102)

the prospect of their death.* The trade of butcher is not practised by any of the natives, but given up entirely to men of foreign nations, whose fate or circumstances have forced to become exiles they enjoy the protection of the laws, but they are not admitted within the class of citizens None of us would practise that sanguinary trade, we should insensibly influence the characters of our fellow-citizens, and make them shut their hearts against every natural impression of communication and love, which you know is the best and most precious of the endowments of nature."

~~~~

CHAP. XXIV.

*While sleep oppresses the tir'd limbs, the mind
Plays without weight, and wantons unconfin'd*

WITH unaltered good-nature and complacency my guide continued walking with me, and said, "You must by this time be inclined to refresh yourself, your walk must have created you an appetite, let us go into this house. . .." I withdrew a few paces, thinking he had made a mistake "Where are you going," said I, "this is undoubtedly the abode of some prince; do you not see the escutcheon over the door ¿"—"Yes," said my friend, "it is the residence of a prince, and that of a good prince too, for he always keeps three open tables, one for himself and family, another for strangers, and a third for the indigent"—"Are there many such

* This author speaks exactly my own sentiments I never could pass a butcher's shop without feeling a sensation of horror, and whenever I see a drove of cattle, or a flock of sheep, leading to slaughter, the necessity of killing them appears to me among the greatest of the miseries of human nature.——*Translator*

tables

tables in the city?"--"Yes; at all princes houses."—"But I suppose they are reforted to by innumerable idle parasites?"—"By no means; for as soon as any individual, who is not a stranger, appears to make a habit of coming too often, he is remarked, and the censors of the city make it their business to examine his character, and to assign some profession or employment for him, according to what talents or abilities he may possess But if he appears only to go there for the sake of eating, he is banished the city, in the same manner as in the republic of bees, all drones are driven away, being thought unworthy of sharing with the industrious."—"You have censors, then?"—"Yes, but they are rather entitled to another name, they are admonishers, who carry the torch of reason in all quarters, who correct and rectify all mutinous spirits, by employing either the eloquence of the heart, gentleness, or address, as occasion may require.

"Thefe tables are prepared for old men, invalids, pregnant women, orphans, and foreigners, here they may fit without a blush, without any painful embarrassment, here they find wholesome food in abundance. This prince, who respects humanity, makes no parade of luxury; he does not employ three hundred cooks for the entertainment of about a dozen persons, he makes no theatrical decorations upon his table, he takes no pride in that of which every man of feeling would be ashamed, I mean, in the display of an extravagant profusion, while so many individuals are in want of bread. When he takes his dinner, he recollects that he has but one stomach, and that it would be making a god of it to present, as the idolators formerly did to their gods, a hundred different dishes, which he is unable to taste."

While we were thus conversing, we traversed two courts, and entered a spacious hall. it was that allotted

(104)

...r foreigners. One long table was already served. In consequence of my great age I was seated in an arm-chair, and I was presented with a dish of wholesome soup, vegetable, game, and fruit. Every thing was prepared in the most simple manner. "Oh!" cried I, "this is delightful indeed! how desirable are riches, and how worthy of possessing them are those who thus employ them in feeding the hungry and needy! I think that conduct bespeaks their high birth and nobility much more than the vain parade of unmeaning magnificence which characterises the princes of former ages. Every thing was accompanied with order and decency, the conversation, which was animated and rational, gave additional charms to this public ordinary. The prince himself came amongst us, his manners were truly noble, not tinctured with the arrogance of high birth and rank, but with complacency and affability, he came up to me, and with a gracious smile asked several questions relative to the seventeenth and eighteenth centuries, desiring me at the same time to be candid. "Ah! prince," said I, "your ancestors of those times were not so generous as you are, they passed their days in hunting, racing, and the luxurious delights of feasting. When they killed a hare, it was not to feed the poor, but to gratify an idle inclination they never raised their minds to any object so worthy of their rank as relieving the wants of the needy, but they expended thousands upon dogs, horses, valets, and flatterers, in short, they acted like courtiers, and abandoned their country's interest."

The whole company listened to me with astonishment they could scarcely give credit to my words. "and yet," said they, "your history does not mention these things of them."—"Ah!" replied I, "believe not our historians, they are, if possible, still more guilty than the princes themselves."

CHAP

(165)

CHAP XXV

*A ———————————
—————————————
—————————————
—————————————
—————————————
—————————————
—————————————
—————————————*

AFTER dinner my guide proposed to take me to the play. I have always been fond of plays, and, if I live a thousand years I shall continue to be delighted with them. I accepted his proposal with great pleasure. "What play do they perform?" said I. "I should like to know what piece is most in vogue at present among you? Shall I see the Persian, the Grecian, or the Roman robes? or will the French dress be exhibited? Will they represent the downfal of some base tyrant, or the assassination of some stupid fellow? Shall I see a conspiracy, or some gliding shadow issuing from the tomb accompanied with thunder and lightning? And pray can you boast of having good actors, for, in all times, they have been as rare as good poets?" All these questions I asked without waiting for one answer, at length my friend found an opportunity of saying something. "Yes," said he, "they take pains, they study, and suffer themselves to be taught by the best authors, to avoid making the most laughable blunders, they are docile, although they are less illiterate than those of your time. I have told you had the utmost difficulty to find one actor, or actress, who were tolerable performers, all those who pretended to perform would

better

better have suited the scaffolds erected for Punch and Harlequin on the Boulevards. Your theatres, in a metropolis which was the rival of Rome and Athens, were shabby and confined, and the performances very ill managed, the comedian, who enjoyed a fortune which he was very far from deserving, if his merits were justly appreciated, dared to be proud, and to molest the man of genius, who was under the mortifying necessity of depositing the fruits of his labour into his hands these men ought to have died with shame for having refused, or unwillingly accepted, the best theatrical pieces, while those which they had received with transport bore that very triumph as a signal of their merited reprobation and fall. but in these days we never hear of such miserable errors

" We have four playhouses in the centre of each principal quarter of the town, they are maintained by government, for they answer two great ends, they serve for the entertainment of the people, and for a school of taste and morality We understand the great ascendancy which genius can assume over sensible minds, therefore we encourage it, we have seen astonishing instances of the power of genius, the hearts of men of feeling may be said to dwell in the works of the great poets, for they have the power of modifying them as they please, how culpable they are, therefore, when they produce dangerous maxims! but when they strike against vice, or serve the cause of humanity, our warmest gratitude is the least tribute of our approbation, the only end our dramatic authors have in view is the perfection of human nature; they all tend to exalt and strengthen the soul, to render it independent and virtuous All those who are good men express the eager desire of assiduously attending at all those performances which excite the feelings of virtue, which encourage in the heart that salutary emotion which

4   disposes

difpofes it to pity, the diftinguifhing criterion of true greatnefs."

While converfing thus we arrived in a fpacious fquare, in the centre of which a fuperb and majeftic edifice was erected; the top of the frontifpiece was ornamented with allegorical figures, among which, on the right, I diftinguifhed Thalia, who was tearing off the mafk with which vice effayed to conceal its deformity, and was pointing it out with her finger that none might be mifled by it, to the left I perceived Melpomene armed with a dagger, who was plunging it in the breaft of a tyrant, and expofing his heart, devoured with ferpents, to full view.

The theatre was in form of a femicircle, by which means the feats were commodioufly difpofed, here every perfon was feated, and this brought to my recollection all the fatigues I was obliged to endure when I wifhed to fee a performance, I was pleafed to find that thefe people paid fo much regard for the eafe and conveniency of their fellow-citizens Neither had they the infolent avidity to admit more auditors than there was convenient room for, there were always fome places left for ftrangers. The audience was brilliant, and the women were elegantly but decently dreffed.

The play opened with a fymphony, which was connected with the nature of the piece that was to be performed "Are we at the opera?" faid I, "for this is a beautiful piece of mufic!" My guide anfwered me thus. "We have learned to re-unite, without any confufion, the performances of both playhoufes, or, to fpeak more properly, we have renewed the alliance of poetry and mufic, which formerly prevailed among the ancients. Between the acts of our dramas we are entertained with mufical pieces and fongs adapted to the play, which excite delightful fentiments of virtue and humanity in the heart,

and

and prepare the mind for the events to be represented. We have excluded all effeminate and all noisy music, which is always void of expression. Your opera was a composition of good and bad, a mixture of inconsistencies, with a few flashes of genius, and was often the subject of censure and reproach of your people of judgment and taste. We have extracted whatever was good, and we have composed"——

As he said these words the curtain was raised, the scene was Thoulouse, I saw its capitol, wherein were assembled its chief magistrates, its judges, its executioners, and its fanatical inhabitants, then the family of the unfortunate Calas appeared, and I could not refrain my tears the venerable old man was seen, with heroic mildness, and with tranquil fortitude, his head silvered o'er with grey locks, coming to meet his hard fate with becoming composure. I saw the fatal instrument of death aiming at his head, which was undoubtedly innocent of all the crimes alledged to his charge. I was charmed with the air of truth which prevailed throughout the whole piece, for it was no longer the custom to sacrifice truth to the improbable lines included in rhyme, the poet had followed every part of this cruel event with exactitude, and his powers had been exerted to seize the true deplorable case of each victim, or rather he may be said to have borrowed their own language, for the true dramatic art consists in faithfully repeating the language which nature dictates. At the end of the performance I was observed by the audience, who pointed to me, saying, ' behold the contemporary of the unhappy century which produced such tragedies ' He has witnessed the unbridled fury with which the mad populace rose up against that innocent man, and the frenzy of their absurd fanaticism !" I could

not

not support their reproaching looks, but concealed my face in my cloak, and blushed for those gay times.

The tragedy of Cromwell, or the death of Charles the First, was given out for the next day, which seemed to give universal satisfaction. I was told, that this drama was a master-piece of genius, and that the cause of kings and subjects had never been represented with so much energy, so much eloquence and dignity. Cromwell was an avenger, a hero worthy of the sceptre which he had snatched from a king who was perfidious and criminal, and every monarch who had been unjust had been unable to read this play without dread and confusion.

The after-piece was the hunting-match of Henry the Fourth, his name was still held in veneration and love, nor could his memory be effaced, though they had enjoyed the happiness of having several good kings since their revolution. In this piece the hero and the man were happily blended, and the vanquisher of the League never appeared so great as in that instant when, in order to save his hosts a little trouble, his victorious arms were carrying a pile of plates and setting them on the table; the people applauded with transport, for while they were applauding each trait of goodness and greatness of soul in Henry, they had the character of their own monarch in view, in which I was told there existed the greatest affinity.

I remained extremely satisfied with the whole performance, and spoke to my guide in the following manner: "I am quite delighted with your actors, they perform with energy, and appear to express the feelings of their own heart, without any thing overstrained, false, or gigantic, in their manner, even the king's confidant acted his part ingenuously."—"The reason of that," answered my guide, "is, that on the theatre, as well as in private or civil stations, every one thinks it their glory and duty

I

to

to execute his office in the best manner he is able, however mean it may be, it becomes glorious by excelling therein. Declamation is highly esteemed among us as a most important, and it is cherished by government as a salutary art. We inherit all your good dramatic pieces, and we have brought them to a degree of perfection which will surprise you. We think it an honour to be able to express that which proceeds from the pen of genius, and what art can be greater than that which describes and conveys all the tints of sentiment even to the very look, voice, and gesture? What energy in its simplicity, how pathetic and harmonious!"—" I suppose the former prejudices against comedians is quite removed, are they still under the censure of ecclesiastical powers? are they degraded as they used to be?"—" No, as soon as they rectified their morals, they ceased to be so. There are some prejudices which are useful, and some dangerous. In your time it was necessary to set some restraint to the propensities of youth, naturally inclined to engage in a profession so alluring, whose basis was libertinism and immorality; but we, by wise regulations, have recalled all those who had incautiously engaged in the profession, and plunged into a forgetfulness of moral rectitude; we have pointed out the way by which they might redeem their forfeited honour, and we have restored them to the class of citizens. It is not many days since our good prelate petitioned the king to grant an honorary hat to one of the comedians, who had, by the energy of his performance, excited the feelings of the whole audience."—" What! does your prelate frequent the theatre?"—" And why should he not, now that it is become a school for morals, virtue, and sentiment? It has been written somewhere, that the father of the Christians was entertained by going to hear, even in the temple of God, the equivocal voices of a set of unhappy beings deprived of manhood, but we never could listen to such deplorable notes, which afflict both the heart and the ear. How could men be pleased with this cruel sort of music! I think it is much more rational and praiseworthy to see the performance of the admirable tragedy of Mahomet, where the heart of in ambitious wretch is exposed to view, where the furor of fanaticism is so energetically expressed, that they excite terror and dread in every mind.

' Look there, you see the pastor of this district, who is returning home with his children, discoursing with them on the subject of the tragedy of Calas! he forms their taste, he enlightens their understanding, he abhors fanaticism, and when he thinks of that arbitrary rage, which, like an epidemic disease, spread desolation over all Europe for more than twelve centuries, he returns his warmest thanks to heaven for having sent him into the world so many centuries later than the unfortunate men of those times.

" There are certain times of the year when we enjoy a pleasure which was altogether unknown to you, we have revived the art of pantomime so much cherished by the ancients we then admire the wonderful hand of nature in having given so many organs, and such admirable resources to man, that intelligent being, the master-piece of creation, by which to express the variety of his sensations. These eloquent men are all expression, and they speak as clearly with their fingers, and with their eyes, as we do with our tongues. It was an observation made by Hippocrates, that it was sufficient to look at the human hand to be convinced of the existence of a Supreme Being; but our able pantomimes reveal still more of the goodness and munificence of God in the formation of the human head!"—" Oh!" said I, " I have certainly nothing mo e

to

(112)

to say, every thing is established in the best manner possible."—" Oh!" this is not all," said my guide, " there remain many more changes for you to see. We have emerged from the depth of barbarity in which you were plunged, though, even in your time, there were a few enlightened minds, but the nation in general was inconsistent and trifling; by degrees great minds have been formed, but there remains still more to be done than has been done yet, we are only arrived towards the centre of the ladder of perfection, patience and resignation will do great things, but I fear it is not possible to reach the summit. A complete state does not exist in this life however, we ought continually to aspire towards it, in order to make things even passable."

~~~

CHAP. XXVI.

Behold the dawn of reason's day!
Britain and France content no more
In freedom's cause fierce rage to pour
Shall both with equal ——— ——— ———
Pursue the same exalted plan,
And vindicate on earth the right of man.

WE left the playhouse without having cause to lament for loss of time, and without any confusion, the passages were numerous and commodious, the streets were completely illumined, the lamps were pending from the walls, by which means their combined lights cast no shade, neither did they shed a dangerous reverberation, which frustrated their purpose, at the same time that they greatly injured the sight, but now the optician no longer
served

served the cause of the oculist. I observed that there were none of those prostitutes who formerly swarmed in every street, who, with their feet in the mud, and their face resplendent as the moon, proposed the enjoyment of pleasures as gross as they were insipid. All those houses of debauchery, where man went to degrade, to debase himself, to load himself with infamy and shame, were no longer tolerated, for it is vain reasoning, that these vicious institutions serve to preserve youth from a worse crime; it is, unfortunately, too well asserted, that all these abominable vices are a link of the same chain

I beheld, at equal distances, the night-guards, who watched over the safety of the public, and prevented the hours of repose from being interrupted. My guide now resumed the discourse. "These," said he, "are the only sort of soldiers we have any occasion for, we no longer have a consuming standing army to maintain in time of peace. Those mastiffs whom you maintained, in order to defend yourselves against the encroachments of strangers, were often ready to turn against your own families, and deprive them of their rights but the torch of Bellona is at length consumed, and for ever extinguished. Sovereigns have, at last, been prevailed on to listen to the voice of philosophy, they are now linked together by the strongest ties, they are become acquainted with their own interests, after so many centuries of error, reason has at last resumed her seat in their souls, they have opened their eyes to those duties which the safety and tranquillity of the people exacted from them, they have made their glory consist in governing wisely, wishing rather to cause the happiness of a small number than to gratify the frenzied ambition of ruling over desolated countries filled with aching hearts, who always detested the usurped power of the conqueror Kings have, with

I

one

one accord, fet limits to their empire, thofe limits which nature herfelf feemed to have affigned, by feparating every refpective kingdom by feas, forefts, or mountains. They now underftand, that the lefs extenfive the territory, the more it is likely to be wifely governed. The fages of each nation have dictated the general treaty, and it was concluded with the unanimous confent of all, and that which during the iron age, and which men without virtue called the fleeping vifions of a good man, has at length been realifed by men of enlightened knowledge and fenfibility. Thofe ancient privileges no lefs dangerous than thofe by which men were difcerned from each other by reafon of their belief, are alfo fallen. We all view each other as brethren and friends, both the Indian and the Chinefe are our fellow-citizens as foon as they tread on our foil. We accuftom our children to look on the whole univerfe as one family, fheltered under the protection of one common father, this opinion muft certainly be the beft, for it has pierced like a ray of light, with an inconceivable rapidity, through all ranks and conditions of men. The excellent books we have, written by men of fublime genius, have had the effect of torches which have enlightened as many more. Men have learned to love and efteem each other. The Englifh nation, being our neareft neighbour, is become our ally. Thefe two generous nations no longer efpoufe the enmity which prevailed among the chiefs. our knowledge, our arts, are all re-united in commerce, which is equally advantageous on both fides for inftance, the Englifh women, full of fenfibility and folidity, exactly fuit the difpofitions of the French men, who are more light and gay in their manners, and our French women have contributed to foften the melancholy and ferious character of the Englifh men. This mutual agreement produces a fertile fource of pleafures, sures, conveniencies, and original ideas, which are happily received and adopted. Another very essential advantage we now enjoy, which is the liberty of the press, to that we owe this happy revolution, it has operated as a torch to enlighten men's minds, and has produced the most salutary effects." I was transported with joy, and embraced my friend who told me these astonishing and consoling events "O! heavens!" I cried, "the happy time is come when men are worthy of thy notice, they now find that their real force consists in their union with each other. I shall now die satisfied, since my eyes have beheld that which they have so ardently wished to see. How delightful it is to forsake life, when we see ourselves surrounded with happy persons who quit this scene like brothers who, after a long voyage, are going to rejoin the author of their days."

CHAP. XXVII.

Ma pri che l'alma in Dio si riconforte
Che altro qu'ur sospir brève è la morte?

AS we were walking on, I perceived a hearse covered with white cloth, preceded by instruments of music, and crowned with trophies it was conducted by men clothed in blue, who held laurel-branches in their hands. "What car is that?" said I to my guide. "It is the car of victory," he replied "Those who have left this life, who have triumphed over the miseries of human nature, those happy men who are gone to rejoin the Supreme Being, who is the source of every blessing, are conquerors, and we hold their memory sacred—they are

carried

carried with respect to their last resting place. The hymn on the Triumph of Death is sung. In lieu of those horror-inspiring heads, with which your death-monuments were decorated, we have substituted others, expressive of the triumph of Virtue over Death, which is only a passage into a better world, and this is the aspect under which we view it. We never afflict ourselves over the insensible corpse of our friends; we weep over ourselves, but not over them. We, in all things, adore the hand of God, who has withdrawn them from this world. Let us be submissive to the irrevocable laws of nature, and willingly embrace that peaceful state which cannot but greatly amend our being. These bodies are reduced to ashes, at three miles distant from the city, there are small furnaces in a perpetual state of heat, allotted only to that use. Two dukes and a prince are inclosed in the same car with a simple citizen. In death, all distinctions cease, and we then return to that equality in which Nature has placed all her children. This wise custom effaces the natural horror of death from the minds of the people, and, at the same time, it humbles the pride of the great, who are not truly so but by their virtues. As for dignities, riches, and honours, the very memory of them passes away. At the instant of their decease, the corruptible matter, of which their bodies were composed, is no longer a part of themselves, it becomes mingled with the ashes of their equals, and we attach no idea of value to these perishable remains. We are unacquainted with those epitaphs, those mausoleums, those lies inspired by pride and flattery, with which your tombs were decorated. Even kings, at their decease, no longer fill their palaces with the vain pomp of pride, they are not more flattered at their death than they were during their life, and their

descent

descent into the tomb is not accompanied with the ruin of a whole city.

"In order to prevent accidents, we have a visitor, or searcher, who inspects every deceased person, and ascertains the certainty of their death before they are removed from the house. This inspector is a man of abilities, who inquires the sex, age, and nature of the disease of which the person died all this is inserted in the public papers, and also the name of the physician who attended him. If, as I have already told you, they find, in the book of reflections, which every man leaves at his death, any great or striking thoughts, they are published, and these are his best eulogiums after his death.

"We have a salutary idea which prevails among us, which is, that the soul, separated from the body, has the liberty of revisiting those places which it delighted to inhabit, and to see those objects most beloved, in silence, it hovers over their heads, and contemplates, with delight, the sincere lamentations of friendship. That tie, by which it was united to sublunary objects, is not dissolved, and it is capable of pleasure in being present, though unseen, and in removing every danger which might await their frail nature. These cherished shades may be compared to guardian angels, and this delightful persuasion inspires in us a certain confidence, either to undertake or execute, of which you deprived yourselves, by receiving, in your deluded minds, all sorts of sad and chimerical ideas.

"You may conceive what respect this belief must inspire in the mind of a young man who, having lost his father, still supposes him present, and the witness of his most secret actions. He addresses himself to him in solitude, and is animated by the idea that he is heard by him, and that he recommends the practice of virtue to him,

I 3 from

from which, if he was ever to deviate, he would say to himself, *My father sees me! my father hears me!*

"The young man dries up his tears, because the horrible idea of annihilation has no access to his soul, he feels, on the contrary, that the shades of his ancestors are waiting for him to enter the eternal abode. Ah! who could deny themselves the hope of immortality! even if it were an illusion, it is one of the most endearing and sacred."

THE ECLIPSE OF THE MOON,

BY A MAN IN SOLITUDE

[This chapter is a digression from the work, and is much in the stile of Dr Young The author composed it originally in French, and thought it applicable to the preceding chapter]

Come, Melancholy! silent power,
Companion of my lonely hour,
 To sober thought confin'd,
Thou sweetly sad ideal guest,
In all thy soothing charms confest,
 Indulge my pensive mind.

Through yon dark grove of mournful yews
With solitary steps I muse,
 By thy direction led,
Here, cold to pleasure's tempting forms,
Consociate with my sister worms,
 And mingle with the dead

Ye pale inhabitants of night,
Before my intellectual sight
 In solemn pomp ascend,

*O tell how trifling now appears
The train of idle hopes and fears,
That varying life attend!*

I INHABIT a small country-house, which greatly contributes to my happiness, it commands two different prospects, one of which extends over vast fertilised plains, which germinate the precious seed for man's subsistence, and the other, more confined, presents to my view the last asylum of the human race, the spot which terminates human pride, and the narrow space, where Death, with undistinguishing hand, heaps up his peaceable victims.

The aspect of this cemetery, far from exciting any disgust, which is only the offspring of vulgar terror, creates in my breast many wise and useful reflections. I hear no more the tumult of cities, which numb all the faculties of the soul. Alone, with my favourite companion, solemn Melancholy, my mind is filled with great and awful subjects. With a fixed and serene eye I contemplate that tomb wherein man sleeps for a time, and revives again, to justify eternal wisdom.

To me, the pompous blaze of day is sadness. With anxious expectation I wait the setting sun, and the soft obscurity of twilight, which gives additional charms to the silence of night, and is calculated to favour the soarings of sublime reflection. Soon as the nocturnal bird has given the shrill accent which precedes his heavy flight through the density of shade, I too, with mournful song, invoke thee, O, majestic shades of darkness, to thee I devote the gloomy hour; let thy solemn sadness exalt my soul above the changing scenes of this life, and discover the radiant throne of sublime Truth.

In the deep silence of this mournful retreat, I lend an attentive ear to distant sounds hail! it is the solitary bird of night, I trace his rapid flight bending towards a pile of human bones—he seeks a resting place among them the pile gives way, and, with a hollow sound, I hear a head roll down, a head which, perhaps, was formerly the abode of ambition, of pride, and of the most audacious projects. Again, he perches on the cold stone, where ostentation had formerly engraved names which the hand of time had erased, and on the grave of the poor, where flowers grew up spontaneously to weave him an humble garland!

In the all-conquering empire of death, how despicable, how vain, are all chimerical titles! The dust of the proud and noble, does it not mingle with that of the humble poor? But I have seen the clay cold bodies of the haughty sons of men, enclosed within a treble coffin, to prevent their bones from mingling with that of their fellow-creatures.

Turn this way, ye scornful proud, behold these tombs! why give a name to that which is nameless? These lying epitaphs do but expose you to a light more disadvantageous than the shades of everlasting night, they are but floating banners, which survive a short period, but are soon engulfed in the waves of oblivion

Oh! how much happier is he who never erected these vain pyramids, these monuments of pride, but who has invariably trod the path of honour and of virtue! His views were centred in heaven while he felt the decline of that frail edifice, which contained his immortal soul, he blessed the hand of Death, so formidable to the wicked, and when we recall the memory of that expiring good man, it is that we may learn to die as he died he saw our tears which flowed, not for him, but for ourselves,

his

his brethren, that is, his friends furrounded his funeral bed. We difcourfed with him on thofe confoling truths with which his foul was penetrated. We directed his attention towards that God, of whofe prefence he was more intimately convinced than we were ourfelves. A part of the awful curtain feemed to be open to his expiring eye ...... he raifed up his head, which already appeared invefted with rays of glory, and held out his hand to us, while, with a fmile, he expired.

But thou! vile wretch, whofe life was a continued feries of crimes, happy only in their concealment, or in having authority to commit them, thy death will not be thus eafy; thy pillow will be ftrewed with thorns, defpicable tyrant! now thou art pale, expiring, prepare thyfelf! Death will be to thee the king of terrors, he will bring thee a bitter chalice, which thou muft drink with all its dregs, thou can'ft not raife thy guilty hands towards heaven, nor extend them towards thy friends on earth, thou haft made all men thine enemies—both heaven and earth abandon and reject thee thou fhalt expire in terror, and launch into a futurity of fuffering and ignominy.

Rejoice ye, who are upright and innocent! this dreadful and awful moment, the bare idea of which appals the wicked, will infpire confidence in your fouls. My heart acknowledges the irrevocable law of diffolution. I contemplate all thefe graves as fo many burning furnaces, wherein matter is diffolved, while the moft precious part of us, our immortal foul, is purified, and for ever feparated from the corruptible part: the earthy remains perifh, but the foul fprings up in its original beauty. Why fhould we feel terror in viewing thofe remains which have been the terreftrial habitation of the foul? their afpect can only recall the happy recollection of their deliverance

the

the antique temple always retains its majesty, even in ruins.

Thus I am penetrated with veneration and reverence for these remains of mankind. I descend upon that ground strewed with the sacred ashes of my brethren the silent calm, the cold quiescence which prevailed, all that I could see in this abode of death, every thing whispered to my attentive ear, "THEY ARE AT REST HERE" I draw near, endeavouring to avoid the painful sensation which the sight of my friend's tomb might occasion, but, Oh! vain precaution, the marks of recentness still remained, and recalled the memory of my friend I paused in silent respect—I lend an attentive ear to catch the sounds of that celestial harmony which he enjoys in heaven. The moon shone in full splendour, diffusing her silver rays over this funereal scene. I cast my eyes towards the firmament, viewed all those numberless worlds, those blazing suns, with which it is bestrewed with such prodigious magnificence, after which they fell in solemn sadness upon those silent graves, where, in one common mass of corruption and decay, lay mouldering the eyes of man, once capable of viewing these heavenly bodies; the heart, the tongue which conversed with me on those sublime and marvellous works, and admired the magnificent architect of so many miracles.

Suddenly, I perceived an eclipse of the moon, which I had not foreseen. I was not sensible of its effects until I found myself environed with increasing darkness I could only distinguish a very diminished point of the shining orb which the shadow of the earth was hastening to intercept—and now, 'tis all eclipsed—the deepest night succeeds.—I pause, unable to discern the objects around me.—I wander, I turn about a hundred times, the door still eludes my stretched out hands in the mean time,
thick

thick clouds render the total darkness still more impenetrable, the winds begin to whistle, a distant thunder echoes from cloud to cloud, and soon approaches upon the lightning's rapid wing—and now my ideas are confused a shivering fit seizes my wearied limbs—I stumble over a pile of bones recently dug up—terror and affright precipitate my steps into an open grave prepared for a deceased person—thus I am received into the humid bosom of my parent earth, and already, in fancy, I hear the dead welcome me to their dreary abode---I am struck with an icy tremor---a cold sweat deprives me of my senses---a lethargic swooning deprives me of life or motion

Ah! why did I not remain in that peaceful state! I was inhumed. the veil between eternity and me would then have been withdrawn---I am not weary of life---I know how to enjoy it---I endeavour to make a worthy use of it, but every thing convinces me that our future existence will be far preferable to this---

At length my senses return, a feeble ray of light began to display the starry vault, the clouds began to assume various shapes by the infused rays of light by degrees they received a brighter influence, and soon they plunged beneath the horizon, while my eyes began to distinguish the moon's disk half disengaged from the dark shadow, at length it resumes its whole lustre, and shines with increased brilliancy, pursuing its allotted course. My courage returns· I spring from the tomb, the prevailing calm of the winds, the serenity of the heavens, the approaching rays of Aurora, revive my spirits, and dispel the gloomy terrors which the events of this night had created.

I stood contemplating, with a smile, that grave which had received me in its bosom Was there any thing hideous in its aspect? It was the earth, my parent and my friend,

friend, ever subservient to my wants living or dead? The phantoms of my credulous imagination all disappeared when reason resumed her sway. It is imagination alone which engenders gloomy visions, my friends! I imagined myself on the brink of death in this adventure. I fell into the grave with that degree of terror, which perhaps is the prop with which nature is supported amidst all the calamities incident to human life. But I fell into a gentle sleep, in which I felt an undescribable luxury. If this was a terrifyng scene, it only lasted a short time, indeed it scarce existed at all for me, as I was unconscious of life during those few minutes; but when I awakened, and enjoyed the calm and pure breezes of the morning air, the serene aspect of day-spring, I quickly banished all puerile terrors, and admitted the purest joy to glide into my heart. Thus, after that transitory sleep called death, when we awake in the full glory and splendor of the Eternal Sun of the World, which illumines the immensity of space, he will change all our terrors into pure delights, by discovering to us the folly of our ill-grounded prejudices and fears, and the inexhaustible source of a new felicity which no vicissitude can ever interrupt.

But, in order to be free from apprehension, it is necessary, O mortal being! to be virtuous while treading the rugged path of life be thou enabled to receive these secret admonitions from conscience. "Fear not, go forward under the all-seeing eye of thy God, who is the universal Father of Men. Let not thy heart be dismayed with dread of his justice; but hope in his clemency; adore his goodness, trust in him as a tender and dutiful son, but let not thy soul harbour the servile fear of a guilty slave

CHAP

CHAP. XXVIII.

Consult the wisdom of each page,
Inquire of every scienc'd sage,
How you may glide with gentle ease
Adown the current of your days,
Nor vex'd by mean and low desires,
Nor warm'd by low ambition's fires,
By hope alarm'd, deprest with fear,
For things but little worth you care.

I Was at this part of my dream when some door, situated very near the head of my bed, by a violent creaking on its hinges made a revolution in my sleep, by which I lost sight of my guide and of the city, but my mind was too forcibly struck with the images with which it had been impressed not to recover them immediately: I soon fell asleep again, and a continuation of the same dream again engaged my senses I was now quite alone abandoned to myself. It was mid-day, and I thought myself in the king's library, but I was some time ere I could be certain of it, so greatly it was changed instead of those four halls of an immense length, which contained many thousand volumes, I only saw a small closet, in which there were several books, very far from voluminous. Surprised at so great a change, I scarcely dared to ask whether some fatal conflagration had devoured that rich collection "Yes," they replied, "but it was a conflagration we ourselves occasioned and gladly set light to."

I must not omit that this people were most affable, and particularly to old men, and that they answered every question which was proposed, not like Frenchmen, who

always

always interrogate while they answer, but in a satisfactory and pleasant manner.

The librarian, who was a man of real learning and sound judgment, approached towards me, and having maturely weighed all the objections, and listened to all the reproaches I made him, held the following discourse

"Convinced as we were by the most exact observations, that the understanding is bewildered by attending to so many different inquiries; we have discovered that a numerous library was the centre of the greatest follies, and of the most ridiculous chimeras. In your time, to the great disgrace of human reason, authors began to reflect after they had written. Those of our time pursue the opposite plan, and we have destroyed all those whose thoughts were buried under a prodigious mass of words or passages.

"Nothing disorders the understanding so much as ill-written books; the first notions being once adopted without having been sufficiently examined, the next become precipitate conclusions, and thus man proceeds from error to error, and from prejudice to prejudice. All, therefore, that remained for us to do, was to lay a new foundation for human learning, this was in appearance a difficult project, but we have only removed every unserviceable pursuit, tending to conceal from our view the essential aim of our researches. We acted in the same manner as the architects did, who, when they built the Louvre Palace, judged it necessary to throw down all the old houses which impeded its prospect.

"In this maze of innumerable volumes, the sciences only circulated and constantly returned to the same point without ever rising above it, while the exaggerated riches of these books served only to discover their real poverty. In fact, what did all these volumes contain? they were in general nothing but continual repetitions of the same things.

"Philosophy has been represented to our sight under the emblem of a statue, ever celebrated, always copied, but never embellished she appears much more perfect in the original, and always seems to degenerate in all the copies of gold and of silver which are made of her. How much more beautiful when carved of wood by the wildest hand, than when loaded with foreign ornaments, which deprive her of her natural simplicity. When men, by giving themselves up to enervating indolence, adopt the opinions of others, their own talents then become servile imitators; they quickly lose originality and invention. How many vast projects, how many sublime speculations have been totally extinguished by the breath of public opinion! Time has only conveyed to our knowledge those trifling brilliancies of wit, which have met with the approbation of the multitude, while those elevated and solid reflections, which were either too simple or too complex to please the vulgar, have been absorbed in oblivion.

"Our days being limited ought not to be consumed in pursuing an unprofitable or puerile philosophy, therefore, we have struck a decisive blow against all the wretched controversies of schools"—"What have you done?" cried I eagerly, "do proceed"—"With the unanimous consent of all the people, we gathered together in a spacious plain, all those books we have judged to be either frivolous, useless, or dangerous, we formed them into a pyramid, which in height and breadth resembled an enormous tower, in fact, it was another tower of Babel. This wonderful edifice was capped with all sorts of periodical works, flanked on all sides with bishop's mandates, parliamentary remonstances, funeral orations,

and

and law suits. It was compofed of five or six hundred thoufand commentaries, eight hundred thoufand volumes of jurifprudence, and about fifty thoufand dictionaries, a hundred thoufand poems, fixteen hundred thoufand voyages, and a thoufand million novels and romances. We fet fire to this enormous pile, as an expiatory facrifice offered to truth, good fenfe, and true tafte. The flames fpread in torrents on all fides, and devoured all the idle nonfenfe of men, both ancient and modern, they raged for fome time, many authors faw themfelves burnt alive, but their outcries did not ftay our hands, however, we found fome fheets of the works of Piron, of De la Harpe, of L' Abbe A———, which, owing to their extreme frigidity, could never be confumed, thus we have renewed, through an enlightened zeal, that which had formerly been executed by a blind and barbarous enthufiafm. However, as we are neither unjuft, nor like the Saracens, who made ufe of the mafter-pieces of literature to heat their baths, we have a chofen collection, we have employed fome able pens to make a felection of all the fubftance of a thoufand folio volumes, of which they have formed one fmall volume in twelves, like thofe able chymifts who extract the virtues of a plant, contract it into a fmall vial, and throw away the drofs.

"We have made abridgements of every moft important work the beft are reprinted, and all of them have been corrected upon the true principles of morality Our compilers are all perfons who are moft eftimable and dear to the nation, they are men of good tafte, and of a genius capable of creating, they know what fhould be chofen and what rejected We have obferved, that good books are only produced in philofophic ages, but in your time, when real and folid knowledge was not fufficiently eftablifhed, it became neceffary to collect the materials for acquiring it. In the beginning, each science must be treated of in separate parts, and every one directs his attention to that which is appointed to him, by this method, nothing escapes due notice, the most minute details are observed. It was necessary you should write a multiplicity of books, and it remained with us to gather all the scattered parts which were worth preserving. Men of shallow parts, and but half informed, are those who always talk most, but the well informed wise man speaks very little, and his discourse is accompanied with good sense.

"This closet contains the books which have escaped the flames, there are but few, but those have deserved to be approved by our generation." My curiosity led me to examine them, and those I found preserved among the Greeks were Homer, Sophocles, Euripides, Demosthenes, Plato, and, above all, our friend Plutarch, but Herodotus, Sappho, Anacreon, and the vile Aristophanes, were burned. I was going to defend the cause of Anacreon, but they gave the best reasons for destroying him, which I shall not undertake to enlarge upon, as they would not be understood by the people of my century.

In the next division, destined for Latin authors, I I found Virgil, Pliny, as well as Titus Livy, intire, but all the works of Lucretius had been burned, except a few of his poetical pieces, his principles of natural philosophy are false, and his morality dangerous. The tedious pleas of Cicero had been suppressed, he was rather an able rhetorician than an eloquent man, but his philosophical pieces had been carefully preserved, and they are thought to be the most precious remains of antiquity. Sallust was wholly preserved, but Ovid and Horace had undergone much curtailing. The Odes written by the latter are very inferior to his Epistles. Seneca was reduced to one

K fourth

fourth part. Tacitus was whole, but, as there prevails through all his writings a taint of melancholy, which casts a shade of sadness over the actions of men, and as human nature must not be clothed in unfavourable colours, the the perusal of this profound author was only permitted to men of good hearts and sound judgment. Catullus and Petronius were entirely deftroyed. Quintilian was remaining in one thin volume.

The third division contained the English writers, and it was there I saw the greatest number of volumes All the philosophers which that warlike, commercial, and politic island had produced, remained entire Milton, Shakefpear, Pope, Young, and Richardfon, ftill enjoyed an unblemished fame Their creating genius was allowed to be unfettered and unreftrained, at the fame time that those of our nation, who dared to be authors, were obliged to weigh every word and fentence. The eminently prolific genius of those free fouls was ftill the admiration of a people in whom real tafte and found judgment were blended The frivolous reproach we formerly made them of being deficient in tafte was now effaced in the opinion of men enamoured of true and fublime ideas, who took the trouble to read, and could meditate upon what they had read. They had fuppreffed all thofe dangerous fceptics who had endeavoured to fhake the very foundation of morality, this virtuous people, influenced by fentiment alone, difdained the vain fubtleties which dared to pronounce virtue an empty name, a chimera.

The fourth divifion was deftined for the Italian authors the Jerufalem Delivered, the fineft of all known poems, was at the head of them all, a whole library of critical pieces againft this enchanting poem had been committed to the flames. The famous Treatife upon Crimes and Punifhments had received all the perfection of which a work so important was susceptible. I was agreeably surprised to find many solid philosophical works sprung from the bosom of that nation, which at length had for ever crushed the talisman which seemed doomed to perpetuate superstition and ignorance amongst them.

I now found myself opposite to the division which contained the French writers I seized with an eager hand the three first volumes, it was Descartes, Montaigne, and Charron. Montaigne had undergone a little curtailing, but, as he was one of the philosophers who had best known the human heart, his writings had been preserved, though some of his ideas are not altogether uncensurable The visionary Mallebranche, the melancholy Nicolle, the unmerciful Arnauld, and the cruel Bourdaloue, had been burned. Every thing relating to scholastic disputes was so totally annihilated, that when I mentioned the Provincial Letters of Paschal, and of the destruction of the Jesuits, the learned librarian made a most considerable anachronism I politely set him right, for which he thanked me very sincerely. I could not meet with those famous Provincial Letters, nor even the history still more modern, which contained a detail of that great affair, which now was become very insignificant indeed! The Jesuits were then spoken of as we now speak of the ancient Druids.

That crowd of theologians, improperly called fathers of the church, those most sophistical, obscure, and irrational writers were all fallen into nought, from which they ought never to have arisen, diametrically opposite to all human reason, they were the very antipodes of Locke, and of Clarke, and seemed, as the librarian justly said, " to have fixed the limits of human insanity."

K 2 I eagerly

I eagerly opened and turned over every book, seeking for writers of my acquaintance. Heavens, what destruction! What numbers of large books all vanished into smoke! Where, where is the celebrated Boffuet, which was publifhed in my time, in no lefs than fourteen volumes quarto? I was told they had all perifhed among the reft. "What!" faid I, "that eagle who foared up to the higheft region—that elevated genius . . . . .' the librarian interrupted me, and faid, " I ay my good friend, inform me what part of his works it was poffible to preferve. I grant he had genius, but he made a moft pitiful ufe it: we have adopted the maxim of Montaigne, who fays, ' we muft not inquire which is the moft learned, but which is the beft learned.' The Univerfal Hiftory of that Boffuet was no more than a mere fkeleton of chronology without life or colouring, and the turns he had given to the very long reflections which accompanied this miferable production, were fo conftrained and extraordinary, that we can fcarcely perfuade ourfelves that the work was perufed during a longer period than fifty years. But his Funeral Orations . . . . . have greatly increafed our indignation againft him: they were truly the language of fervile flattery. Does it become a minifter of the God of Peace, of the God of Truth, to afcend the pulpit in order to fing the praifes of fome morofe politician, of an avaricious minifter, of an ill famed woman, or of a murderous hero,—who, while as a poet he is wholly engroffed with the defcription of a battle, does not beftow one figh upon that moft dreadful fcourge which caufes fo much devaftation upon the earth?

"At this moment he is very far from fupporting the rights of humanity, or of prefenting to an ambitious monarch, through the facred organ of religion, the forcible and awful truths with which he ought to be acquainted

he

he rather aims at celebrity, and hopes to have this remark made of him ' *That man speaks well, he publishes the praises of the dead* how much more then will he not give incense to those kings who are not yet deceased' This Bossuet is indeed no favourite with us, for, setting aside his own private character, which was haughty and cruel, a subtle and ambitious courtier, it was he who first caused funeral orations to be held in esteem, which have since multiplied like funeral torches, and, like them, exhale, as they pass, a pestiferous odour. This species of writing has always appeared the most frivolous, and the most dangerous of any, because it is at the same time the most false, the most insipid, and uninteresting, it always contradicted the public voice, whose echoing cries often resounded in that very church, where the orator himself, while he was declaiming against pageantry, laughed within himself at the false colouring with which he vainly daubed his idol.

" You there see his rival, his modest and gentle vanquisher, the amiable and tender Fenelon, author of Telemachus, and several other works which we have carefully preserved, because in them are found the rare and happy union of reason and sentiment. To have composed Telemachus at the court of Louis XIV was a proof of the most admirable and astonishing virtue the monarch certainly did not understand the book, and that is the most favourable supposition which can be formed to his honour in this work there are many things wanting, a more extensive knowledge, and more profound reasoning, but what noble expression, what forcible truths accompany his simplicity Next to this charming writer, we have placed the works of the good Abbé de St. Pierre, whose heart was sublime, though his pen was feeble seven centuries have given to his great and noble ideas all desirable maturity; he was accused of being a visionary, but it was rather his accusers who followed chimerical pursuits than himself. His dreams are now become realities."

Among the French poets, I saw Corneille, Racine, and Moliere, but the criticisms which had been written upon their works were all burned. I asked the librarian the question which will be asked seven centuries hence, " To which of the three would you give the preference?" —" We understand very little of Moliere in these days," answered he, " the manners he described, are quite done away, but we think he has attacked ridicule rather than vice, and among you there was more vice than ridicule. As for the two tragic poets, whose representations were of a nature to be more durable, I know not how a man of your age can propose such a question. He who eminently succeeds in drawing the human heart from real life, he who elevates, who enlarges the soul, who has best known the force of jarring passions, who has sounded the abyss of political craft, no doubt had more genius than his more harmonious rival, who with a stile more pure, and more exact, is less forcible, less striking, and has neither his penetrating quickness, nor his sublimity of thought, his ardor of imagination, his sound reasoning, or his wonderful diversity of character. To this may be added, that Corneille directed his sole aim to morality, he exalted the minds of men to the love of every virtue, to liberty! Racine, on the contrary, having enervated all his heroes, and represented them as the most effeminate personages, enervates his spectators in like manner without pleasing them. True arte consists in the art of beautifying the most trifling things, in this instance, Corneille was inferior to Racine. Time, that sovereign judge, who equally annihilates both eulogiums and criticisms, time, I say, has pronounced and removed these two writers at

infinite

infinite diftances from each other the one is a genius of the firft order, the other, if you fet afide a few beautiful points borrowed from the Greeks, is no more than a man of great fenfe and profound erudition, according to the judgment paffed on him even in his own century In your time there was no energy, nothing was pleafing unlefs highly finifhed, and a truly great ftile is ever accompanied with harfhnefs, you placed the chief merit of a man in his ftile, as it ever happens among all corrupted and weak nations."

Here I likewife found the terrible Crebillon, who has given thofe terrifying colours to vice which fhould always characterife it. This people allowed themfelves fome times to read his works, but they never could confent to fee them reprefented.

It may be fuppofed, that I found my friend La Fontaine ftill equally cherifhed, and always read with pleafure He is the firft of the moral poets, and Moliere, who knew fo well how to make a juft eftimate of his works, had foretold his immotality It is true, that fable is the allegoric ftile of a flave, who dares not fpeak freely to his mafter, but, as it qualifies fomewhat of the harfhnefs of truth, it ought long to be cherifhed on this globe, given up to all forts of tyrants fatire may be ftiled the only weapon of defpair.

In this century, our immutable fabulift was placed far above Boileau, who pretended to dictate to all Parnaffus, and who, void of invention, of genius, of energy of grace, or fentiment, had been no more than an exact and cold verfifier. Several other fables had been prefented, among others, thofe of De la Motte and thofe of Nivernois.

Rouffeau, the poet, made a very wretched appearance fome of his odes and cantatas had remained, but as for his sad epistles, his fatiguing harsh allegories, his Mandrake, his epigrams, being all productions of a depraved heart, it may be easily imagined that such stuff had met the fate they so long had deserved. I cannot here enumerate all the salutary mutilations which many celebrated works had undergone. I saw none of those frivolous poets who had only flattered and pleased the taste of their own times, by spreading over the most serious objects that deceitful varnish of wit, which prevents the operations of reason. All those sallies of a light and heated imagination, now reduced to their real value, had evaporated, like those sparks which glisten most when they are extinguishing.

All those romancers, either historical, moral, or political, in whose works one melancholy truth only was to be found here and there by chance, which might have been united, and rendered more forcible by their union; all those writers who had never seen and judged of things through the medium of truth; those who had been misled by a systematic spirit, and had seen or followed none but their own ideas, all these writers, deceived as they had been, either by possessing a sort of genius they did not follow, or by not possessing any, had either disappeared, or had been subject to the pen of a judicious critic, which was no longer the instrument of envy or of gain, but of just discrimination.

Wisdom and the love of order has presided at this useful overthrow. Thus, in those thick and impenetrable forests, in which the boughs of trees, by meeting and interweaving, obstruct the traveller's path, where an eternal and unhealthy gloom would for ever preside, if the industrious hand of man did not remove, by applying the axe or the fire-brand, those impediments to the soft and beneficial rays of the sun. Then the natural beauties

ties are seen to revive, which had so long been drooping, deprived as they were of the envigorating heat of that great father of vegetation. Darkness is dispersed, re-animated verdure returns to recreate the traveller's sight, who now may traverse the various windings of the wood without dread or fear. I perceived in a corner a curious book, which, upon examination, I found worth reading; the title of which was this—USURPED REPUTATIONS, in it were explained the motives and reasons which had decided for the extinction of several works, and for the contempt annexed to the pen of some writers, who had been admired in their own times. In this same book the wrongs of all those contemporaries of great men, who had suffered from the unjust jealousy of their adversaries, were avenged and redressed.

At length I fell upon a Voltaire. "O heavens!" cried I, "how much he has lost of his good plight! Where are those twenty-six volumes in quarto, emanated from his bright and inexhaustible pen? If this celebrated writer could return upon earth, how astonished he would be!"—"We have been obliged to burn a great part of them," said the librarian. "You know that this famous genius paid a heavy tribute to the weakness of human nature. He penned his ideas with precipitation, ere they had time to come to maturity. He gave a decided preference to every thing energetic and bold rather than to the slow discussion of truth. He was like a swallow, who, with a rapid graceful flight, lightly grazed the surface of a deep river, drinks, sips without stopping. Thus he, aiming at genius, but only is a man of wit. It cannot, however, be denied that he possessed the first, the noblest, and greatest of all virtues, the love of humanity he struggled hard in defence of the interests

of

of mankind he detested and stigmatised persecution, and tyrants of all kinds he introduced on the great scene of life the most rational and pathetic morality he has described heroism under its real colours. In short, he was the greatest of the French poets. We have preserved his poem, though the plan of it is servile, but the name of Henry the IVth will ever immortalise it We are particularly enamoured of his beautiful tragedies, in which the characters are drawn with a pencil so natural, so easy, and so varied We have preserved all those of his prose pieces in which he is neither a buffoon nor cruel, there indeed he is truly original but you know, that during the last fifteen years of his life he retained but few ideas, which he continually represented under an hundred different forms, he perpetually repeated the same things. he waged war against those persons whom he ought to have contemned in silence he was so weak as to suffer himself to write the most bitter and grossest invectives against Rousseau, and he was so strangely misled by his furious jealousy that he wrote without judgment. We have been obliged to burn all those wretched productions which would have disgraced him in the most distant generation. Jealous of his glory, even more so than he was himself, we have endeavoured to preserve his reputation as a great man, by destroying one half of his works "

" Gentlemen," said I, as I continued to examine the books, how charmed! how delighted, I am to find J J Rousseau whole and entire What a wonderful work is his Emilius! What charming sensibility of soul throughout every part of that beautiful novel of Eloisa! what force of thought! what extent of reasoning, what depth of political skill, in his Letters! what sublimity! what

what vigour in his other productions! how he thinks and how he teaches to think! every part of his works are worthy of attention."—" It is thus we have judged of them," answered the librarian, " the pride of man in your time was truly mean and cruel." he added, " Indeed it was not properly understood, your minds were so frivolous that you did not take the trouble to examine it. Your philosophers themselves were a people ... . but I believe we are all agreed upon our opinion of this philosopher you understand me; I need say no more."

" While looking over the books of the last shelf, I with pleasure perceived several works, formerly very dear to my countrymen, viz. The Spirit of the Laws, Natural History, Belisarius, the Works of Linguet, the eloquent Discourses of St Servan, of Dupaty, of Le Tourneur, and the Conversations of Phocion. I here found the innumerable philosophical works which the age of Louis XV had produced The Encyclopedia had been reprinted upon a better plan. Instead of that pitiful taste which inclined them to reduce every thing into dictionaries, that is to say, to mince all the sciences into small pieces, every art was presented whole, at one view, each different part might be embraced, as upon an extensive canvas represented with order by the hand of an able artist. They were all connected together by a simple and methodical clue, which rendered them still more interesting. Every work against the Christian religion had been destroyed, as having become totally useless.

" I now inquired for the historians, and the librarian held the following discourse " It is our painters who have now taken this branch in hand. Facts naturally fall under the exertions of the pencil, from their physical

certi-

certitude. What is understood by history? It is only the science of facts. Reasoning and reflections are all produced by the historian who has first penned them. But facts, you will say, are innumerable. Yes there are endless details of superannuated fables: for though the events of each century are the most interesting of any to their contemporaries, yet it is those of all others which are in general the least understood. A multiplicity of ponderous folios have been written to prove the existence of some antique foreign facts, while the attention of men was drawn from the present events much more worthy of notice, a spirit of conjecture was seen to shine at the expense of exactitude: many men have even undertaken to write universal histories (so little were they acquainted with their own weakness) more senseless even than those honest Indians who supposed the physical world rested on a basis of four elephants. In short, history has been so disfigured, and so altered by false representations, so loaded with puerile reflections, that a romance, given as such, is far preferable to those histories, where the reader may be compared to a person sailing upon an ocean without a rudder or compass. We have made rapid extracts of each century by describing them in colours, but we have omitted to represent any of those personages who have not really influenced the destiny of empires. We have also omitted those reigns, in which there is nothing to be recorded but battles, and examples of furious revenge. We have thought it necessary to be silent on those subjects, and not represent to future generations any examples but those capable of honoring the last: it is dangerous to register all the excesses at which crime is capable of arriving. Guilt so multiplied is an excuse for many, but while we see but few outrages

com-

committed, we are not tempted to commit more. We have treated human nature in the same manner as that respectful son treated his father, whose shame he was fearful of exciting, and therefore threw a veil over the disorders occasioned by intoxication."

I drew near to the librarian, and, whispering, asked him for the history of the age of Louis XV a Supplement to that of Louis XIV. by Voltaire He handed it to me, saying it had been reprinted in the twentieth century by a faithful historian, who was unwilling to omit any of the particulars of those strange times, but represented things in their true point of view Indeed, I had never perused any thing so curious and singular as this work appeared at this time. My curiosity and astonishment redoubled at every page. I here learned to reform several of my opinions, and I now understand that, in general, the age in which we live is that which is most remote from our comprehension I laughed, I very highly admired, but I wept almost as much I cannot at this time say more. The present events may be compared to that sort of meat pastry which is only to be relished after it has had time to cool.

CHAP

CHAP. XXXI.

Let sage instructions, to refine the soul,
   And raise the genius, wonderous aid impart,
Conveying inward, as they purely roll,
   Strength to the mind, and vigour to the heart.
When morals fail, the stains of vice disgrace
   The fairest honours of the noblest race

COMING from the library, a person who was there with me, but who had not spoken during three hours, accosted me, and we engaged in deep conversation: we fell upon the subject of men of literature "In my time," said I, "I was not acquainted with many, but those I did converse with were in general mild, candid, modest, and men of probity. If they were subject to those failings incident to human nature, they were counteracted by so many valuable qualities, that it was almost impossible not to be attached to them, and none but persons insensible to the charms of friendship could be otherwise The characters of many others have been disfigured by envy, ignorance, and calumny, for every public personage is exposed to the senseless discourses of the vulgar, who, blind as they are, always pronounce their opinion with boldness The great, who were in general void of talents, as they were of virtues, were jealous of these men, because their abilities attracted the notice of their countrymen, and therefore they appeared to despise them Besides all this, these writers had to contend with the vitiated taste of the public, who, though enriched by the labours of these inestimable men, were covetous of their praises, and would sometimes pour contempt on a master-piece of human genius, and fall in ecstacies at some low piece of buffoonery. In short, they

(143)

they needed the highest degree of courage to continue their laborious pursuits, in which the pride of man pre-'ented a thousand difficulties, but they have braved the insolent contempt of the great, and the senseless speeches of the vulgar; their noble efforts have been crowned by the hand of fame, who, while she was just to their merit, was equally just in branding their adversaries with merited infamy."

"This is an exact character of them indeed," said my new acquaintance. "Men of letters, however," continued he, "are now the most respectable and respected of our citizens. All men experience and are desirous of the pleasure of having their feelings roused and excited; it is the greatest delight of the mind. To them devolves the care of developing this principle of all virtues; for can there exist any in a heart where there is no sensibility? By designing and painting pieces the subjects of which are sometimes majestic, pathetic, or terrific, they extend or create the dispositions to those peculiar passions, and dispose men, while they perfect their sensibility, to all the great virtues of which it is the eternal source.— We think," added he, "that the writers of your times have surpassed those of the age of Lewis XIV as to morality and deep and useful researches. They have dared to describe the faults of kings, the misfortunes of the people, the ravages of the passions, the efforts and struggles of afflicted virtue, and even the triumph of vice. Ever faithful to their calling, they have had the courage to insult those bloody trophies, which error and slavery had consecrated to tyranny. Never had the cause of humanity been pleaded with more energy, and although, by an inconceivable fatality, they lost their cause for a time, still these respectable pleaders have retired with glory.

Thes.

"Those powerful rays of light, which had emanated from the pen of these courageous and noble souls, were preserved and transmitted from age to age; they may now be compared to some small particle of seed, which, having fallen from the hands of the sower, remains obscure and trampled under foot by the ignorant multitude, till, by a sudden gust of wind, it is blown upon some favourable and happy soil, where it takes root, grows up, and becomes a lofty tree, whose rich foliage becomes at once both an ornament and shelter.

"If we are better enlightened as to that which constitutes real grandeur, and despise the pageantry and ostentation of sovereign powers, if we have directed our attention towards objects more worthy of the attention of man, it is to literature we are indebted. But your writers have been outdone by ours with regard to courage. If any of our princes were to deviate from the laws, we should witness the revival of that tribunal, formerly so famous in China, which caused the names of those sovereigns who had lived unworthy their high office to be engraven upon brass; thus his shame and disgrace would be handed down to the latest posterity. In the hands of such historians history becomes the infallible wreck of false glory, the sentence pronounced against illustrious criminals, and the trying furnace, in which the hero disappears, if ever he deviated from his duty as a man.

"Dare those masters of the world still complain that all those who surround them have the appearance of constraint and dissimulation, while they have with them those silent, independent, and intrepid orators, who can instruct without offending them, and have neither favours to obtain from the throne, nor displeasure to fear. These noble writers have certainly fulfilled their destination better than

than any class of men, some have fulminated against superstition, others have supported the rights of man, some, again, have dug deep in the fertile mind of morality; others have displayed virtue to our view under the garb of the most endearing sensibility. We have overlooked the weaknesses which, as men, they were unavoidably liable to commit; we only notice the innumerable discoveries they have made, the ray of light they have thrown upon every acquisition in the sciences; they may be termed a moral sun, which will continue to enlighten the world until the extinction of the universal luminary!"

Having listened to this discourse, I spoke thus: "I should be very happy to be in company with some of your great men, I have always had a particular inclination for good writers, I love to see them, and, above all, to hear them."—"It happens very fortunately," said my friend, "that the doors of the Academy are this day to be opened, a man of letters is to be received as member."—"I inquired if he was to replace a deceased member?"—"What!" said my friend, "and is it necessary that real merit should wait for the decease of a member, in order to assume the place he is entitled to?"—"The number of our academicians is not limited, every talent ensures its own reward; their labours are crowned; and there exists a sufficient number of rewards for the respective productions of every member."

CHAP.

CHAP XXX.

——Inter sylvas Academi quærere verum

To search for truth in Academic groves

WE continued our walk towards the French Academy. The name had been continued, but how very different its situation! It was no longer in the palace of Kings. Oh! astonishing revolution of a few centuries! A Pope usurps the throne of the Cæsars! ignorance and superstition prevail in Athens! the fine arts have fled into Russia! and now, that same spot, that hill, which formerly was covered with thistles and brambles, and afforded pasture to the humble and patient ass, is become the faithful image of ancient Parnassus, the abode of genius, and the residence of the most famous writers! Its former name of Montmartre was abolished, but it was from pure complaisance for the existing prejudices. This respectable spot was overshadowed with venerable words, and was consecrated to Solitude: it was forbidden, by an express law, to cause the tranquillity to be disturbed by any discordant sounds. the quarries of white plaister, for which this place was famed, were now exhausted: the earth had produced a new bed of stone, to serve for a foundation to this noble asylum. This mount, favoured as it was by the sun's softest rays, and by a beneficial soil, produced lofty trees, whose summits, shooting forward, meeting and crossing each other, formed a delightful shade; and in other places they grew at proper distances, through which the eager eye of Contemplation might elevate itself to heaven.

I ascended with my guide, and perceived here and there various hermitages, delightfully situated at short
distances

diſtances from each other, and equally calculated for the enjoyment of ſocial intercourſe, or for temporary retreat. I inquired whether theſe groves were not the delightful and intereſting abodes of their eminent philoſophers — "You will ſhortly be informed," ſaid my guide, "let us haſten, the hour draws nigh" and indeed I preſently ſaw a number of perſons arrive from different parts, not riding in gaudy coaches, but walking. Their converſation ſeemed animated and intereſting. We entered a ſpacious hall, which was very ſimply decorated. Here was no oppoſition to my entrance, no Swiſs porter ſtanding at the gate with a heavy halbert in his hand, but this was the peaceful ſanctuary of the Muſes, and I was ſuffered to accompany theſe good people. This hall, though of vaſt extent, was extremely ſonorous, by that means the moſt feeble voice might be diſtinctly heard in the moſt remote parts. The good order which reigned in every place was no leſs remarkable. Several rows of benches, at different heights, ſurrounded the circumference of the hall, this people knowing that the ear ought to be unmoleſted at the academy, as well as the eye at an exhibition of paintings. I contemplated all theſe changes with delight. The number of ſeats for the academicians was not ridiculouſly limited to forty, but the only particularity I obſerved was, that over each chair I ſaw a waving ſtandard, on which the titles of each work, which had diſtinguiſhed its reſpective owner, were engraved in large letters. Here every perſon might take his ſeat without any introduction, and with this law only, that they ſhould diſplay the ſtandard on which the liſt of their writings was inſcribed. It may be ſuppoſed that none of them dared to ſet up the white ſtandard, as it was the cuſtom, in my time, for biſhops, dukes, marſhals, and preceptors, to do. Still leſs did any one dare to produce before the scrutinizing eye of the public the title of any indifferent work, nor was there ever the smallest appearance of plagiarism or servile imitations. All their works offered a progressive improvement in the career of literature, and the public never was satisfied with any work which was not superior to its preceding. My guide pulled me by the sleeve, saying, " I see you look at every thing with astonishment, but it will soon be increased You remember those charming retreats which attracted your notice when you came here, these are the abodes of those who have caught the enthusiasm of poets, or the impulsive influence of genius. Our academicians are like your Carthusians of old, it is in solitude that the genius extends and strengthens itself, there it springs forward from the common, to open for itself a new path It is when an author communes with himself that enthusiasm and energy spring up in the soul when he digs in that profound mine for treasures, which are often unknown to the possessor Friendship and solitude, O! what powerful inspirers! What more need be desired by those who wish to study nature and truth? Where are their sublime voices to be heard Is it in the tumult of cities, amidst that crowd of passions which imperceptibly assail our hearts?—No it is in the midst of rural scenes that the soul revives and re-envigorates? It is there the true Majesty of the Universe is felt, that eloquent and peaceable Majesty which powerfully inspires energetic expressions, strikes the sentiments, gives a high colouring to the imagination, and elevates the soul above itself.

" In your time men of letters scattered themselves abroad in the circles of insignificant trifling women, and their ambition was directed towards the equivocal smile of approbation of these frivolous judges They sacrificed to
the

the futile power of fashion those sublime ideas, which would have done them honour; they debased their souls, in order to please the taste of the times, by adopting a set of trifling, low opinions, unworthy of a man of genius. Instead of looking forward to the awful series of future ages, they were the slaves of a temporary depravation of style; they were in pursuit of ingenious idle..ces, and stifled the interior voice of reason: but with us they enjoy that happy easy competency, which is all the riches we desire; we do not go to them in order to interrupt them, or to spy out all the emotions of their soul, or to boast of having seen them; we have more respect for their time, which ought not to be frivolously expended, and, ever attentive to all their wants, they are relieved at the first signal."—"If things are thus," said I, "you must have a great number of printing-houses; but you must likewise have a number of persons who assume the appearance of genius, merely as an honorary title to conceal their indolence or their real weakness of intellect."—"Oh! no; this is an enlightened abode, where the least blemish is quickly discovered; the knave and the impostor avoid these places; they cannot face the man of genius, whose penetrating eye discountenances falsehood. As for him, whose presumption would so far mislead as to draw him hither, notwithstanding his incapacity, there are some charitable persons who would soon endeavour to restore him to a right opinion of himself, and dissuade him from a project so greatly to his discredit. In short, the law . . . . . .' Here our conversation was interrupted by a general silence, which suddenly prevailed throughout the assembly. My whole soul flew quickly to the seat of hearing, to catch every word; I perceived one of the academicians preparing to read a manuscript which he held in his hand, and, with a very pleasing manner, which was worth noticing, he began. But, O! ungrateful perfidious Memory! how couldst thou be so unkind as not to allow me to retain the substance of that most eloquent discourse which the academician pronounced? The force, the method, the manner of style, have escaped me; but the impression of it remains deeply engraven in my soul. Never did I feel myself so transported. The countenances of all the auditors expressed the same emotions as those I felt: it was one of the most delightful enjoyments my heart had ever experienced. What depth of reasoning! What beautiful images! What truths! What heavenly fire! How sublime his thoughts! The orator spoke against envy, the sources of this fatal passion, its horrible effects, the infamy it has spread on the laurels with which many great men would otherwise have been crowned; all the detestable vileness and injustice of it were so forcibly expressed, that, while we deplored the fate of the unhappy victims of that blind passion, we also shuddered at the idea of possessing a heart infected with its poison. Here the mirror was so adroitly presented to each particular character, their meannesses were displayed under such varied ridiculous forms, the human heart was sounded in a manner so new, and so striking, that it was difficult not to see oneself in his descriptions, which, while they characterised the disadvantageous side, it was impossible not to form the laudable design of immediately abjuring such pitiful weaknesses; the dread of bearing the least resemblance to that odious monster envy produced a most salutary effect. I saw— O most edifying spectacle! O moment unknown in the annals of literature! I saw those persons who composed the assembly look at each other with a mild and cordial aspect, I saw the academicians mutually embrace, shed tears of joy, while they were pressed to each other's

bosom

bosom with the most sincere friendship. I saw (would it ever have been expected?) the authors dispersed every where in the hall, emulous to give proofs of attachment to each other, acknowledging the talents of their brother authors, and swearing an eternal and unalterable friendship. It was like a family of brothers, who had substituted that honourable kind of applause to our stupid clapping of hands.

When every one had enjoyed these delicious moments, when they had all expressed themselves on the various sensations which the discourse just pronounced had excited, and pointed out those passages which had been most striking, another member of this respectable society arose, with a cheerful smile, the buz of applause was heard through all the assembly, for he had the reputation of being a Socratic jester. he raised his voice and spoke thus.

"Gentlemen,

"SEVERAL reasons have induced me to give you
"this day a very curious extract of what I suppose our
"academy to have been in former times, that is, towards
"the eighteenth century. The cardinal, who founded
"the academy, and whom our predecessors have praised
"beyond all bounds of moderation, to whom were attri-
"buted the most profound and best-intentioned views in
"our establishment, would never have instituted it but
"that he made the most detestable verses, which he him-
"self idolised, and wished to be admired by every one.
"This cardinal, by inviting all men of literature to
"assemble in one body, and subjecting them to regula-
"tions ever unknown to true genius, only displayed his
"despotism. This founder had so little idea of a society
"of this kind, that he thought forty places would suffice,

"there-

" therefore Corneille and Montesquieu, according to these
' circumstances, might never have found room for ad-
" mittance. This cardinal likewise imagined that genius
" would remain obscure, if titles and dignities were not
" brought forward to raise it. When he formed this
" strange opinion, he surely had no other person in view
" than such poetasters as Colletet, and those other poets
" whom he supported through vanity.

" It became then a custom, that those who had money
" instead of merit, or titles instead of genius, should come
" and take seats beside those whose names were cele-
" brated by the voice of fame all over Europe. He
" himself set the first example of this incroachment,
" which was soon followed by many like him, void of
" merit. Those great men, who attracted the whole
" attention of the age in which they flourished, and had
" reason to expect the veneration of posterity, having
" filled the place of their assemblies with glory, were
" soon to see the gate besieged by a gold laced puppy,
" who, because his name was accompanied with a title,
" and his coat ornamented with an honorary ribbon,
" dared to suppose he conferred honour to the humble
" man of genius, by whose side he was placed.

" There were seen generals, vanquishers, and van-
" quished, mitred heads, who had not yet written their
" mandates, gownsmen preceptors, financiers, who
" wished to be thought wits, and, being at best no more
" than the decoration of the scene, thought themselves
" the actors there were scarce eight or ten of the forty
' who shone with their own merit, and yet it was only
" by the death of one of the academicians that another
" member might be chosen to fill the vacancy, which
" choice frequently left the place more truly empty than
" if no choice had been made. Nothing could be more

laugh-

"laughable than to see this academy, the fame of which
"extended to the two extremities of the kingdom, hold-
"ing its assemblies in a small hall, both narrow and low:
"there, upon arm chairs, which had formerly been red,
"were seated these grave academicians, who looked
"weary of their functions ere they had begun them, in
"indolent attitudes weighing a set of syllables, gravely
"examining the words of some sorry piece of poetry
"or prose, and, after all, pass a favourable judgment
"upon the least tolerable of the two but observe,
"gentlemen, that no mistakes were made when they had
"any medals to share in the absence of their fellow-aca-
"demicians, for they always kept the whole. Would
"you believe it, the prize given for the highest degree of
"merit was a gold medal, instead of a branch of oak,
"and upon this medal was engraven this laughable in-
"scription TO IMMORTALITY—and this immortality
"passed the next day into the crucible of the refiner, and
"that was the most substantial advantage which remained
"to the crowned champion and would you believe still
"further, that this little champion sometimes lost his
"senses with ridiculous pride, and that the judges had
"no other functions to perform but to distribute these
"useless prizes which no one even took the trouble to in-
"quire to whom they were given

"The hall was only open to authors, but the unlet-
"tered multitude might gain admittance by means of
"certain tickets signed by some great personage. The
"day began by a fine mass, performed by the opera
"band, at which a trembling priest pompously declaimed
"the panegyric of Louis the IXth (though I cannot
"well say why), praised him for more than an hour, al-
"though he certainly was not a good king, and when
"the orator entered upon the subject of the Crusades,

"he

"he displayed his powers, and the refinement of his
"rhetoric: this, in general, incensed the wrath of the
" archbishop, who laid the orator under an interdict for
" having dared to speak good sense. In the evening ano-
" ther eulogium was given, but as it was generally on
" some profane subject, the archbishop did not pronounce
" his opinion on the matter it contained. It must be
" observed, likewise, that the hall of Genius was guarded
" by a number of fusileers, and gigantic Swiss, who
" understood not a word of French. Nothing was so
" comical as to see the encounter between one of these
" learned, with meagre aspect, and one of the guards,
" whose enormous stature seemed to repel their entrance.
" These days were usually called public assemblies; the
" public, indeed, did make their appearance, but it was
" to remain outside the door, which was very ill-requi-
" ting their complaisance in coming to hear them.

" In the mean time, the only liberty which the nation
" was entitled to, was that of pronouncing decisively
" upon their pieces of prose or verse, and of hissing one
" author, or applauding another, and very often to laugh
" at them all.

" The academical rage took possession of every one,
" they all were devoured with the ambition to be 'royal
" censors,' and afterwards academician. The days and
" years of the members of this august assembly were
" numbered by the competitors, they calculated the de-
" gree of vigor they seemed to possess, and mortality never
" descended quick enough for the wishes of the rival—
" they are immortal! said they: one would mutter to
" himself, on seeing another elected, ah! when shall I
" be so happy as to make thy funeral oration, at the end
" of the great table, and declare thee a great man, con-
" jointly with Louis XIV. and the chancellor Seguier:
" when

" when thou wilt be forgotten, and sleep in a coffin loaded
" with epitaphs?

" At length by the successful cabals of the rich, in an
" age when gold was held in higher estimation than every
" thing else, they effectually removed all the men of let-
" ters from this place, so that the ensuing generation
" saw the forty chairs filled by the *fermiers-généraux*,
" wherein they slumbered as much at their ease as did
" their predecessors, and they were still more dextrous in
" the management of the medals; and then arose the
" well known proverb 'it is impossible to gain admit-
" tance at the academy without an equipage.' Men of
" letters in despair, not knowing how to recover their
" usurped domain, began a formal conspiracy; they
" called in their usual weapons, epigrams, songs, ballads,
" &c. they exhausted all the arrows of satire, but, alas!
" they all proved impotent; their hearts were become so
" callous, that they were insensible even to the most
" piercing darts of ridicule. The gentlemen-authors
" had in vain expended their "bon-mots," if they had
" not been assisted by a serious indigestion, which one
" day seized all the academicians as they were returning
" home from a most splendid feast. Apollo, Plutus, and
" the God of Digestion, are three divinities who are always
" at variance. This disorder, added to the titles of
" financier and academician, so entirely overpowered
" them that they all died; by this means the men of
" letters were restored to their ancient domain, and the
" academy was saved." . . . .

The whole assembly burst out in loud exclamations and
laughter. Some members came and asked me in a whis-
per, if this was an exact relation? "Yes," said I, "it
is nearly all true; but, when we look at the distance of
seven hundred years back, it may certainly be allowable

to

to ridicule the dead. However, I have heard the academy acknowledge, even in my time, that a separate member, taken individually, claimed more merit than the whole collective body of the academy. Nothing could be added to such a confession; the misfortune is, that so on as men assemble in a body, their minds become contracted, as Montesquieu himself acknowledged."

I walked through the hall, in which were suspended all the portraits of the academicians both ancient and modern. I contemplated the portraits of those who are to succeed the present members; but, that I may not vex any person, I shall beware of mentioning their names. I cannot refrain, however, relating a fact which will certainly give great delight to hearts of sensibility, who love justice, and detest tyranny; it was the portrait of Abbe St. Pierre, which I saw re-instated and restored to its rank with all the honours due to his prerogative; he was placed between Fenelon and Montesquieu. I highly praised an equity so noble, and expressed all my approbation of this delightful author. The servile meanness with which the academy had so long debased itself, by bending under a foreign yoke, was now totally effaced. I no longer saw the portrait of Richelieu, nor that of Christina, nor that of . . ., nor that of . . ., which, though only in painting, were most certainly misplaced.

I descended the hill, looking back several times to those shady groves, the residence of those eminent men of genius, who in silence, and in the contemplation of nature, laboured to form the hearts of their fellow-citizens to virtue, to the love of truth, and of the sublime—and I could not refrain exclaiming to myself HOW GLORIOUS TO BE WORTHY OF BEING ADMITTED A MEMBER OF SUCH AN ACADEMY!

CHAP

CHAP. XXXI.

Say, thro' the air, the seas, or the earth,
What others find, a being, who lives
Above, how high progressive life may go!
Around, how wide! how deep extend below!
Vast chain of being! which from God began,
Natures ethereal, human, angel, man,
Beast, bird, fish, insect, what no eye can see,
No glass can reach, from infinite to thee,
From thee to nothing——

WITHIN a small distance of the enchanting abode of the Muses which I had just left, I perceived a spacious temple, to which I approached filled with reverence and admiration, the following inscription which I saw engraven on its front, here excited my curiosity, AN ABRIDGEMENT OF THE UNIVERSE. "Behold the king's closet," said a man who was standing by me! "Not that this edifice particularly belongs to him, it belongs to the state, but we give it that title to shew the esteem we have to his person, and particularly as our sovereign, after the example of the ancient kings, exercises physic, surgery, and the arts. That happy time is returned, when men in power, who possess those funds necessary for great experiments, are flattered with the glory of making discoveries important to human nature, and therefore hasten to raise the sciences to that degree of perfection, which will be the infallible consequence of their zealous researches. The most considerable persons of the nation make use of their wealth to extract all the secrets of nature, and gold, which was formerly the source of vice, and the reward of idleness, is now a fund that humanizes and ennobles the hearts of men."

I entered

(158)

I entered, and was seized with a delightful surprise! this temple was the animated palace of Nature all the productions which she brings forth were assembled here with great profusion, but not without great order and regularity this temple was erected with four wings of an immense extent, and surmounted with the largest dome my eyes ever beheld

On every side I saw figures of marble with peculiar inscriptions, viz TO THE INVENTOR OF THE IN-CLINED PLANE—TO THE INVENTOR OF THE TURN-ING WHEEL—TO THE INVENTOR OF THE LEVER—OF THE PULLEY—THE WEDGE AND THE SCREW, &c. &c

Every sort of animal, of vegetable, and of mineral, were placed within these four wings, so as to be discovered at first sight. What a prodigious and marvellous assemblage!

In the first wing I saw every tree and plant, from the tall cedar down to the humble hyssop

In the second, every flying bird and insect, from the towering eagle to the wanton fly

In the third, every quadruped and crawling insect and reptile, from the docile elephant to the conceited glow-worm.

In the last, every fish, from the great whale to the elegant little gold fish

In the midst of the dome were all the various sports of nature, monsters of all kinds, the most strange, the most wonderful and rare productions for when nature deviates from her usual laws, she discovers a greater depth of intelligence than when she follows her accustomed rules. On every side were seen large entire pieces taken from the mines, and presented the secret elaboratory wherein Nature works those metals which man have rendered both useful and dangerous Several long layers of
land

and artfully dug up, and dexteroufly placed, prefented the whole interior of the earth, and the wonderful order fhe obferves in the different beds of ftone, of clay, or of lime, which fhe herfelf arranges.

How great was my aftonifhment, when, inftead of a few dried bones, I difcovered the immenfe whale, the monftrous hippopotamus, the terrible crocodile, &c. &c. whole and entire. In this arrangement, all the gradations and varieties with which nature accompanies her productions, were obferved thus the eye might follow without difficulty the whole fcale of beings from the largeft to the leaft the lion, the tiger, and the panther, all in the fierce attitudes which characterife them The voracious animals were reprefented as fpringing fiercely on their prey the energy of all their motions, and that powerful breath of life which animated them, had been nearly preferved. Other animals, of a milder afpect and ingenious nature, were feen with almoft the fame countenance as when living craft, induftry, patience, all thefe were expreffed by art the natural hiftory of every animal was engraven befide him, and that which would have taken too much time to write was verbally explained by thefe ingenious men.

That fcale of beings, formerly fo much difcuffed and doubted, and which feveral of our philofophers had judiciously fufpected to exift, had at this time been evidently proved It was now diftinctly afcertained that every fpecies, by a gradual progreffion, were clofely linked together, that by the moft delicate but evident avenues, from a rough hewn ftone to a plant, from a plant to an animal, and from an animal to man, the chain was uninterrupted, that, in fhort, the fame caufes of growth, of duration, and of deftruction, were common to all Thefe philofophers had difcovered that man was the nobleft work of nature,

that

that all her operations tended to his improvement, that she had patiently elaborated this important work, making various diftant effays in order to attain the gradual term of perfection, and that the human fpecies was apparently the laft effort referved for her glorious workmanfhip.

This cabinet of wonderful productions was far from being a chaos of confufion, or an undigefted mafs where objects were fcattered, and crowded one upon the other without offering any precife idea; but the gradation was wifely arranged, and that which ftill increafed the riches, the order, and regularity of this collection, was a preparation which had lately been difcovered to preferve thofe infects which have fprung from corruption. I felt myfelf oppreffed with the weight of fo many miracles. I embraced at one view the whole luxury of nature. How much I admired its great author at this moment! what homage I paid to his omnipotence, to his wifdom, and to his goodnefs ftill more precious and admirable! how great was man, while walking in the midft of fo many marvels collected by his own hands, and which feemed all created for himfelf; for he alone enjoys the advantage of feeling and perceiving them. That proportioned connection, thofe various fhades ever obferved, and ever regular; thofe apparent vacancies ever confiftent with nature's laws, that gradual order, that plan which admits of no intermediary, all this, after the profpect of the heavens, is the moft awful and magnificent fpectacle upon this globe, which in itfelf is no more than an atom, when compared to the whole immenfe univerfe.

"By what means,' faid I, " have fuch aftonifhing things been executed?"

" It is the work of feveral of our kings," they replied. " curious of rending the veil by which the bofom of nature was obfcured, and jealous of doing honour to the title of
intelli

gent being, they were animated with this fublime and generous emulation, and never fuffered their zeal to abate in this laudable purfuit. Inftead of enumerating all the battles gained, and the cities taken by affault, or an innumerable variety of unjuft and fanguinary conquefts, it is faid of our kings, ' He has made fuch and fuch difcoveries in the immenfe ocean of things; he has accomplifhed fuch a project favourable to mankind.—THE PUBLIC MONEY IS NO LONGER EXPENDED BY MILLIONS, IN ORDER TO SLAUGHTER THOUSANDS OF MEN IN A CAMPAIGN. It is, on the contrary, employed in augmenting the real riches of the ftate, in extending the genius and induftry of the people, in augmenting their refources, and in completing their happinefs.'

" Many fecret and important difcoveries have been made by men in all appearance uninformed and unintelligent; they have fometimes alfo been loft foon as made, but we are convinced that our refearches would always be crowned with fuccefs, were we to perfevere in them. In the vaft bofom of nature a thoufand refources are found; it is there they muft be fought, her fecrets lie deep, and by perpetually agitating the chain of ideas we at laft ftrike upon that ray of light which we thought the moft diftant. thus being affured of the poffibility of making the moft aftonifhing difcoveries, we have endeavoured not to lofe time. We do not attribute any thing to the power of chance, it is an obfolete word in our language. Chance is but a fynonymous term for ignorance, we make ufe of thofe inftruments beft calculated to make Nature difcover her moft hidden treafures, fuch as labour, fagacity, and patience. Man has learned how to employ the gifts he has received to the beft advantage, having once conceived the elevated point of knowledge which he might attain, his ambition gave him wings to foar up still higher into the infinite region opened to him. We have discovered that the life of one man is too limited for researches, therefore we have re-united the powers of each individual, and they have had a wonderful success. One man has perfected what another began, the chain is never interrupted, every link is united, and thus it will endure to the extent of ages this wonderful chain of ideas, and of continual labours, will one day embrace and enclose the whole universe. In your days all your laudable enterprizes had but one motive in view, the self-interested desire of personal glory, but here it is the interest of mankind which softens every difficulty, we no longer bewilder ourselves with senseless systems thanks to the folly of your times, they are all exhausted and destroyed we now direct our steps by the torch of experience our aim is to know the secret movement and spring of all things in nature, and to extend the dominion of man by giving him the means of executing every enterprise which may aggrandize his being.

"We have a few hermits, who live in forests, but it is only to study the nature of herbs and plants, and they repair hither on certain days to impart the useful discoveries they have made. We have erected some towers upon the summit of mountains, from which continual observations are made upon the heavenly bodies, all corresponding to each other. We have formed artificial torrents and cataracts, in order to attain sufficient force to produce the effects of motion. We have established aromatic baths for the recovery of persons grown decrepid by age and infirmity, which cause the renewal both of their strength and powers, for the author of our being, no doubt, has given those salutary plants, and the knowledge of their uses, in order to entrust to man's industry the care of preserving his health, and the precious, but

frail,

frail, web of his days. Even our walks afford us a useful tribute of knowledge, we meet with none but fruitful trees to recreate our eyes and gratify our smell, instead of your useless linden trees, your steril chesnut, and grubby elms. We graft and innoculate our wild trees, that our labours may be equal to the liberality of nature, who only awaits the helping hand of man, for whom the great Creator has reserved all her exhaustless stores. We have also some very extensive "menageries" of all sorts of animals, many species of which we have found in the wild recesses of deserts, entirely unknown in your time. We mix their breed, on the result of which we make our observations. upon this head we have made some very extraordinary and useful discoveries. some sort of breeds are much increased in size, and more prolific. In short, we have observed, that the pains taken to improve nature are rarely fruitless. we have also found several secrets which had been lost in your time, because your authors were given to write a multiplicity of words, rather than, by dint of laborious study, to raise the wonderful inventions we have now discovered. We possess, as the ancients did, the art of making the malleable glass, the *specular lapis*, the Tyrian purple used for dying the garments of emperors, the mirror of Archimedes, the Egyptian art of embalming dead bodies, the machines with which they erected their obelisks, the shirts in which dead bodies were consumed to ashes upon the pile, the art of melting stones, the inextinguishable lamps, and even the Apician sauce.

" Take a walk in those gardens wherein you will find botany arrived at the highest degree of perfection. Your blind philosophers complained that the earth was covered with poisons. but we have discovered them to be the most active remedies which could be employed for various disorders. Providence has been juftified, and would be fo in every point, if our underftandings were not fo weak and con'racted. The voice of complaint is no longer heard all over the earth, no lamentable accent is heard to exclaim, that the calamities of life furpafs its bleffings, that every thing is ordered upon the worft plan; but, on the contrary, we all cry with one accord, that every thing is eftablifhed upon the beft and happieft plan. The worft effects of poifons having been difcovered and defcribed, we no longer fear them.

"We have extracted the juices from all plants with fo much fuccefs, that we make various liquors capable of penetrating into the pores and mixing with the fluids, thereby re eftablifhing conftitutions, and rendering bodies more robuft and fupple. We have acquired the fecret of diffolving the ftone in human bodies without burning the entrails. We have a cure for the phthifick and all pulmonary diforders formerly pronounced mortal but the beft of our exploits is, that of having exterminated that abominable hydra, that difgraceful and cruel fcourge, which attacked the fource of life and generation; the human fpecies groaned under this dreadful diftemper, and were on the brink of deftruction, we have difcovered that happy fpecific which was to reftore him to pleafure, and to life, a ftill more defirable good."

In my walks through this valuable affemblage I was accompanied by the Buffon of that century, who added demonftrations to words, and we examined every object of natural hiftory, to which he joined his own reflections

But that which furprifed me moft was a clofet full of optics, where they had fkilfully re-united every accident of light, it was one con inued magic. They prefented to my fight a variety of landfcapes, fome particular profpects, palaces, rainbows, meteors, illumined cyphers,

feas

ſeas which had no existence, but the illusion was more striking to my senses than if they had really existed, it was the abode of enchantment the whole spectacle of the creation, created in the twinkling of an eye, would not have excited a more quick and exquisite sensation. They also presented some particular sort of microscopes to me, through which I discovered a multiplicity of new beings, which had always escaped the eyes of our modern observers. None of these wonders were fatiguing to the eye, the power and operations of art were so simple, and at the same time so subtile. Every step advanced in this spot I found objects capable of satisfying the most ardent curiosity, which became more inexhaustible, the more food it found to devour. Often I exclaimed, "Oh, how great is man! but how trifling and insignificant those who, in my time, were stiled great, when compared to these!"

The science of accoustics also was raised to a very high and wonderful degree of perfection, so much so, that they knew how to imitate all the sounds articulated by the human voice, the cry of every different species of animals, and the various notes of the feathered race, by some particular operation upon certain springs. By this wonderful invention, a man might imagine himself in some wild forest in the midst of lions, tigers, bears, and wolves, the imitation was so exact, that the most intrepid mind might be betrayed into sensations of fear, for it was like the distant echo of those discordant sounds, but when the warbling of the nightingale succeeded, every particle of air was filled with delightful melody, 'strains most grateful to the ear.' This imitation was so delicately natural, that the imagination might fancy the amorous fluttering of their wings, and the eyes in vain sought for the little objects capable of producing such sounds. Men have endeavoured to imitate the melody of birds, but all their efforts have never been crowned with any success equal to that which I heard at that moment; surprise succeeded to an excess of pleasure, and filled the hearts of all present with a delirium of transporting sensations.

This people, who always had some good end in view, by encouraging the prodigies of any curious art, knew how to make these deep inventions produce the greatest advantages. As soon as any young prince discovered an inclination towards combats, or any martial disposition, he was led to a large hall, to which the appellation of *Hell* had very justly been given; immediately a person, who superintended the machinery, set fire to several springs for that purpose, and all the horrors of an engagement were produced. The shrieks of rage, and those of pain, the plaintive groans of the dying, the sounds of terror, and the bellowing of that dreadful thunder-signal of destruction and death. If the feelings of nature were not roused, if his soul was not struck with horror, if his countenance remained calm and immoveable, he was confined in this dreadful place; and this scene was represented to him every day, that his ferocious propensities might be gratified, but not at the expense of suffering nature. The steward of this cabinet, taking me by surprise, began to play all those terrible engines, by which this whole scene was laid open to my senses. "O heavens!" I exclaimed, "spare me, spare my ears, spare my feelings!"—"What!" said he, "does it not please you?" —"This can please none but devils," I replied.—"And yet, in your time," said he, "this diversion was very common, and that which kings and princes were passionately fond of; this you called an opera; and to this entertainment you all resorted, as well as to that of the chace, which was equally the passion of all, kings, princes, nobles of every

every degree, after having for many hours followed this inhuman diversion with the most unfeeling barbarity, were addressed in long epistles of praises and congratulations by the best poets of the age, for having spread terror among the poor inhabitants of the air and forests for thirty or forty miles round. Such were the noble subjects which inspired these sons of the Muses a battle, where thousands were slaughtered by their fellow-creatures, would often produce the highest panegyric upon the ambitious monarch, who was the unfeeling cause of so much mischief and devastation."—" Ah!" cried I, " mention not that epidemic disease alas! it had every symptom of madness and folly A monarch, sitting cowardly on his throne, would, with a word of command, send thousands to be sacrificed, and this obedient flock, by order of its shepherd, would joyously march to receive the stroke of death In those days of illusion, no circumstance, though of the most disastrous nature, had the power of opening their eyes, no catastrophe could break the magic talisman, but a little blue or red ribband, a staff, an enamelled cross, or some such bauble, was sufficient to spread the frenzy amongst all ranks of people, others were mad at the sight of a cockade, or of a few pieces of money This cruel disorder must have taken a long time to eradicate, but I have always thought, that, sooner or later, the balm of philosophy would heal these wounds so disgraceful to human nature."

From this place I went into the closet of mathematics, which was very rich, and very properly arranged. All those useless trifles, which seemed best calculated to amuse children, every thing proper only to encourage an idle or useless speculation, or whatever seemed above the limits of the human understanding, were totally banished from this place. I saw all sorts of machines invented for the relief of man in laborious works, and capable of much more force than thofe known in our times with thefe the heavieſt loads appeared to lofe half their weight, for they might be ufed in various ways, and on different occafions. "You fee," faid they, "all thefe obelifks, thefe triumphal arches, thefe palaces, thofe bold monuments, which aftoniſh the human eye, the inftruments we have made ufe of, which were perfect, have perfected our architecture." In fact, I found here in detail every exact inftrument, either for geometry, aftronomy, &c &c.

All thofe who had attempted any bold or new experiment, even if they had failed (for inftruction often follows, though fuccefs may not be attained), had their bufts erected in marble, environed with their fuitable attributes.

One of the profeffors obferved to me, " that feveral marvellous and fingular fecrets were entrufted only to a few wife men, who were capable of making a proper ufe of them, that there were many things very good in themfelves, of which it was very eafy to miftake the ufe, that the human mind was not yet arrived at that high ſtate of perfection which it was to attain ere it made great and wonderful difcoveries, without making a dangerous ufe of them"

CHAP.

CHAP. XXXII.

See, nature taste the varied scene imbibes
With the rich lustre of the rainbow's hues!
See, from each pencil varying beauties rise,
While the proud canvas glows with mingling dyes
See, fancy gives to every mimic form
New power to fascinate, new grace to charm,
While on each finished, each attractive part,
Nature stands wondering at the touch of art

AS the arts were all united under the same roof, I very soon arrived at the Academy of Paintings. I traversed some very spacious saloons ornamented with pieces executed by the first masters, each of them presented subjects of instruction equal to what might be found in a book of morality. That collection of mythology so long repeated, continually and eternally the subject of every piece, was now totally forgotten. the artful ingenuity of these tales had, it seems, given them a right to be tedious The best inventions become common in time, thus it was with the gross flatteries of those adulators who had deified Louis XIV Time and truth had devoured these lying canvas, and had placed the verses of Boileau and the prologues of Quinault in their true places. It was forbidden to represent falshoods, those men, called amateurs, who prescribed laws to the genius of artists with a sum of gold, no longer called Genius was now free, it followed none but its own laws, and never debased itself. In these galleries of paintings were no longer seen either the dreadful representations of bloody battles, the shameful debaucheries of the fabulous gods, and still less a variety of sovereigns surrounded by all those virtues in which they were most deficient No

subjects

(170)

subjects were represented but those calculated to inspire sentiments of sublime virtue. Those Pagan divinities, as absurd as they are scandalous, no longer engrossed the pencils of those artists, whose precious time was employed and destined to transmit to posterity the most important facts; such as fell under this denomination, were all those capable of giving a noble idea of mankind, such as clemency, generosity, public interest, courage, contempt of luxury, &c.

I saw several pieces representing those beautiful subjects worthy of being recorded; those sovereigns who possessed greatness of soul were immortalized. The generous ardour of the noble Saladin; Henry the Great sending provisions to the city he was besieging; Sully slowly counting out a sum of money which his master destined for his pleasures; Louis XIV on the bed of death, saying, *I have been too fond of war*; Trajan, tearing his garments to bind up the wounds of a poor man; Marcus Aurelius alighting from his horse, while going on a pressing expedition, in order to take the petition of a poor woman; Titus distributing bread and medicines to the sick; the Chevalier de St Hilaire, who when his arm was shot off was directing the attention of his weeping son to the great Turenne, then wounded and lying on the ground; the generous Fabre receiving the chains of a galley-slave to release his father, &c. These generous subjects were neither thought too gloomy nor too sorrowful. There were none of those vile courtiers who would ridicule the morality of these pieces. The public, on the contrary, were grateful to these painters for having collected those sublime traits which raised human nature; this mode of writing history they had very justly observed to be the most useful. All the arts had conspired in favour of humanity, and this happy correspondence had cast the brightest ray of light

on

on the sacred effigy of Virtue, who is thereby become more amiable, and her features, continually embellished, formed a public school of instruction, as successful as it was pathetic, for it was not possible to resist the voice of fine arts, unanimous in rewarding and crowning the efforts of the free and generous citizen.

All these pieces attracted the eye, equally by their execution as by their subjects. The painters had united the Italian style of feature to the Flemish colouring, or rather, they had surpassed them both by a more profound study. Honour, the only specie worthy of great men, by animating their labours gave an early reward here nature seemed reflected, as in a mirror. The friend of virtue never could contemplate these delightful pictures without rapture, but the guilty and vicious durst not lift their eyes towards them, lest these inanimate figures were to address them in the language of accusation and reproach they deserved.

I was informed that these pieces were to be exposed to public examination, and prizes given according to the particular merit of each artist, and all strangers were invited to this exhibition. Every year, four different subjects were given, that every artist might have sufficient time to bring his work to the highest perfection. The general voice of the people soon decided for the most perfect, and this universal approbation was always attended to as the most equitable. The other less successful candidates for fame likewise received that praise which was their due, they were not so unjust as to discourage their pupils, nor were the professors acquainted with that unworthy and ungenerous jealousy which was the cause of the exile of Le Poussin, and of the premature death of Le Sueur. These academicians had conquered that dangerous and fatal obstinacy, which, in my time,
would

would not even allow their disciples to follow any particular style of drawing but their own. They did not disgrace the genius of those pupils who might have raised themselves to a high degree of perfection, by keeping them all their lives as copyists. Disciples were no longer oppressed under the weight of a ruling scepter, which only served to render them more timid; they were not obliged to restrain their genius by following the tardy progress of a capricious master, of whom nothing was to be obtained without flattery but they were suffered to overtake him, if their genius would allow them; and the teacher was always the first to be proud of the improvements of his pupils.

There were several academies of drawing, of painting, of sculpture, and of practical geometry. These arts, so dangerous in my time, by favouring luxury, ostentation, avarice, and libertinism, were now of greatest use, because they were only employed in giving lessons of virtue; and that by these various embellishments, the city wore an air of dignity and majesty, and afforded those agreeable acquisitions, which encouraged such simple and noble pursuits, which, by a secret association of ideas, exalt the souls of the people.

These schools were opened to the public, under whose particular inspection the students prosecuted their studies. Here every person found access, and had the liberty of giving their opinion; but each respective master continued his visits. Here were no titled apprentices of such or such an artist, but they professed to imitate every able master in general. By thus avoiding even the shadow of slavery, so fatal to the masculine and independent spirit of genius, they had succeeded in perfecting the art, and the arts to a degree so eminent, that they raised themselves above the greatest masterpieces of antiquity. Their
works

works were so highly finished, that the remains of Rubens or Raphael were no longer sought for but by a small number of persons, and those were antiquaries, who have always been an obstinate people

I need not say that every art and every profession were equally free. It belonged only to the seventeenth and eighteenth centuries, of barbarism and tyranny, to give fetters to industry, to exact a sum of money, under the appellation of a patent, from him who would exert his talents, instead of giving him that reward due to his exertions. In these times, such a body as they called an academy was only a burlesque society, where men's passions were set in a violent ferment. These persons always had a multiplicity of endless affairs, to which, by being confined, they necessarily became troublesome to their neighbours. It is thus in prisons, those who are oppressed by the weight of their chains communicate to each other both their rage and vices. By attempting a separation of interests, the freedom which ought to reign in such assemblies was totally lost. Being under that constraint which prescribed even the style of drawing to which they must be confined, they neglected every effort of genius, and plunged themselves into disorders of every kind. The indigent was unable to raise himself from his miserable situation, because every means of exalting his genius was barred against him, and that gold alone could open a passage for him, while the monarch, in order to enjoy an insignificant tribute, had destroyed the most sacred liberty, and had caused every effort of courage and industry to droop in obscurity.

Among these people, who were enlightened upon the first principles of the rights of the people, every one followed that employ to which his particular taste inclined him, which is a sure method to succeed. Those who had no inclination for the fine arts followed other purfuits more adopted to their faculties, for nothing of mediocrity was fuffered in what related to genius the glory of the whole nation feemed attached to thofe talents which diftinguifhed men as well as empires.

CHAP. XXXIII.

*Ah! wilt thou then recall thofe fcenes of woe,
And teach again my fanatic tears to flow?*

I Paffed into a private hall, in which the genius of each century was reprefented under emblematic figures. All the peculiar features which diftinguifhed them had been carefully depicted. Thofe of ignorance were drawn under the figure of perfons clothed in black, with gloomy enfigns, the chief figure, whofe eye was hollow, and deeply tinged with red, held a torch in hand, in the back ground, a pile was feen, and priefts clothed in furplices, furrounded by feveral wretches, who were blindfolded, devoting themfelves to the flames. At a little diftance, a fanatic enthufiaft without any virtue, but an ardent imagination, appeared eager to inflame the minds of his fellow citizens under the pretence of religion, and was mifleading a crowd of perfons, who, like a flock of fheep, were blindly hurrying headlong down a precipice. Kings were feen quitting their depopulated territories, miftaking the flight of their own imagination for the voice of heaven, calling them to inhabit deferts and woods, thereby leaving their fubjects to the mifery of an ill-governed nation. A monftrous giant, whofe feet extended to the two extremities of the earth, walking upon the

heads

(175)

...ads of men, shaking ... torches, which were so many signals for homicide... ...olding in the other hand the palm of martyrdom, which reached up to the clouds, such was the figure representing fanaticism in another part of the piece.

Others, less violent, ... contemplative, given up to mystery and illusion, ... plunging into the marvellous ... ...they seemed to take pains to ... ... with which they were environed; the ... Platonic rings, the Pythagorean numbers ... verses, with the powerful ceremonies of ... and all the ingenious and stupid illusions which the human mind has created.

Another was seen with a ... in hand, consulting a calendar, and calculating the fortunate or unfortunate days upon his lengthened ... ...onomy was depicted a cold taciturn gravity, he turned ... the conjunction of two planets, for him, time present had no existence, and the future was his tormenter. His form of worship was extracted from the ridiculous science of astrology, and he was embracing that phantom as his unerring guide.

Again, I saw another figure all covered with steel, whose head was buried in a brazen helmet, clothed with a coat of mail, and armed with a long spear; he breathed revenge, and longed for private combats. The hearts of these heroes were harder than the steel which covered them. It was iron, which alone seemed to have the right of deciding upon the opinions of justice and truth. Near this figure were seen many others of the same kind in the background, where several judges and heralds were rewarding the vanquisher, and raising the vanquished. Another personage, of an extravagant appearance, was busied in building and erecting columns without observing the rules of proportion, and covering them with ridiculous ornaments

ments he was a barbarous architect without taste or judgment, and he mistook his grotesque style for a delicacy of work unknown among the Greeks or Romans. His logic was accompanied with the same disorder, it was nothing but perpetual cavils and abstracted ideas. A group of somnambulators were talking and acting with their eyes open, but plunged in a profound dream, and never had two connected ideas but by the greatest chance.

Thus I took a survey of every age, but it would be tedious to give a detail of all the figures I saw. I could not help taking particular notice of the eighteenth century, which had been that of which I had the most knowledge. The painter had represented it under the figure of a woman her haughty and delicately beautiful head was loaded and fatigued with the richest and most precious ornaments, her neck, her breast, and her arms, were covered with pearls and diamonds, her eyes were full of fire, and uncommonly brilliant, but a forced smile gave an air of constraint to her mouth; her cheeks were extremely ruddy, but it was the glow of a hectic fever rather than that of health her words, as well as her looks, were artful and seducing, but all was false in both. She had upon each hand two very long ribbons of a rose colour, which appeared like ornaments but these ribbons only served to conceal two iron chains, by which she was closely confined. Her movements, however, seemed perfectly free, she could gesticulate, jump, and make a thousand gambols, which power she took care to use with excess, in order (as I thought) the better to disguise her slavery, or to make it seem easy and agreeable. I attentively examined this figure, and took notice that her magnificent robe was hanging in rags at the bottom, and all covered with mud and filth. Her bare feet and legs were plunging deep in a thick mire, and her extremities

ties were as abominably hideous as her summit was fine and dazzling. In this piteous state she was very like a courtezan walking the streets after the close of the evening, behind her were several children, whose pale complexions and meagre looks bespoke misery and famine; they were devouring a piece of black bread, and raising their piteous looks and cries towards their mother, who strove to hide them under her robe, but the little wretches were clearly discovered through the holes. At the end of the piece were several superb castles, marble palaces, beautiful parterres, and spacious forests filled with stags and fawns, the huntsman was seen at a distance sounding his horn, surrounded by dogs and hunters, but the country was but half cultivated, and a variety of unfortunate peasants were represented harassed with fatigue, and dropping down upon a gavel of corn a number of men were surrounding some, forcing them to inlist, and carrying away the beds and provisions of others.

The character of every nation was faithfully depicted and expressed By the various colours of a thousand different hues, by the insensible gradation from light to the darkest shade, by the sad and gloomy countenance, the jealous and revengeful Italian was known. There was a mixture of seriousness and gaiety in his aspect, but in the outward lines of his features there was an expression of softness, which seemed the effect of the melody of a concert to which he was attentively listening, and the painter had wonderfully seized that facility of giving an instantaneous suppleness to his countenance, for which the Italian is so distinguished The back ground of this piece was filled with pantomimes, who were making grimaces and comical gestures.

The Englishman was represented in an attitude rather haughty than majestic. situated upon the summit of a rock, he appeared as commanding the ocean, and was making a signal to a ship in full sail to depart for the new world, and to return from thence laden with treasures. In his countenance was an audacity, which seemed to say, "That civil and political liberty were both equally cherished by his nation." The waves, which were dashing against the foot of that rock on which he was standing, and roaring with the tempest, was the kind of harmony most grateful to his ear. His arm appeared ready lifted to seize the weapon of intestine commotion, but it was in defence of his liberty, while he smilingly arrested his looks towards a scaffold, upon which were the ensigns of a recent execution—it was that of his sovereign.

The German appeared unappalled and deaf to the concussion of the elements; and while the thunder roared and the blue lightning flashed, he seemed either to brave the storm, or to be insensible of it. On all sides of him, eagles were tearing each other with violent fury, but for him it was a spectacle at which he was unmoved; his thoughts seemed concentrated within himself, and he contemplated with an eye of indifference, or philosophy, his future destiny.

The Frenchman, full of noble and exalted graces, appeared under the most finished form; there was nothing original in his countenance, but much greatness in his manner; and his physiognomy expressed both imagination and quick sense: he smiled with an air of cunning, bordering upon craft. His whole figure was uniform and consistent. The colouring of this piece was fine, but the bold strokes of character, and the beautiful effects of light and shade, were not so conspicuous in this painting as in the others. The eye was fatigued by a multiplicity of trifling minutiæ, which crowded each other to no effect. A vast number of little creatures were carrying tambourines

and

and other inftruments; and were taking much trouble to produce a great noife, by which they thought to imitate that of the cannon, but it was an activity and petulance of a moment, and it was feeble and ineffectual, as it was of fhort duration.

CHAP. XXXIV.

In lighten'd France! no more I view
With cold contempt thy glittering coaft,
To active worth is honour due,
The fetter'd mind has caufe to boaft

SCULPTURE, the younger fifter of Painting, prefented a no lefs beautiful appearance, and difplayed all the wonders of her chiflel. It was now no longer proftituted to a fet of infamous fons of Plutus, who debafed the art, by engroffing it to carve their venal figures, or other fubjects equally defpicable. Thofe artifts who were penfioned by government confecrated their talents to merit and virtue. In thefe galleries were no longer feen, as heretofore, the bufts of kings upon the fame line with thofe of the infidious flatterers, who had deceived and defrauded them, but if a man, of whatever condition he might be, had been worthy to attract the notice of pofterity, by a career full of glory and memorable incidents, if any had been famed for fome great and courageous action, then the artift took upon himfelf the care of difcharging the tribute of public gratitude. He fecretly modelled one of the fineft traits of his life, and prefented his work, by which the artift immortalized himfelf, by immortalizing the great or good man. This reprefentation of virtue was always striking, and needed no commentary. All subjects which conveyed no language to the soul, were absolutely prohibited in sculpture, consequently there were no fine pieces of marble, or other materials, put to improper uses. All licentious pieces were banished. This was a part of our legislation which this good people could not comprehend, while they read so much in our histories of our attention to religion and morals, that fathers of families exposed before the eyes of their children such scenes of profligacy, under the frivolous pretence of their being master-pieces of art, calculated as they were to inflame the coldest imaginations, and to precipitate the minds of young people, liable to all sorts of impressions, into innumerable disorders. they lamented this custom, thus established among us, of publicly and criminally depraving the hearts of men ere they were half formed.

An artist, with whom I have been conversing, informed me of all these changes. He told me, that in the nineteenth century, there being a great want of marble, the artists were allowed to make use of those innumerable ignoble busts of financiers, flatterers, and commissioners, which served as so many blocks ready prepared, they were much better carved than before, and presented more valuable subjects. From this gallery I passed into the next, which was no less curious, by the variety of good pieces it contained. Here I found a collection of all sorts of engravings and designs, for though they had attained a high degree of perfection in this art, they had preserved every performance of the preceding ages, to serve for comparisons, for the imperfections of these works are soon discerned, and therefore they are not dangerous like bad books, whose poison is concealed under the most artful clothing.

This

This gallery owed its origin to Louis XV. but it was very differently arranged to what it had been. It was no longer a small closet, in the centre of which a table was placed, which would scarcely admit a dozen persons, and to which it was impossible to gain a seat, even after having paid several different times, which closet was never opened but once in the year, but now it was free of access every day, and entrusted to persons who were paid with punctuality, that the public might be gratified at all times. In this spacious hall were found all the pieces engraven, which had been carved in marble, it contained an abridgment of all the master pieces which had been immortalized and made known to the world. These people are as happy in the art of engraving as in typography, which, like the latter, had procured a great advantage to its admirers, by multiplying its proofs; and by this means, strangers may procure copies, which are sometimes superior to the original, with which they decorate their dwellings, as the most interesting representations of virtue and heroism. There were none of those pretended amateurs, no less trifling than ignorant, who, at the expense of their peace, and of their purse, were in constant pursuit of an imaginary perfection, and were always the dupe of their own folly.

I surveyed, with an eager eye, all those folios, containing the easy symmetry and perfection of nature, which engrossed all my attention, as much on account of their exact dimensions as for their beautiful colouring. The subjects were all admirably designed, but more precision had been given to every thing relating to arts and sciences; as for instance, all the plates belonging to the Encyclopedia had been newly engraven, and the strictest exactitude had been attentively observed, for therein must consist their chief merit, as the smallest error in them becomes of consequence.

sequence I found a magnificent and regular course of natural history, engraved in a masterly stile; and as this science peculiarly engages the senses, it is to the exactitude and beauty of its engravings, that the student owes a great part of his conceptions This art was in the highest estimation and perfection, and was become of infinite use to the state, by the commerce of engravings which is carried on with all foreign countries, and of those artists it might be with truth said, *under their hands, copper becomes gold.*

CHAP. XXXV.

Exulting in her prince rever'd,
　Whose mild parental virtues grace
The sacred throne by glory rear'd
　On Freedom's adamantine base.

I Quitted those rich galleries with real regret, but my insatiable curiosity was such, that I was anxious to see every thing. I therefore returned to the centre of the city I saw a multitude of persons, of every age, and of both sexes, who were directing their precipitate steps towards a portico of majestic appearance, and decorated with elegance I heard on all sides persons, who in their conversations to each other were saying, " Let us hasten our pace! Our good king is perhaps already ascended the throne, and we shall not be able to see him to-day!" I followed the crowd, but I was surprised to find that he was not surrounded with a ferocious guard, who had wont to impede the eager desires of the multitude to see their sovereign. I entered an immense hall, supported by a colonnade, and upon a nearer approach, I obtained a sight

of

of the throne, than which, nothing can be conceived so beautiful, so noble, so august, and so consoling: here royalty appeared under the most favourable aspect, my tears flowed with sensations of pleasure and joy. Here I saw no thundering Jupiter, nor any terrible apparatus, or instruments of vengeance. Upon the throne, I saw four statues of white marble, representing Fortitude, Temperance, Justice, and Clemency, supporting a chair of white ivory, which was only raised from the ground, in order to facilitate the distinct sound of the voice. This seat was surmounted by a canopy suspended by a hand, the arm of which seemed to issue from the roof. On each side of the throne were two marble tables, upon which were engraven, on one side, the laws of government and the limits of the royal power, and on the other, the duties of kings, and that of subjects. Fronting the throne, was seen a painting, representing royalty under the emblem of a woman suckling a child. The first of the steps, which served to ascend the throne, was in the form of a tomb, whereon was engraven, in large characters, the word ETERNITY. It was under this stone that the body of the deceased monarch was deposited until his successor died, and then he was removed to give place to the next. From this tomb the last sovereign continually reminded his reigning successor that he is immortal, that the dream of mortality would quickly terminate, and that, after that term, nothing will remain of him upon earth but his fame. This spacious place was filled with people, and at length I saw the monarch clothed with a purple mantle, which hung gracefully upon his shoulders. His diadem consisted of a wreath of olive branch, which was the ornament with which he always appeared in public, which inspired respect and veneration. When he ascended the throne, nothing was heard but acclamations of joy, to which the good king was never indifferent; but as soon as he was seated, the most respectful silence pervaded the whole assembly. I lent an attentive ear of expectation; his ministers read with an audible voice all the proceedings of importance during the last session. if they disguised the truth, the people were present to confound the calumniator, here nothing was forgotten, and a strict account was given of the manner in which the laws and ordinances had been executed, and the audience always terminated by an exact account of the price of provisions the monarch listened, and either approved or remitted the business to the next day's more ample examination, but if, from any part of the hall, there arose a voice of complaint, it was attended to, and of whatever condition he might be were he of the lowest class, he was desired to draw near, into a circle appropriated for petitions, or remonstrances, at the foot of the throne; there he explained his grievance, or proposed his ideas. if justice was on his side, he was attended to and applauded, and the sovereign cast upon him a look of benignity; if, on the contrary, he had nothing to propose but what was absurd or selfish, he was dismissed with ignominy, amidst the hootings of the multitude Thus every one might present themselves without any fear but that of meriting the derision of the public, if their views were self-interested or unprofitable

The monarch was always accompanied by two great officers of the crown, whenever he attended any public ceremony, they walked on each side of him, the one carrying a gavel of corn upon a pike, and the other a branch of a vine, in order that he might never forget that those were the two supports of the state, and of the throne. The king's baker followed with a basket of bread, which he distributed among the indigent who claimed his assistance;

affiftance, this bafket was the certain thermometer of public want, for when it was unfupplied, the minifters were difmiffed, and replaced by others, but it always was full, and thereby attefted the abundance of the country.

This auguft affembly was held once a week, and lafted three hours. I retired from this place with a heart penetrated with refpect for the king, almoft equal to what I had felt for the Deity. I felt for him the affection I fhould feel for a father, and honoured him as a protecting god.

I difcourfed with feveral perfons of all I had feen and heard, and expreffed my furprize, which they could not underftand, as all thefe things appeared to them very fimple and natural. "Why," faid they, "do you attempt to compare the prefent age to that in which you lived, which was truly extravagant, in which falfe ideas was imbibed upon the moft fimple matters, where pride affected greatnefs, where oftentation and pomp held the place of every virtue, which was only looked upon as a phantom, and the offspring of imagination?"

CHAP. XXXVI.

―――――― *A found*
Of madd'ning joy burfts on my ear!
From fhore to fhore its ecchoes bound,
Its new-born Freedom's voice I hear!
Arous'd at Superftition's death,
In Gallia's world fhe pants for breath!
Fierce fpouts a vo'tice the finifh'd ftrife,
She breaks her bands—fhe fprings to life!

"MAY I dare afk you what form of government you have? Is it monarchical, democratical, or ariftocratical?"—"It is neither," replied my friend, "it is a
rational

rational government, calculated for men. Monarchy is no more. All monarchical states, which were so unprofitable, have dwindled into despotism, and are lost therein, as a great river loofes itself in the ocean, and despotism itself will soon be lost in its own ruins this was foreseen in your time, and has been literally accomplished.

"After having measured the distance of the sun from the earth, having weighed all the spheres, and having acquired so much knowledge, it were too much to have also discovered the simple and fruitful laws which are calculated to govern rational beings, it is true, that pride, ambition, and interest, presented a thousand obstacles, but where would there have been a greater triumph than to have found out the means of making these passions subservient to public utility? The ship which ploughs the seas, commands the elements, at the same time that she obeys them being subjected to a double impulse, she constantly re-acts against them. This is the faithful image of the state, which, while carried away by tempestuous passions, receives their motion from those same passions, and ought to resist the tempests they cause—all the art rests with the pilot. In your time, political knowledge was very circumscribed, and yet you foolishly taxed the Great Author of Nature for those misfortunes which he had given you intelligence and courage sufficient to avert, had you exerted them. Nothing was wanting to awaken the multitude from the lethargic inaction, but a powerful voice, *whispering liberty*. If the cruel hand of oppression overwhelmed you, it was the weakness of your minds which taught you to crouch under it, and even to flatter your oppressors. *Liberty and happiness belong to those who have courage to seize them*. This universe is one continued revolution, but the happiest of them all has reached the hight of maturity, and we enjoy its fruits.

"Emerged

"Emerged from oppression, we have been very far from restoring all the forces with every spring of government, and all the rights and attributes of power into the hands of one man inftructed by our paft misfortunes, we would not have been thus imprudent, had even Socrates or Marcus Aurelius returned on earth, we fhould not have entrufted them with arbitrary power, not through any miftruft of them, but that we might not debafe the facred character of free men. Is not the law the expreffion of the general will? and how is it poffible to confide fo important a truft to the hands of one man? Will he be free from human frailties, and if he were exempt from them, fhall man renounce that liberty which is his deareft and moft valuable prerogative?

"We have experienced how much an abfolute fovereignty is contrary to the real interefts of the nation. The dreadful catalogue of the evils produced by a monarchy, fome of which I will enumerate, have been a fufficient leffon to us. All the forces of the terrible turning wheel of defpotifm progreffively multiplied, in order to levy innumerable taxes. a mafs of confufed laws, all contradictory to each other, the poffeffions of individuals devoured and abforbed by the deep cavilings of the law, whole cities filled with privileged tyrants, the venality of offices; of minifters, who conducted themfelves in feveral parts of the kingdom as conquerors do upon a fubdued country; a fubtle hardnefs of heart, which was capable of arguing in favour of inhumanity, a fet of pampered officers, whofe dignity would have been debafed by attending to the complaints of the people, but would rather infult their misfortunes. Such were the effects of that vigilant defpotifm, which re-united and gathered all the powers of the nation in a mafs, in order to make an improper ufe of them, fimilar to thofe burning lens which collect all the

rays

...s of the sun, to kindle therewith every object near them. France, the most beautiful country in the world, favoured with all the riches of nature, was in a state of desolation, misery, and distress of all kinds, in every city, in every town or village, an innumerable multitude of beggars, whose pale and haggard countenances bespoke famine and oppression. All these evils were known but not remedied, self-interest and covetousness overcame every sound and evident principle, and authorised the general depredation.

" Would you believe it? our revolution has been accomplished without difficulty or bloodshed, and by the heroism of one man, whose soul deserved to be called great. A king philosopher, who was worthy of the throne, since he knew how to contemn its grandeur, more zealous for the happiness of his people than for the phantom of power, desirous of the esteem of future generations, offered to restore all the ancient prerogatives, and to establish new ones. He felt that in an extensive kingdom, all the provinces should be re-united under general laws, and modified by particular ones, according to its soil, its situation, its particular commerce, and respective interests. So in the human body, besides the general circulation, every part has a particular one suited to its form, by this means, every province flourishes for itself, and is no longer absorbed by the court and metropolis. Never do the blind decrees, emanated from the throne, carry distress and trouble into places and abodes which the eye of the sovereign has never penetrated. Every province, every county, is the depositary of its own happiness and safety they find every thing within themselves, their fruitful soil produces all sorts of blessings, and whatever misfortunes happen, there is a remedy at hand, which is administered

by

by those who are interested in their success, by the love they have for their country.

"Thus you see sovereignty is totally abolished, the chief continues to be called king, but he does not absurdly suppose himself capable of supporting the whole weight of government, under which his ancestors were overwhelmed. The assembled states of the kingdom are entitled to the legislative power the administration of political and civil affairs is entrusted to the senate, and the monarch watches over the execution of the laws he proposes every useful establishment or plan. The senate is answerable to the king, and both king and senate are responsible to the states, who assemble every two years. At this assembly every thing is decided by a plurality of votes: their business consists in making new laws, in disposing of vacant charges, in the redress of public grievances: other unforeseen or peculiar circumstances are reserved for the monarch's decision.

"Our monarch is most happy, and his throne is strengthened by the surest basis, for liberty is its safeguard. Persons who, in a despotic state would have had no opportunity of shining, are now among the most eminent men, and they owe their virtues to that wonderful spring of great actions. Here the citizen forms a part of the state, and contributes with zeal to every thing calculated to raise its splendor.

"Every decree, formed by the senate, is accompanied with its motive and its views. We cannot conceive how, in your enlightened century (as it is called), your magistrates dared, in their haughty stile, to dictate a set of dogmatic decrees, in the same manner as your theologians dictated in matters of religion, treating the law as if it were divested of reason, as if it were unnecessary for the people to be informed of the motives of their obedience

These gentlemen, who called themselves the fathers of their country, were totally ignorant of the great art of perſuaſion, which requires no effort, when properly applied, and ſoftens every difficulty, but, on the contrary, they continued their plan of conduct without any fixed deſign, ſometimes by ſeditious cabals, ſometimes they became the vileſt ſlaves, and, with unceaſing adulation, offered the incenſe of flattery to the monarch, other times they would perplex themſelves about trifles, and ſoon after receive a bribe from the rich criminal, or ſell the liberty of the people to gratify their avarice

" You may ſuppoſe that we did not fail to make a ſtrict reform in this magiſtracy, who had been from their youth accuſtomed to that degree of inſenſibility which made them diſpoſe, without remorſe, of the life, fortune, and honour, of the citizen, they were bold in the defence of their own privileges, but timid and backward in the public intereſt, and, towards the latter end of their reign, the rich were ſaved the trouble of corrupting them, for they were fallen in a perpetual ſtate of apathy to every thing but gain. Our magiſtrates are very different to thoſe they really deſerve the title of the fathers of the people, with which we very juſtly honour them.

" At preſent the reins of government are entruſted to perſons who are ſteady in the purſuit of a fixed wiſe plan the laws themſelves reign over us, and no man is exempt from or above them, and this was not the caſe in your Gothic times. The general happineſs of the nation is founded on the ſecurity which each individual enjoys they do not fear men, but they reſpect the laws, and the ſovereign himſelf ſees them impending over his head upon any deviation his vigilance renders the ſenators ſtill more attentive to their duties the confidence he repoſes in them softens all their labours, and his authority gives all the strength and vigour necessary to their decisions. Thus the sceptre, with the weight of which your kings were oppressed, is light and pleasing in the hand of our monarch. Our king is no longer the pompous idol of the state, gorgeously apparelled and placed above the rest of his fellow-creatures, but he is a beneficent being, ready to sacrifice all his possessions for the good of his people. We possess a prince who is pious and just, who fears the Supreme Being, who bears the continual remembrance of the interests of his country in his heart and mind, who stands in awe of the divine vengeance, and of the blame of posterity, and who looks upon a good conscience and an unblemished and glorious reputation, as the highest degree of felicity. He sets less value on brilliant talents and extensive knowledge than on the sincere desire of an upright heart, which cherishes virtue, and loves to do good to his subjects. We have conciliated that which appeared impracticable and incompatible, that is, the good of the state, and the happiness of individuals. Formerly it was thought that the public good of a state was necessarily separate from that of its members. We have abolished that barbarous political maxim, founded upon ignorance of the most useful laws and upon a contempt for the poor, who are generally the most useful members of the nation. There existed in your time the most cruel and inhuman laws against crimes which would not have been committed but through the institution of those laws. Despotism is calculated to inspire every thing criminal, dishonourable, and degrading to human nature, by irritating and contracting the mind, it corrupts the heart, and absorbs the spring of every virtue. Our king has all the power and authority necessary to do good, but is limited

when

when he would commit injustice the national character is represented to him under the most favourable aspect, our valour and fidelity for our prince, he is well acquainted with, as well as our aversion for a foreign yoke, this raises his esteem and love for his subjects, and mutually excites the love of his subjects for their king At court, there are censors who have the right of removing from the king all those whose want of principles might incline him to irreligion, libertinism, falsehood, or to the fatal art of turning virtue into ridicule. That class of men is no longer known amongst us, who, under the title of nobility, were continually surrounding the throne with vain flattery and fawning, and disdained the profession of any laudable pursuit or trade but that of a courtier, who lived in idleness, while their vain pride and folly were satisfied with pomp and splendour, and the soldier shed his blood with a noble courage and intrepidity at the hazard of his life, which was far more valuable than that of those inglorious parasites Such a description of men, under our republican form of government, would have been very offensive to the other orders, all citizens are equal, it is merit, genius, virtue, and labour, which creates the only distinction between them.

"Amidst the various precautions we take care that our monarch may not forget the poor, we have established a solemn fast every year, which continues three days, during which the king suffers hunger and thirst, and sleeps upon straw, and this terrible and salutary fast impresses in his heart the most tender commiseration for the necessitous, therefore, in times of public calamity, he feels all their sufferings, and gives orders for their relief Our sovereign, however, has no need for the experience of any physical sensation to influence his mind towards good,
but

but this is a sacred law which has always been repeated and followed. After the example of the monarch, every minister, and all those who, in any degree, hold the reins of government, think it their duty to feel want, pain, and misery, and thereby they are better disposed to relieve those who, by their situation in life, are subject to the hard necessity of enduring them. To this I replied, "All these changes must have taken a length of time to bring to perfection, and have been painful and difficult. What efforts must have been made! what struggles against despotism and corruption!" The philosopher, with mildness replied, "It is not more difficult to do good than evil. Human passions are the most terrible obstacles; but when minds are enlightened in what relates to their real interests, they then become just and upright. I think the whole world might be governed by one man, if all men's hearts were disposed to toleration and equity. It was well known and expected, notwithstanding the inconsistency of your century, that natural reason would be highly improved and enlarged, this is become sensibly evident, and the happy principles of a wise form of government, have been the first fruits of this blessed revolution."

CHAP. XXXVII.

*Blest is the prince, who on the solid base
Of pure religion builds his upright sway
Who tempers human power with heavenly grace,
And points to all his people virtue's way*

THE more information I acquired, the more I wished for, I therefore continued my inquiries, and exercised the patience of all the persons I spoke with. Coming down from the hall, where the throne was erected, as it was formerly called the palace, I spoke to an agreeable looking man, who was next to me, in the following manner "Sir, I have seen the monarch seated on his throne, but I have a great wish to see the king's sons, if he has any: will you inform me where the heir-apparent, who, in my time, was stiled the dauphin, may be seen?"—He very politely answered in the following words "We are fully convinced that the happiness of the people greatly depends on the education of those who are placed above them, and that virtue may be taught, as well as vice communicated, we therefore watch with peculiar precaution over the youthful years of the princes, but more particularly over the heir to the throne he is never at court, lest he should there meet some vain adulator who would endeavour to persuade him that he is more than other men, who are no better than vile insects in comparison to him, his high destiny is always concealed from his knowledge Soon as he is born he is marked between the shoulders with the signet of royalty by which he may always be known. He is placed under the care of persons whose discreet fidelity has been found equal to their probity. They take an oath before the Supreme

Being

Being never to reveal to him that he is destined to be king; this oath they hold most solemn, and never dare to violate it.

"Soon as he is old enough to be removed from female attendants, he is taken abroad, he travels in order to prepare his physical education, which ought always to precede the moral, he is dressed like the son of a plain countryman, and is accustomed to the most ordinary food, and early inured to habits of sobriety, in order that he may learn hereafter that his economy must serve as an example, and that a false prodigality ruins the state, and dishonours the extravagant dissipator. He successively visits every province, where he becomes acquainted with all the country labours, the various manufactures, and the productions of every soil; he sees and examines into every thing; he enters the labourer's cottage, eats at his table, unites in his labours, and learns to respect those useful members of society. He enters into familiar conversation with every man he meets, his character and disposition thus unfold themselves without any restraint, and he thinks himself as far from the throne as he is near it.

"Many kings have become tyrants from ignorance of the real state of the poor rather than from a bad heart. Thus if this young prince was given up to the flattering ideas of future unlimited power, he might, though possessing a good and upright heart, (such is the unfortunate propensity of human minds) seek to enlarge the limits of his authority, at the expense and bloodshed of his subjects. It was in this that many sovereigns have made the grandeur of royalty to consist, and consequently their interests and those of the nation were ever opposite.

"As soon as the young prince has attained the age of twenty, and even before that age, if his heart is formed, he is led to the great hall, where the throne of his father is placed he is left among the crowd as a simple spectator every order of the states are on that day assembled. The monarch rises suddenly, and calls the young man three times with a loud voice he is astonished, and advances with a timid step towards the throne, and trembles as he ascends the steps The king receives him in his arms, and declares, in the presence of all the citizens, that he is his son, and with a voice full of majesty and sweetness, he addresses him nearly in the following words " *Heaven has destined you to bear the weight of royalty, these twenty years have been employed in endeavouring to render you worthy of it do not then disappoint the hopes of this great people, whose eyes are directed towards you. Yes, my son, I expect from you the same zeal which I have always felt for the good of the nation*" What a moment for the young prince ! What a crowd of ideas enter his soul! then the monarch points out to him the tomb of his predecessor, that tomb on which he finds engraven in large characters the word ETERNITY, after which he continues in the same tone of voice " *My son, all our labours, all our efforts, have had this happy moment in view. You are now standing on the remains of your great ancestor. you are to be his reviver, take an oath to be just as he was. I soon shall descend to the grave, and shall occupy his place, remember, that I shall accuse you from beneath this tomb, if you make an ill use of the power committed to you Remember, my dear son, that the eyes of the Supreme Being and of the whole kingdom are opened upon you, and that none of your actions, or even of your thoughts, will escape their notice If at this moment any emotion of pride or ambition prevails in your soul, it is not yet too late to overcome them, you may forego the diadem, descend from the throne, and return amongst the people you will be more truly great, and more respected* as an obscure citizen than as a vain, inglorious monarch. Let not your young heart be flattered by the chimera of authority, but with the delightful idea of having the power of doing good. I promise you, for a recompense, the love of this people, who are harkening to us, my tenderness, the esteem of the whole world, and the assistance of the Supreme Monarch of the Universe. It is he, my son, who is the true sovereign: we are no more than mere machines, who are sent to fill this high station upon earth, in order to fulfil his august designs.

"The young prince, moved and agitated, scarcely dares to cast a timid eye upon this great assembly, whose looks and attention are wholly fixed upon him. The whole extent of his duties, thus exposed to his view, excites a momentary pensive gloom, which he soon represses, and acts like a hero: he has been taught that the truly great man ought to sacrifice himself for the good of his fellow-creatures; and that, as nature has not prepared for men any happiness without alloy, he to whom the nation has entrusted the happy power of doing every sort of good, ought to remedy the defects of nature, in bestowing happiness wherever it is wanting. This noble idea penetrates and enflames his heart; he takes the oath in the presence of his father, which he calls the shade of his great ancestor to witness: he receives the sceptre, which he himself is bound to respect, as well as the meanest of his subjects: he then adores the Supreme Being, and he is crowned. The orders of the state salute him, and the people, with transports of real joy, speak thus to him: "*Oh thou, who art now gone from amongst us, thy fellow-creatures, who hast dwelt familiarly with us, let not the vain illusions of grandeur make thee ever forget either thyself or us, when thou art on the throne of thy fathers!*"

"Our prince must never afcend the throne until the age of twenty-two, unlefs the monarch dies before the end of that time; for we think it abfurd and contrary to reafon to fubmit to a child, and for the fame reafon the old fovereign abdicates at fixty, if he lives till then, becaufe the art of reigning requires activity and fupplenefs in the organs, and a fenfibility of foul, which the weight of years extinguifhes. Befides, we always fear that the long habit of power may caufe that contracted ambition to fpring up in his foul, which is called avarice, for that is in general the laft fad paffion which man has to ftruggle with. The crown always devolves in a direct line of fucceffion, and the fexagenary monarch continues to be ufeful to the ftate by his counfels, or by the example of his former virtues. The two years which elapfed between this public acknowledgment and the time of his majority, were paffed in various trials he is always addreffed by ftrong and impreffive metaphors if they wifh to prove to him that kings are not unlike other men, but that, on the contrary, they have the fame weaknefs of body, and are fubject to the fame infirmities, that they are equal to others, and that they have no advantage over other men, but by thofe virtues they may acquire, that it is the choice of the people which conftitutes the bafis of their grandeur and authority, they caufe a young porter to be brought forward, of the fame age and ftature with the king's fon, they wreftle together, and the latter is ufually vanquifhed, notwithftanding his advantages over the former, in point of beauty and form, and he is forced to acknowledge his defeat The young prince is then raifed up, and is thus addreffed " *You fee that no man is by nature fubject to another, that none are born flaves, that kings are born men, and that the human fpecies has not been created for the pleafure or fport of a few families. Even the Almighty himfelf*

does

does not govern by violence, but by the laws of nature, over men whom he has endowed with free will it is therefore presumption to aim at making men slaves by exercising undue tyranny over them." Then the wrestler who has vanquished him, says to him with humility, "I may be stronger than you, in which there is neither glory nor boast, but real strength of mind consists in equity, and greatness of soul is true glory. I render you homage as my sovereign, and when I am oppressed by tyranny, to you I shall fly for relief I will then call upon you, and you will save me from the unjust and powerful man......"

"If the young prince commits any fault, or imprudence, on the very next day he finds it published in the newspapers, which sometimes astonishes and vexes him, upon which he is spoken to thus *There is a tribunal famed for integrity, which watches over, and writes down all the actions of princes Posterity will know and judge of all that you have either said or done it therefore depends on yourself to give cause for favourable representations.*" If upon this the young prince looks back upon his fault with humility, and repairs it, then the next day's news give information of it, as being the proof of a happy disposition, and it is accompanied with every eulogium to his noble mind and goodness of heart which they deserve.

"But that which is most strongly recommended, and impressed by various images on his mind, is a continued horror for pomp and luxury, which is only calculated to ruin the state, and degrade their sovereigns These gilded palaces are only like theatrical decorations, in which gilt pasteboard represents solid gold, and pleases the child, who supposes he sees a real palace, but we are no longer children. Pomp and parade have been introduced by

pride

pride and policy, they served to inspire respect and fear. By these means subjects acquired servile minds, and have accustomed themselves to slavery but kings have never been debased by making themselves equal to their subjects, for what are all those vain ceremonies of grandeur in comparison with that open and sincere affability which attracts the love and esteem of every one for his person! The monarch is in no respect different to other men, as J J Rousseau has justly said, 'If he wishes to enjoy the purest of all enjoyments, let him render himself worthy of being beloved'

"In short, not a day passes but he is reminded of the existence of the Supreme Being, of his watchful eyes, open upon the whole world, of the just fear of that Being, which ought to accompany all his actions, and of the respect he ought to have for his providence, and confidence in his infinite wisdom. The most hateful and impious of all beings, no doubt, is an atheistical king. I would rather be in a ship battered by a storm, and steered by an intoxicated pilot, chance might save me, but under such dominion I never could be safe.

"Our prince is not allowed to marry until he is twenty-two he then makes choice of a wife among his own countrywomen We never suffer a foreigner to ascend the throne, for they often bring with them a disposition and manner totally different from our national character, while they corrupt our own nation, and thereby we are governed rather by Spaniards, Italians, or Germans, than by the descendants of our own great ancestors

"The king does not insult the whole nation, by supposing that beauty and virtue are not to be found but in a foreign land. If, in the course of his travels, his heart has been struck with the virtue of an amiable girl, who, with

a sina sincere attachment, returned his affection, even before she knew him to be heir to the crown, she is allowed to ascend the throne with her lover, and becomes both dear and respectable to the nation by her tenderness, and by her merit, in having gained the heart of a hero By this we derive a two-fold advantage. We infpire to all the young girls the love of goodnefs and virtue, by giving them, in perfpective, a reward worthy of all their efforts, and we avoid all thofe family wars, which are quite foreign to the intereft of the ftate, and often have defolated all Europe

"On the day of his marriage, inftead of expending money in extravagant feafts and fuperb entertainments, in fireworks and illuminations, the prince gives money for fome work of public utility, as a bridge, an aqueduct, a high road, a canal, or a theatre, and this public monument bears the prince's name. The benefit is for ever remembered, but thofe unreafonable profufions were foon forgotten, as they left no traces but of dreadful accidents and misfortunes. Thus the people, fatisfied with the generofity of the prince, are not even tempted on this occafion to repeat the well-known ancient fable of the frog, who, from the bottom of the ditch, had caufe to lament the nuptials of the fun."

CHAP.

CHAP XXXVIII.

If her worship'd woman we entranc'd behold,
We praise the Maker in his fairest mould
The pride of nature, harmony combin'd,
And light immortal to the soul refin'd!
Depriv'd of charming woman, soon we miss
The prize of friendship, and the life of bliss

THE affable and complaisant man, who was so kind as to inform me of all these things, continued in the same style of open candour "You must know," said he, " that our women have no other portion in marriage but their virtues and their charms therefore they have an interest in perfecting their moral characters, and we, by that wise part of legislation, have abolished the hydra of coquetry, so fruitful in vices and ridiculous irregularities "—" What! no portion!" I exclaimed, " women no property of their own! and what man will espouse them?"—" Women have no portion, because they are by nature dependent on our sex, who are their strength and glory, from which lawful empire nothing ought ever to exclude them, and it is much less painful than that to which they are liable from their own sex, besides, it is nearly the same thing a man who marries a woman without receiving any fortune, may also have his daughters provided for without giving any We do not see a girl, proud of her portion, seem to confer a favour on the husband she accepts Every man is bound to provide for the wife he chooses, and she is happy to owe every thing to her husband, to whom she is always disposed to shew the same fidelity and obedience. This law being universal, no one feels the weight of it. Our women have no distinction but that which they derive from their husbands all submissive to the duties which their sex imposes on them, their honour consists in following those austere laws, which can alone ensure their happiness.

"Every citizen who is not defamed, though he were of the lowest class, may look up to the daughters of men of the highest rank, provided she give her consent to his pretensions, and that he makes use of no art to seduce her affections, or that there be no disproportion of age. Every citizen, though without exactly following the same business, are in that state of natural equality necessary to render that connection happy. Thus there is no condition in life so distant by rank, but what may be united by the ties of Hymen. When a woman is married, the paternal power and civil authority can no longer reach her. Our marriages are always fortunate, as they are not corrupted by interest, and this simple law has banished from among us a variety of vices and trivial customs, such as slander, jealousy, idleness, pride, and envy for a rival, and all such wretched meannesses. Our women have cultivated their understandings, instead of seeking for the gratification of their vanity, and all their riches consist in the moral virtues, which they acquire in a high degree, and all necessary talents, among which music and dancing are no longer the principal. They have learned economy, the art of pleasing their husbands, and of educating their children. That extreme inequality of rank and fortune, which is so destructive to all political societies, is banished from among us. The last citizen in point of rank or profession, may, without a blush, be allied to the first, who feels no shame at the alliance. The law has united all men as much as possible, instead of creating those injurious distinctions, which have only produced pride on one side, and hatred on the other;

other, and it has abrogated all such as were calculated to disunite all the children of one family, for we look upon the whole nation as being such.

"Our women are such as they were among the ancient Gauls, amiable, sincere, and simple in their manners. We respect and consult them in all our affairs. They do not affect to be wits, for which they were so often ridiculed in your time, neither do they take upon themselves to pronounce their opinion on men of genius; but they are satisfied with having good sense, which is a quality far preferable to those artificial sallies of wit, and frivolous amusements of idleness. Love, that fertile principle of the rarest virtues, presides at, and watches over the interests of our country; for it becomes dearer to us children, in proportion to the degree of happiness they enjoy within its bosom. Here the women are very great gainers; instead of those vain and fastidious pleasures, which they pursued through vanity, they have all our tenderness and esteem, and enjoy a felicity much more solid and more pure in the possession of our hearts than in those voluptuous enjoyments, the pursuit of which brings lassitude and disquiet. Entrusted with the care of the first year's education of their children, their time is sufficiently engaged, for they never have any other preceptors, and our women being more vigilant, and better informed than they were in your time, are better acquainted with the delightful pleasure of being mothers, in the true sense of the word."

"And yet," replied I, "notwithstanding all your perfection, man is always man, he still has his weaknesses and all his imperfections. If the torch of discord were ever to succeed the torch of hymen, how then would you manage? Is divorce permitted among you?"—"Undoubtedly, when it is founded on lawful reasons, for instance,

instance, when both parties desire it. The incompatibility of dispositions is sufficient to dissolve those ties. Marriage is a state in which no person should engage but with the desire of being happy; it is a contract which ought to have nothing in view but the mutual felicity of both parties, produced from peace and a reciprocity of kindness and mutual endearments. We are not so senseless as to wish to force two persons to live together whose hearts are naturally disinclined to each other; it would be renewing something like the dreadful torture introduced by Mezentius, of fastening a living body to a corpse. Divorce is the only convenient remedy, as it restores to society two persons who were lost for each other. But, would you believe it? the greater the facility of employing this remedy, the greater their fear is of having recourse to it; for they think there is a kind of disgrace in not being able to support together the miseries of this temporary life. Our women, who are virtuous from principle, are delighted with domestic pleasures, which are always endearing; when sentiment is blended with duty, nothing is then painful, but every thing tends to strengthen the tie of affection."

"Oh!" cried I, "How grieved I am at being so old! I would immediately marry one of your amiable women. The manners of our's were so haughty and disdainful! they were in general so false hearted, and their education so neglected and full of error, that he who married was thought to commit the greatest folly. The dispositions even of the best of our women discovered an immoderate inclination for pleasure and coquetry, and an indifference for every thing but themselves; they played off sensibility, but possessed no degree of it except towards their lovers; they had no taste but for voluptuousness and extravagance; as for modesty, it was not even known but to turn it into ridicule: therefore every wife man, having to choofe of two evils, preferred celibacy as the leaft. The difficulty of bringing up their children was another motive againft marriage, for men could have no wifh of leaving pofterity in a ftate which overwhelmed them with rigorous oppreffions. Thus the captive elephant, being once fubdued, overcomes his own nature, and refufes to give himfelf up to the natural inftinct of all animals to procreation, that he may not leave his pofterity in flavery. Even hufbands, in the midft of their tranfports, were careful to prevent the natural productions of their union. Thus man avoided the propagation of his own fpecies, as it could only tend to prolong their miferies! Many poor virgins, fixed in the ftate of celibacy, languifhed, drooped, and died upon their ftems, like thofe flowers, parched up by the fun, which fade away in their bloom, for want of the genial influence of falutary rains. The generality of them dragged on a weary life, pining with defire of being united to the man who had engaged their affections, and often expofed to make the facrifice of their honour in order to obtain him. In fhort, the number of perfons who lived in celibacy amounted to a moft alarming number, and what made the misfortune ftill more deplorable was, that reafon feemed to juftify this attempt againft humanity. However, let me entreat you to give me the confolation of hearing the delightful and affecting picture of your prefent morals. How have you been able to remedy fuch great evils, which feemed to menace the annihilation of the human fpecies?"

My companion raifed his voice, and with a noble and dignified manner, lifting up his eyes to heaven, faid, "Great God! if man is wretched, is it not by his own fault? He either becomes a voluntary exile, and remains buried within himfelf, or, by a miftaken activity, con-
fumes

fumes his exertions upon frivolous objects, while he neglects those pursuits which might procure satisfaction to his mind. When Providence destined man for society, she wisely accompanied every evil which might befal him with an exact proportion of remedies for each. Thus we are under a mutual obligation of succouring each other, and that is the natural, and ought to be the general, wish of human kind."—" How happened it to be so frequently interrupted?"—" I repeat to you, that our women are wives and mothers, hence do they derive all their virtues. Our women would be dishonoured, were they to daub their faces with paint, to take snuff, to drink liquors, pass their nights in dancing or gaming, sing licentious songs, or behaved with the least familiarity towards men they have a surer way of attracting them, gentleness, modesty, the simple graces, and that noble decency, which ought to constitute their greatest pride. They suckle their own children, which they do without effort, for nature not being checked by fashionable pursuits, they have that abundance of food for their children which is intended for them, and all the affection which renders that duty delightful. The children are early strengthened by being taught to swim, to raise up heavy weights, to be good marksmen, in short, to excel in all bodily exercises, for their physical education, according to our judgment, is of the greatest importance, and, therefore, we form their constitutions long ere we suffer their minds to receive any impression

" The mother seizes the dawn of her son's young ideas, and as soon as the organs of his mind are capable of obeying her will, she reflects on the manner in which she may form his soul to virtue, she makes use of the most beautiful allegories and affecting fables, not to throw a veil upon truth, but in order to render her more amiable and
fasci-

fascinating to his inexperienced heart: and, in order to change his sensibility into humanity, his pride into greatness of soul, and his curiosity into a thirst after useful knowledge, she watches over every gesture, and attentively listens to every word spoken in his presence, that his heart may be preserved from any unfavourable impression. Thus she guards him against the pestiferous breath of vice, which so frequently tarnishes the fair flower of youth.

"The education of every child varies according to the employ destined for him in society, for we are totally delivered from the pedantic yoke of classical educations, as they were called, and from the ridicule of teaching children that which they must inevitably forget when they come to years of maturity. Every art has its peculiar difficulty, and, in order to excel, it is necessary to give up an attention and study of many years to each. The mind of man is incapable of admitting more than one object at a time, notwithstanding the recent discoveries which have, in some measure, enlarged its contracted span, therefore he must sedulously follow that study to which he fixes his mind, and not aim at a superficial knowledge of many. In your time a pretension to universal knowledge was only thought ridiculous, but in our's it is regarded as the height of madness.

"When the youth has attained a more advanced age, when his heart has been taught to feel the tie of union existing between him and other men, then, instead of those frivolous acquisitions, which were crammed without choice or judgment into the head of the young man, his mother, with that mild eloquence so natural to women, will teach him what is meant by those words, virtue, morals, and good order; to effect this, she waits for the time in which nature, adorned in her brightest array,

speaks

speaks to the moft infenfible of hearts when the envi‑ gorating breath of fpring returns to beautify the woods, the vallies, and the meadows 'My fon,' fays fhe, preffing him to her maternal breaft, ' behold thefe green fields, thefe trees crowned with rich foliage a fhort time back they were all dead, they were ftripped of their beautiful ornaments, and were petrified with the cold which contracted the bowels of the earth but there reigns a beneficent Being, who is our common Father he will not abandon his children, his abode is in the heavens, from whence he looks with paternal affection on all his creatures By his decree the fun darts his rays, the trees revive, the earth gives her increafe of grafs deftined for the food of cattle, who, in return, contribute to your nourifhment and clothing —' And why do we enjoy thefe bleffings? Is it that we love the Lord with all our hearts?' ' No, my dear child, it is becaufe he is all-powerful and good all that you fee is the work of his hands, and that which you fee is but the leaft part of his works, it is nothing compared to that which is hidden from your perception. That eternity, for which your foul is created, will be an infinite chain of furprife, joy, and admiration. His benefits and his greatnefs are without bounds He cherifhes us, becaufe he is our Father he will daily increafe his favours to us, if we are virtuous, that is to fay, if we follow his laws O! my fon, how fhould we forbear to adore and blefs him!"

"At thefe words both the mother and fon offer up their mingled vows to heaven in humble adoration It is thus fhe inculcates in his foul the idea of the Deity, and that fhe ftrengthens his mind with truth evident to his fenfes, fhe may then reft affured that fhe fulfils the defign of the Creator But that is not all our mothers keep a conftant watch over every paffion which might be prejudicial to their children's peace of mind; and to the tenderness of a parent she unites the watchfulness of a friend.

"You have seen at what age our young men are admitted to the communication of the two points of infinity. Such is our education, it is all given and received by sentiment. We abhor that spirit of dispute which was so prevalent in your time, and was so prejudicial to the peace of society, and to the good qualities of the heart; it impeded every avenue to the finer feelings, and sowed the seed of all vices: even good sense itself, what is it, if unaccompanied by sentiment? the most profound reasoning is deprived of half its power, if incapable to move the heart, for it is there alone the impression ought to be made, in order to be durable; that eloquence which abounds in striking images, in moving and awful truths, is the only eloquence we cherish; it is that which lends to the imagination those fiery wings, by which it is enabled to soar above itself, and to seize the object of its pursuit, because the heart is gratified while the mind is enlightened.

"Neither is our philosophy severe, for why should it? Is not virtue more honoured by being represented under cheerful and pleasing appearances than by gloomy and fearful images? We are of opinion that we ought to receive and enjoy, with gratitude and pleasure, those blessings, emanated from the beneficent hand of our Creator, rather than turn away from them. Pleasure is only another name for virtue, for there is no pleasure for the guilty. Far from endeavouring to destroy the passions, those invisible movers of our being, we regard them as precious gifts, which ought to be treasured up with care. Happy that soul who possesses strong passions! for they constitute his glory and true greatness

On

Our wife men cultivate their understanding, and reject all prejudices; they acquire all useful and agreeable sciences, and adorn their minds with all knowledge; this task being accomplished, he only attends to and follows the dictates of nature, under the guide of reason, and it is reason which leads him to happiness.

CHAP. XXXIX.

Oh freedom! sov'reign boon of heav'n,
Great charter with our being giv'n,
For which the patriot and the sage
Have plann'd, have bled thro' every age!
High privilege of human race,
Beyond a mortal monarch's grace
Who could not give, who cannot claim,
What but from God immediate came!

I Now questioned my conductor on the subject of the taxes; I inquired how they were levied, "for, however perfect," said I, "your legislation may be, still I think it cannot be maintained without public taxes?" To this my kind friend made no other reply than taking me by the hand, and leading me into a wide square, where I perceived a strong chest, twelve feet in height; it was supported upon four wheels, and was sheltered from the weather by a double lid, raised at some distance from the chest, which was divided into two compartments. On one side were engraven the following words. " TRIBUTE DUE TO THE KING AS REPRESENTATIVE OF THE STATE," and on the other, which was the least compartment, " VOLUNTARY CONTRIBUTIONS." I saw several persons, who, with cheerful countenances,

threw

threw into an opening, contrived for that purpose, little sealed-up packages, in the same manner as we formerly threw our letters in a general post-box. I greatly admired this easy manner of paying the taxes, and addressed many ridiculous interrogations upon this subject, which caused me to be gazed at as a stupid old man come from a remote country, but the affable indulgence of this good people never left any of my questions unanswered. I must acknowledge that such kind people, and, above all, such *loyal* people, are only to be met with in a dream.

My companion, who never left me, spoke to me nearly in the following words "That strong chest which you see is the receiver-general of our finances. It is there that every citizen comes to deposit the money which he owes for the support of the state. In one division we are all obliged annually to give the fiftieth part of our income. The labourer or dependant, who has no income but what he earns for his daily sustenance, is dispensed from this tax, for how is it possible to take any part of that bread which requires a whole day's labour to obtain? In the other division is deposited all voluntary offerings destined for useful purposes, all tending to the public good. This side is sometimes richer than the other, for we love to be free in our gifts, and to have a laudable motive for our generosity, that is, the love of our country, and of the public weal. As soon as our sovereign has given out an edict, which appears useful, and worthy the approbation of the public, we, his people, are seen in crowds bringing our tribute of love and gratitude to him. In this manner we acknowledge every worthy act, which proves the love of our monarch for his children he need but propose, and we provide the means of executing his good projects. In every district of the city, and in every town in the country, there is such a chest, which receives the tribute of the country people; I mean of those who are in easy circumstances, such as the wealthy farmer, and all who enjoy a certain state of affluence."

"What," said I, "is it left to the people's own honesty to pay the tax? I suppose there are many who unperceived omit to pay it"—"Oh! not at all," he replied, "you need not fear any neglect of that kind, for what we pay, it is with our free consent, nothing is exacted from us but what is founded upon equity and reason, and there is not one among us who does not make it a point of honour to pay exactly this most sacred and lawful debt. Besides, if any man who is able to pay dared to omit it, we have a sure means of knowing it by consulting a book, wherein all the names are written of every family, and it would soon be discovered that he has not thrown in his packet sealed and signed, as they all are, he would be forever disgraced, forsaken by society, looked upon as a thief, and the appellation of bad citizen would accompany him to his grave.

"These instances are extremely rare, for the voluntary gratuities usually amount to much more than the annual contributions. Every citizen knows, that when he gives any part of his revenue to the state, he is serving himself. But why need I say so much on a subject, while I have the power of convincing you by facts? You shall now judge of our loyalty; this is the day when all the annual contributions of a faithful people, towards a benevolent sovereign, are brought together from all parts of the kingdom. Come to the king's palace, the deputies of each province are expected this day." I had scarce walked a few paces, when I saw several men who were drawing little carts, which contained several small chests crowned with laurels. The seals of these trunks being broken,

broken, they were weighed in order to afcertain what quantity of money they contained All fums were paid in money, and the general produce of every article was always fixed and publicly made known to every one, that no perfon might be ever defrauded. In like manner was the income of each individual made public, by their annual contributions, which were thus reviewed every year and advertifed, by which means the whole revenue of the ftate is known This treafure is depofited in the royal treafury, under the fafeguard of the comptroller of the finances.

This was a day of rejoicing the people with acclamations went to meet each tribe on the roads, which were all filled with tables and provifions to refrefh the travellers and deputies from each province, who thus met with cordial friendfhip, and made prefents to each other, while they drank fuccefs and happinefs to each other with unfeigned wifhes, the health of the fovereign was likewife pledged, accompanied by the firing of cannons in the palace, which were anfwered by thofe of the capitol, as the interpreters of the king's moft hearty thanks to his people. It was on thefe occafions that the people all feemed like one family, in the midft of which the king appeared furrounded by them, and anfwered their acclamations of joy with that tender and affable manner which infpires unbounded confidence, and returns love for love, he was ignorant of the art of treating politically with a people of whom he thought himfelf the father. His vifits never ruined the cities through which he paffed, for he never coft his people any thing but acclamations of joy, which are a much more brilliant and flattering reception than all the pompous and extravagant pageantry which formerly attended the vifits of princes.

"Thofe

"Those whose office it is to superintend the payments of taxes, though invested with power and authority, they never abuse it to oppress the people; they, on the contrary, take charge of every petition to carry them to the king, whereby he has an opportunity of examining into and reforming every abuse. These stewards or superintendants travel into every city, and erect a monument wherever they have been instrumental to the destruction of any abuse of power; and there cannot be a more instructive history than what may be derived from these monuments, which prove that the sovereign has learned the true art of governing.

'I think your comptroller of the finances must be a man of much more integrity than any in my time, who were like the dog in the fable that carried his master's dinner, accompanied by temperance and example, who were faithful to their trust until prompted by the latter. How is it, that this man has the double virtue of guarding the finances, without appropriating any part of it to himself?'—"It is because he has not the preposterous desire of building palaces and castles, or of aggrandizing all his former valets, or cousins of the fifth or sixth degree. neither is he as prodigal of money, as if he held the revenues of the whole kingdom in his hand. indeed, those who are the depositories of the public funds cannot make any use of the money under any pretence whatever; for it would be a high misdemeanor to receive any money from them; whatever expenses they pay are discharged with bank-bills signed by the king himself. All their own private expenses are defrayed by the state, but they have nothing of their own; they can neither sell nor buy, nor erect buildings. They are maintained both in necessary and superfluous articles by the state, therefore, if they have any degree of honour, they will be moderate in their expenses."

"And pray who is your prime minister?"—"Can you doubt it? It is the king himself. Can the duties of royalty be fulfilled by proxy? The warrior, the judge, the merchant, only act as his representatives. In case of sickness, absence, or any particular contingency, if the monarch entrusts any person with the execution of his orders, that person is always his friend: no other sentiment can oblige a man voluntarily to take so great a burden upon himself, and it is the public esteem only, which can give him this momentary power; he is rewarded by the friendship of his king, for, like the great Sully, he knows how to speak the truth to his master, and, in order that he may serve him more effectually, he sometimes irritates him by combating his passions. In his friendship he cherishes the man equally as much as he is interested for the glory of the monarch, who, while he shares his labours, also partakes of the veneration of his countrymen, which is, no doubt, the most honourable inheritance he can leave to his descendants, and the only one of which he really is ambitious."

"In speaking of taxes, I forgot to ask if you still allowed amongst you those periodical lotteries, in which the poor people in my time lost all their money?"

"Certainly not: we do not abuse thus the credulous hopes of men. We do not levy a tax so cruelly ingenious on the indigent part of citizens, who, weary of the present, lived only in the hopes of future ease, and cast the price of his sweats and labours in that fatal wheel, from whence he always expected a fortunate revolution in his favour. The hand of the cruel goddess disappointed his hopes each time, his ardent desire of the prize prevented his making use of his reason, although

the

the cheat was palpable, for as the heart is dead to life ere man is dead to hope, every one hoped to be the favourite of fortune at last These superb edifices, where the poor man came to intercede for bread, had been built out of the fruit of his labours. The luxury and splendor of royal palaces and churches were paid with his contributions, and yet he never could be admitted within them. Always a stranger, always repulsed, the poor man was not even allowed to sit on that seat which his labours had erected Priests who enjoyed high salaries inhabited those places which, in equity, ought to have lodged him as an asylum"

CHAP XI

Comme[illegible] [illegible] [illegible]
[illegible] [illegible]
A[illegible] [illegible] a large [illegible],
[illegible] her [illegible] for [illegible],
[illegible] gods [illegible],
Gives the full [illegible] [illegible]

Commerce gives [illegible] world again,
By commerce may [illegible],
Then barbarous [illegible] enlighten as they [illegible],
Arts, the rich traffic of the soul!
May travel thus from pole to pole,
And gild the world with learning's brighter [illegible]

"I CONCLUDE, from what you have told me, that the French have not any colonies in the new world, and that every part of America forms a separate kingdom although re united under the same legislation Is it not fo?"—" We should be madmen indeed, if we wished to transport our dear countrymen more than two thousand leagues from us: to what purpose should we separate ourselves from our friends? Our climate is certainly equally as good as that of America. We have every necessary production in common with them, and some indeed of a more excellent nature. Colonies have the same effect upon nations which country houses have upon individuals who possess town residencies, the former generally ruins the latter.

"We have a kind of commerce, but it is a barter of those articles which are superfluous. We have wisely banished three physical poisons, of which you made a constant use, snuff, coffee, and tea, this powder with which you Frenchmen stuffed your noses, deprived you of the little memory you possessed, and you destroyed your stomachs with drinking hot liquors, which, by hastening its action, brought on a debility of the nervous system. The only commerce we carry on, is the interior trade, founded chiefly upon agriculture, which is the most useful of all, for in relieving the wants of man, it did not administer to his pride. No man amongst us is ashamed of cultivating his field, and we endeavour to raise agriculture to the highest state of perfection, even the monarch himself has several acres of land which are cultivated under his own eye, and with us that crowd of titled gentry, who passed their days in idleness, is no longer to be seen. It was foreign traffic which was the offspring of that destructive luxury which afterwards gave rise to that immense inequality of fortunes, by which a small number of individuals appropriated to themselves all the money of the kingdom. The oppressed peasant, ceasing to be a proprietor, was forced to sell the field of his fathers, and to fly far from his native soil, where he ended his days in misery

misery and opprobrium; and all this was frequently in consequence of the ambition and vanity of a woman, the wife of his lord paramount, who must forsooth adorn herself with ornaments bought with the patrimony of ten families, for the insatiable monsters even despised the victim whom they stripped—all their aim was to accumulate

"We began by destroying those enormous companies, which absorbed all the private fortunes, which annihilated the generous ardor of a whole nation, and struck wounds as fatal to morals in general, as they were to the state. I dare say it was extremely agreeable to drink chocolate, to eat sauces highly flavoured with spices, to use sugar and pines, to drink rum, and to be clothed with the beautiful muslins of the Indies, but, in fact, was the gratification of these propensities of sufficient moment to cause you to forget the incredible assemblage of evils which your effeminacy occasioned in both hemispheres? On the coast of Guinea you broke through all the sacred ties of blood and nature, you armed the father against the son, which you pretended was in the name of christians and of men. Blind, barbarous people! you learned by a too dearly bought experience what miseries the thirst of gold could create among you, this avidity after riches banished all moderation, justice and virtue were regarded as chimeras; avarice, with pale and haggard looks, was seen ploughing the most solitary parts of the ocean in quest of riches, and strewing the vast and profound recesses of the deep with dead bodies, a whole race of men were sold, bought, and treated like the vilest of animals, kings became merchants, and shed the blood of thousands for the sake of a frigate, in short, gold issued from the mines of Peru like a scalding stream, overrunning all Europe, withering and parching the very roots of happiness, and after having
tormented

tormented and exhausted the whole human race, was driven like a current into the Indies, where superstition in one hemisphere buried deep into the bowels of the earth that which avarice had extracted from the other with so much labour. This is the faithful description of all the advantages which foreign trade has introduced into the world.

"Our vessels are now better employed than in making the tour of the globe in order to acquire cochineal and indigo. Do you know where our mines are? They are in industry and labour. Every thing which may serve to assist the intentions of nature is encouraged with care, but, on the contrary, every thing which tends to pomp, ostentation, vanity, and the childish desire of gratifying some idle whim, is severely proscribed. Those useless and dangerous diamonds and pearls, so much sought for in your time, are thrown into the sea, for we have no use for them. All those beautiful and precious stones which rendered the hearts of men as impenetrable as themselves, are banished far from us. You thought yourselves very ingenious in your refinements of luxury, but it was only in superfluities, for you were not even voluptuous, and you had no more of grandeur than its bare shadow. Your miserable and futile inventions were limited to the enjoyment of a day. You were no better than children enamoured with brilliant objects, incapable of satisfying your real wants, ignorant of the art of being happy, you tormented yourselves, and mistook the shadow of happiness for the reality.

"When our vessels leave our ports, they do not carry with them that dreadful dealer of destruction and death, in order to seize those fugitive prizes on the free extent of the waters, which have an equal right with our own to sail on the bosom of the deep. The echo of the waves no longer afcends to heaven with the lamentable fhrieks of a fet of furious infenfate beings, who were contending for a paffage over immenfe defert iflands, which the Creator had given in common to all. We vifit remote nations, but, inftead of bringing away any of their productions, we procure far more ufeful benefits from them, we extract from their legiflation, from their phyfical exiftence, and from their manners, all that is worthy of notice. Our veffels ferve us in confirming our aftronomical difcoveries. we have more than three hundred obfervatories which we have erected in remote countries, in order to examine every different appearance of the heavens in each. Aftronomy is become an important and ufeful fcience, becaufe it publifhes in a moft magnificent and awful manner the glory of the Creator, and the exalted dignity of that being who is the work of his hands . . . . . but now that we are on the fubject of commerce, let us not forget to mention a traffic of the moft fingular kind. You muft be extremely rich, for you have no doubt placed your money upon life annuities, and particularly in tontines, as it was the cuftom in your youth. This kind of lottery was really a moft ingenious invention, thus to gamble with lives and deaths, and enjoy an increafe of revenue juft before one defcends to the grave. you, I think, muft have a very handfome fortune, as you have furvived all your affociates. This was an infatuation in which they loft all recollection of either father, mother, children, brother, or fifter, coufins or friends, in order to double their revenue. They left all their property to the king, and then enjoyed a fecure peace, by living only for themfelves."—" Alas!" I replied, " do not remind me of our difgraceful cuftoms, thefe fad privileges completed our growing depravity of manners, and diffolved all ties of nature and confanguinity,

guinity, which, till then, had ever been respected
This barbarous refinement which publicly encouraged
every species of selfishness, which contracted every citizen within himself, and made every man a solitary
being, dead to all but himself, has many times excited
tears of apprehension for the future state of the nation.
I perceived that all private fortunes were by degrees consumed for their proprietors, while they served to swell
the mass of excessive opulence with their ruins, but the
fatal stab which was given to public morals was that
which grieved me most, there no longer existed any ties
between those who ought for ever to have been attached
self interest, already so fatal in itself, was now armed
with a weapon sharper than ever, and received from sovereign authority the keys of those barriers which it never
would have usurped for itself."—" Ah! good old man,'
said my friend, " it is happy for you that you have been
sleeping all these years, else you would have seen all these
mortgagers and mortgagees of the state sufficiently punished for their mutual imprudence, but since that time
the political world is better enlightened, and makes no
such mistakes. The world is now united, and the citizens enriched without ruining their descendants."

CHAP

CHAP. XLI.

O thou! who, 'mid the world-involving gloom,
　Sitt'st on yon solitary spire!
Or slowly shak'st the sounding dome,
　Or hear'st the wildly warbling lyre,
　　Say when thy musing soul
　　Bids distant times unroll,
And marks the flight of each revolving year.
　Of years whose slow consuming power
　Has clad with moss yon beaming tower,
　That saw the race of glory run,
　That mark'd Ambition's setting sun,
　That shook old Empire's towering pride,
　That swept them down the floating tide,
Say, when these long unfolding scenes appear,
Streams down thy hoary cheek, the pity-darting tear?

I FOLLOWED my guide into the house of one of his friends, of whom he had promised to request the favor of shewing me his library, I saw but very few volumes; among which I took particular notice of one which was entitled *Universal History*, it being, as I thought, of too small a size to contain all the events recorded in history. My friend smiled at my surprise. As the book was far from being voluminous, I sat down in a corner of the room to peruse it—its contents were nearly as follows

"How many flourishing empires have successively rested on this globe, of which there now remains no traces but their names! and even these would not have been preserved in the memory of man, but through the pen of historians. Yet why desire to raise the veil which conceals the remembrance of so many acts of violence? Why speak of Nimrod, that ferocious hunter, who, thirsting for con-
　　　quest,

quest, was the first who discovered the art of subjugating men, under the specious pretence of submitting them to the laws? He learned to reduce them in the same manner as he had overcome the beasts of the field, and was the first to discover the most fatal of all secrets, *i. e how easy it is for one man to oppress the feeble human race.* Belus, Ninus, and Semiramis, in ascending the throne, did but manifest the fastidious pride of power, they maintained the sceptre in their hands by violence and terror, and struck humanity with a thousand wounds. This sad catalogue of effeminate or barbarous kings, who had been equally fatal to their people, either in peace or war, terminated with the infamous Sardanapalus, who, surrounded by his women, slumbering in voluptuousness, at length awakened from the lethargy in which his enervating pleasures had thrown him the din of arms by which his ears were assailed, could only extract from him the last act which completed his cowardice, he fell by his own hand, while his rebellious captains invaded his vast dominions. Thus the empire of the Assyrians, which had flourished on the earth during twelve hundred years, and had caused all Asia to dread its power, became at length the scene of anarchy, and was totally dismembered.

"This list of potentates were replaced by others, who, from their superb cities of Nineveh and Babylon, continued to spread carnage and destruction over the earth. The cities of Egypt were ravaged, all Palestine was desolated, Jerusalem burned to ashes, by these monsters of ambition, who drove whole nations before them, like so many wandering tribes, and, by their destructive victories, enslaved those beings whom the God of nature had created free. These conquests impressed so much terror in the minds of the vanquished nations, that they supposed the conquerors

conquerors to be gods, and accordingly altars were raised to them, incense and divine homage were offered them as to the sovereigns of the universe; thus fear creates meanness, and the affrighted man, forgetting to use his reason, no longer finds his equal in the terrible man, armed with power, and preceded by the weapon of death.

"Cyrus, great even in his infancy, gave very early proofs that he possessed a soul equal to his future high destiny. The knowledge of his exalted fate neither surprised nor affrighted him; his character was truly great and lofty, and formed for the enterprises assigned him. He united the three empires of Assyria, Media, and Persia, and he removed the frontiers of his kingdom to a greater distance than any of his predecessors.

"However, the ambition of his successors was not satisfied; they attempted to aggrandise this already terrifying colossus. Having heard of the growing fame of Greece, thither they sent their armies, which, like the overflowings of an immense ocean, poured in on every side upon this feeble part of Europe; but mad ambition, at least this time, received its merited punishment, by the loss of innumerable soldiers.

"The Grecians, who had maintained their freedom by having vanquished this vast deluge of armed soldiers, soon sharpened against themselves those same weapons which had dispersed their enemies. Their states, which ought for ever to have been united, became a prey to jealousy and discord; their orators, whose eloquence rendered them the more dangerous, enflamed the minds of the people, and kindled the torch of civil war among them, which they carried even to Persia. At length, fatigued with so many contrary emotions, the Grecians began to desire that interior calm which generally succeeds to violent commotions; every thing seemed to prepare them to an univerfal and profound peace Alexander however appeared, and the world, though ready to fall into a peaceful flumber, was now again a prey to all thofe convulfions occafioned by the ravages of war. The ambitious prince wept over the conquefts of his father, impatient to fhed human blood, he feared leaft there fhould not remain any more nations for him to conquer, Eager after that murderous glory, which he miftook for the real, he thought a prince could never truly reign but by making all men flaves, and with that haughty courage, which is the only virtue thefe enterprifing men poffefs, he afcended the throne of Macedonia. His reign wore the impreffion of his ardent character, which fignalifed itfelf by carrying defolation into all Greece, Perfia, and the Indies His fatal genius traced a reeking path on the map of the world, which the eye can fcarcely conceive Still he wifhed to conquer, but nations were wanting to gratify his thirft for conqueft he fhuddered to find his power limited ; and while he refolved to return, in order to conquer other countries, Death, in mercy to mankind, cut off, in the flower of his age, the hopes and eager ambition of this dreadful fcourge of humanity, and the world, that before was only fubject to one mafter, now beheld thirty fovereigns contending for the fpoils of the univerfe, which a few hours before were at the difpofal of one man.

" Mankind were plunged in deeper horrors by thefe difcords. All thofe extenfive countries, vanquifhed by the victorious arm of Alexander, to which his fucceffors dared not even in idea to pretend, were ravaged, and the fucceffive generations continued to be a prey to thefe endlefs wars ; and, while thefe fucceffors were mutually haftening each other's ruin, the children of the hero,

his

his lawful heirs, were deprived of that immense succession.

"Among so many kings, whose only aim was conquest, and the destruction of the human species, there appeared one at length who was the friend of men, of philosophy, and of the arts, Ptolemy Philadelphus. He was the first who seemed penetrated with this great truth, that when mankind have once shaken off the shackles of ignorance and barbarism, their only source of happiness and glory is in the sciences. This sovereign could pass his time with delight in meditating in the midst of an immense library, which he cherished as the precious deposit of human knowledge, and which he continually enriched with those productions, the most glorious to the human mind, which he caused to be collected from the most remote countries. Ah! why were these precious volumes, wherein were collected the re-united discoveries of the highest antiquity, reserved to perish by the hand of a barbarian, who, in a fit of inebriation, consumed in an instant the laborious researches of thirty centuries!

"While the successors of Alexander continued plunged in intestine divisions, that power, fated to contend with and to overthrow all nations, was springing up from the bosom of Italy. Those haughty kings of Greece were soon exterminated by the Romans, who themselves became a prey to anarchy in their disputes with their consuls, their decemvirs, and military tribunes; but they, like unto those found constitutions which acquire strength by every violent attack, reared their lofty heads from amidst their internal civil discords, which are frequently so salutary to a state, and, though scarcely out of danger themselves, they meditate the conquest of the world.

"During five centuries the neighbouring nations of this growing power struggled in vain to maintain their ascen-

ascendency they were at length obliged to bend under that yoke, the extent of which was not then known. The Romans, thirsting for conquest, extended their victorious arms to the African shores in quest of new enemies. Their ambitious rival, who, like themselves aspired to the monarchy of the whole universe, in spite of her treasures, and of the genius of Hannibal, was destroyed, and her ruin was the forerunner of the fall of Corinth and of Numidia.

"Even the immense continent of Asia was forced to open her cities before these invincible conquerors. Secure of victory, they flew to encounter their enemies, and the Roman eagle spread his haughty and triumphant wings over every discovered sea and country.

"It was patriotism which inspired the love of glory in their breasts. This was the prodigious seed, from whence sprung those masculine virtues, which charm and amaze, and encouraged them to devote themselves for the good of their country, of which these are the only instances in history. A long succession of heroes, who sincerely loved their country, exalted the Roman republic to a most flourishing state, and she became the mistress of the world. But when all nations were subjected to her power, that same spirit of ambition which had caused her greatness, created the desire of enjoying unlimited sway. Sylla and Marius seized the reins of power, and trampled under their feet the liberty of their country. Even Cæsar, on the banks of the Rubicon, turned his warlike courage against his country, and the greatest and most culpable of men, triumphantly established despotism upon the ruins of expiring liberty; for which his memory was sufficiently punished, he being the original cause of that succession of horrible reigns, which proved the degree of depravity to which human nature was capable of descending

"How-

"However, under Augustus the laurel of Apollo was suffered to flourish; a short interval of peaceful calm soothed the turbulent passions of the Romans, and made them suppose it was possible to be happy under the dominion of one man; but tortures and executions soon awakened them from their lethargy, to the full extent of their error; it was then too late to break their chains, therefore they ingenuously sought for arguments to justify their slavery. They could not become more vile, more disgraceful to human nature. This vast and superb Roman empire was now become the scene of bloodshed and slaughter, a land of victims and executioners, of ferocious cruelty, and base pusillanimity; and these horrible calamities were only interrupted by the reigns of three of these emperors who were worthy to be called men, Titus, Antoninus, and Marcus Aurelius, who gave a temporary truce to the outrages committed to human nature.

"Such an empire seemed inevitably to hasten to its dissolution, internally consumed as it were by the devouring flame of despotism, by the barbarous avarice or lethargic stupor of its emperors, for in a despotic government, whether the chief is stupid or sensible, merciful or cruel, still he is the chief. But who could have foreseen the new revolution which was to renovate the face of the earth? Who could have expected that overflow of the human species, which was to bring the germ of so many new nations, and renew the antique but debased generations of the universe?

"In the northern forests, amidst mountains and vallies eternally frozen, were concealed those nations which were to overthrow the giant colossus of the Roman empire, to restore the inhabitants to a state of reflorescence, by mixing with them, and lay the foundation of those various kingdoms which at present exist in Europe. They were, no doubt, originally invited by the mild aspect of a serene and temperate climate, having accidentally discovered those countries hitherto unknown, and essayed the soft influence of the kinder elements. These innumerable hordes abandoned their haunts, and traced out the path for other nations, still more northern, who successively, and for a length of time, poured in upon all Europe, with the unrelenting fury of the tempestuous waves, inundating a vast extent of land.

" Many centuries elapsed ere these innumerable legions were exhausted they were like a torrent, sweeping all that obstructed their passage. These barbarians began by dismembering all the western empire, and from their ruins they formed several kingdoms, into which they introduced barbarous customs, many of which are not yet annihilated

" At this time the Goths overrun a great part of Asia and all Europe, in order to establish themselves in Spain

" The Anglo Saxons issued from the wild forests of Germany, sailed over to Britain, to rescue it from its oppressors, and afterwards invaded and possessed it.

" The Francs, another people of Germany, were called in to assist the Gauls, who were struggling to disengage themselves from the yoke of the Romans, and, after having avenged, they reduced those they went to defend.

" Rome, that famous city, which had plundered and ravaged so many nations, at length experienced the same fate her palaces, her beautiful structures, were all destroyed by the flames, and the furious rage of the conquerors suffered but a few remains of its ancient grandeur to testify the extent of its punishment

" But all these invasions were nothing in comparison to the victorious course of Attila The parching blaze of an inflamed comet, shedding its fiery influence over one half of the globe, would not have been a more dreadful scourge to humanity. With gigantic strides he ran his destructive race, ravaging all Macedonia, Mœsia, Thrace, and Italy. All these countries were devastated, the inhabitants were forced to fly before the victorious arms of the merciless conqueror, and the human species, unable to find an asylum upon earth, were reduced to take refuge on the shores of the Adriatic. These fugitive and trembling tribes gave rise to Venice, that beautiful city, which will soon deserve to be called *the superb*.

" The western empire here received its last shock, and Rome and Italy, which had been reunited to the empire of the east, were again snatched from it, and soon experienced an accumulation of new disasters.

" But now an unknown and dreadful scourge sprung up in the east. How shall we describe this terrible Mahomet? at first despised, but afterwards adored, by his own people. This wonderful man, who united the quickest intelligence to the most audacious courage! Is he an enthusiast, or an impostor? What shall we say of him, when we behold him crushing one part of the east, and laying the foundation of the powerful kingdom of the Caliphs? Equally dreadful by his sword as he is powerful by his tenets, influencing and seducing the minds of that people, whom he subjugates by his arms, a legislator and a sanguinary warrior, raising the arm of a barbarian with the eloquence of a great man, making an equal use of religion and of arms, while victory places him both on the throne and upon the altar, prescribing laws, for a long succession of future ages, to a multitude of people, whose existence or submission he cannot even expect.

" The unhappy western empire was lacerated on all sides, and daily experienced fresh wounds. Italy was attacked by the Lombards. Spain was overrun by the Saracens, who threatened France and other nations with their conquering power. The swarm of barbarians, far from being exhausted, were ravaging the most flourishing parts of Europe. At length there arose in France a man, worthy to be called great, full of ardour, and possessing the genius of a politician with the energy of a hero, born amidst storms and tempests, and destined to disperse them. Charlemagne was sent to subdue the Saracens, to make all Germany tremble, and to strike a mortal blow to the Lombards in Italy, and while he quelled the disturbances of his kingdom, he placed the Imperial crown of the western empire upon his own head. But this diadem was too weighty for his feeble successors thus the empire of Charlemagne was divided, and the feudal government reared its hundred monstrous heads

" Here the philosophic eye may trace the epoch of Helvetian liberty. How delightful it is to see those courageous men shake off the yoke of tyrants! and, after having learned to combat, learn also to establish a form of government, admirable for its wisdom, and, in its happy effects, evincing to the whole world, that it is possible for a state to enjoy a pure morality, and to live without ambition, without jealousy, the heroic preservers of their own liberties, satisfied with the bare necessaries of life. They set the example to all nations, but, alas! it is an example more admired than followed.

" The new western empire was now again torn asunder, and that of the east totally disappeared. The last eruption of the barbarians, fated to overpower Europe, suddenly precipitated itself, like a torrent, over Constantinople, and became masters of the whole empire of the east, which they possess to this day.

" In

"In our days, and even during a system of equilibrium, we frequently see a crowned head, either by its power or weakness, agitate and set in motion every neighbouring sovereign. Their interests are divided and subdivided by the least shock, and frequently he who gives the first impulse can scarcely guess at what point the movement will stop. In former days, however, it was still more astonishing to behold a pilgrim, though without a crown, set those wonderful emigrations in motion, known under the name of Crusades. To see an enthusiast have the power of persuading kings to abandon their thrones, and an innumerable multitude of subjects to forsake the soft influence of their native soil. A troop of vagabonds, disgracing the Christian name, and, reeking with the blood of their fellow creatures, thus prostrating themselves before the sepulchre of Jesus Christ.

"A second eruption of this nature, headed by a sovereign of France, occasioned similar excesses. Constantinople was taken and pillaged, and the virtues of Louis IX. were deprived of that salutary influence over his kingdom, which they would have had in an age when other opinions had prevailed.

"This religious epidemy did not cease until two million of Europeans had found a grave in the east.

"At this time appeared those warlike Tartars, headed by Genghis Kan. From the remote parts of Corea he spread the torch of war into the heart of Persia and the Indies, overleaping the cloud-capped mountains of Caucasus, of Taurus, and Imaus. Since the age of Xerxes the world had not witnessed such formidable armies. He reduced under his power one half of China and of Indostan, the best part of Persia, the frontiers of Russia, and all Tartary. The treasures of Asia were at his feet, and no conqueror ever spread his glory and his victories to so vast an

extent.

extent. The entire conquest of China was completed by his children. This empire, situated at the extremity of Asia, which boasts the highest antiquity, possessed laws and arts, and knew how to trace the revolution of the planets in the heavens, whilst we Europeans existed only as wandering tribes, without civilization, without laws. These glorious conquerors submitted themselves to the government, police, and arts, of the nation they had vanquished, a striking instance of the majestic ascendency of good laws, and of the natural impulse which barbarous nations feel to assemble in societies under the mild influence of civil life. These legislators seemed to have perfected the system of morality, if not that of good policy; and if the perfection of a government may be calculated from its effects, the government of China is most perfect. It rests on the immutable basis of the love and respect of the subjects for their sovereign; it produces population, peace, and prosperity, the subordination of each respective state, and resembles the paternal authority of a father in the bosom of his family. Possibly a love for the marvellous, and, above all, the pleasure of satyrising the manners of our own country, may have embellished the language of these high raters of that foreign nation, and have adorned it in those colours, which the admiration they wished to inspire in others enabled them to exaggerate. If, however, the famed tribunal of history is not fabulous, and if it really consists in keeping a register of all the public events, if those generous historians are truly and philosophically enlightened, and prefer exile and death, rather than to fail in transmitting to posterity the public faults and personal vices of princes, this nation may certainly boast of having found the most salutary curb, either against despotism or the weakness of monarchs, and her historians are

more

more respectable, and more useful, than the writers of any other nation

"The torch of civil wars and revengeful animosity still prevailed, caused by the grand schism of the west, and while Edward and Philip engaged in the most bloody battles, a scourge more fatal even than war was ravaging all Europe That murderous plague, which had travelled over the whole world, and after having depopulated Asia and Africa, spread its baneful influence over all France and England, by which a fourth part of the unfortunate race of man were swept off from the face of the earth.

"The prosperity of the popes, who had claimed the right of arbitrating between the divisions of kings, and who would have been worthy of the respect and veneration of the whole world, had they only employed their ascendency in pacifying every dissention, made them imagine that the fate of ancient Rome was revived in their favour. They had frequently essayed the dreaded power of the fulminations of the church, and these spiritual thunderbolts, in their sacred hands, had inspired the same terror which had formerly accompanied the rapid flight of the Roman legions. They distributed their bulls with the same authority as the Roman emperors had published their decrees The court of Rome, like the Roman republic, cited, judged, and punished the private faults of princes at her tribunal How majestic and venerable, if justice and humanity, issuing from the bosom of the ancient capital of the world, had thundered against the ambition of kings, and repressed the disorders of Christendom ! But Rome, while she affected moderation, knew how to flatter and terrify the passions of princes, to abridge their power, and keep them in a dependent mediocrity, and to enflame them against each other, in order to benefit by the spoils of all. Kings

stripped

stripped themselves of their diadems, to lay them at the feet of the holy see, and become tributaries to the pope, in the same manner as, in the days of Roman grandeur, the monarchs of various countries vied with each other in requesting the alliance of the Romans, and thought themselves honoured by the title of their freedmen

"Such was the profound ignorance of princes, and, but for the blow of the latter heresies, which by kindling anew the torch of war created an energic impulse in the minds of men, so favourable were the circumstances, that the clouds of ignorance, by their increasing opacity, gave Rome a near prospect of becoming sole mistress of the universe, aided by the impenetrable shade of night, into which the world was ready to be enveloped.

"The throne and kingdom of France was once more exalted by a wife and political king Charles V. is one of the few, whose memory is rendered precious by the recollection of his virtues; he again annexed respect and love to the title of monarch, and his wisdom and goodness are rendered the more illustrious by the misfortunes which his son occasioned.

"Tamerlane, after the example of Alexander, and Genghis-Kan, conquered all ancient Persia, and desolated the Indies, Bajazet himself fell under his victorious power, and was made his prisoner.

"Constantinople also was forced to surrender to the Turks The Ottoman empire, established by the power of victory, acquired strength and splendor, and extended from the Archipelago to the Euphrates.

"At this time the feudal power was extinguished in France Louis XI. an absolute, barbarous, perfidious, and artful prince, dishonoured the throne, and made the very name of king odious to the nation. The conquest of Naples by Charles VIII. and the flight of Alexander VI.

to

to the castle of Saint Angelo for refuge, are two facts, which from their awful lesson, engrave a deep impression in the immensity of events.

"The incestuous nuptials, and the infamous and abominable pleasures of that pontiff, polluted with innumerable crimes, though disgusting to the friends of virtue, ought for ever to live in the memory of posterity, in order to impress that execration and horror, with which his name must ever be accompanied.

"England at this time groaned under disastrous civil wars, which, however, had this salutary effect, that they stamped the national character with that active and impulsive energy, which was to germinate that spirit of freedom for which they are distinguished, and seemed to announce that the tree of liberty would shortly flourish in their soil, though nurtured with the blood of thousands

"The sixteenth century was rendered illustrious by a succession of the grandest events

"Gustavus Vasa, by shaking off a foreign yoke, merited, and bore the glorious name of THE DELIVERER OF HIS COUNTRY.

"The powerful Charles V. was the sole sovereign of Spain, of Germany, and of Italy, and both as a warrior, and a politician, he bore the sway over all Europe.

"Francis I oppressed by misfortunes, but magnanimous even in his captive state, excites a kind of affectionate interest in the heart, which seldom exists in favour of vanquished kings but he was a lover of the fine arts, and transplanted them from Italy into France, and this merit alone seems to absolve him from his faults, which were various

"Henry VIII. was a cruel despot, but he exalted his nation by the ascendency of his genius, and taught her to poize and appreciate the power of her neighbours

"Leo X.

" Leo X was surrounded with great men, he impressed their genius with that power, by which they soared up to celebrity He idolized the fine arts, and by them his pontificate is immortalised.

" As soon as the schism of Omar and Aly had for ever separated the Persians from the Turks, when Asia and Africa had experienced that revolution in their religion, which was to sow the seeds of enmity between them, there suddenly appeared an orator, named *Luther*, who, by his thundering eloquence, acquired that astonishing dominion over the minds of men, by which he snatched one half of Europe from the Romish pontiff, and kindled the first sparks of philosophy.

" But the greatest of these events, was the discovery of a new world, fated to change the whole face of the earth.

" America was reduced by a handful of cruel monsters, who spread terror and devastation wherever they appeared, sprinkling their footsteps with the blood of the human race, in order to conquer that land which produced the gold for which they thirsted. Never had the eye of heaven, in its greatest wrath, witnessed such atrocious cruelties, accompanied with an insensibility so barbarous. They have stamped the disgrace of the ancient world, and it will be difficult ever to erase the ignominy attached to that bloody stain.

" Cortez conquered Mexico, and Francis Pizarro took possession of Peru, and from this new world was brought the most dreadful scourge, which attacked the source of pleasure and of life, as a punishment for those repeated outrages to human nature, and man seems to acquire strength and age but for his greater misfortune.

" Spain was now in possession of one half of the world, and Portugal acquired the coasts of Asia and Africa.

" Russia,

" Ruffia, which had hitherto been feparated from Europe, now began to prove her exiftence, and her immenfe empire became important to the other powers of the world.

" And now the degenerated race of Genghis-Kan, which had been driven from China, produced, from among the loweft clafs of people, a man capable of forcing his way to the throne, and of eftablifhing a new dynafty

" The celebrated Sha Abbas, after the fchifm which had defolated all Perfia, but confolidated the national genius, impreffed the empire with a character of greatnefs, of fplendor, and of felicity, till then unknown in the annals of the world

" The conquefts of the Ottomans were aftonifhing Selim the Invincible fucceeded the powerful Mahomet II and Solyman, the fucceffor of Selim, exerted his victorious arms againft both Chriftians and Perfians with equal fuccefs. His empire extended from Algiers to the Euphrates, and from the Black Sea to Epirus.

" In Spain appeared that Philip II. who fixed the attention of all Europe by his preponderating power; he fomented divifions in all the neighbouring ftates, he afpired to the poffeffion of all the gold of the new world, and, with one glance, could, from the folitude of his clofet, embrace the whole extent of his dominions from Mexico to Sicily He, in the battle of St Quentin, ftruck France with one of the deepeft wounds fhe had ever encountered. Such was the depth of his diffimulation, that he deceived even the court of Rome itfelf, and it was his cruel fanaticifm which gave birth to the famous republic of the Seven United Provinces.

" From amidft lakes and marfhes, this infant ftate reared up her timid head, fupported by courage, induftry, and commerce, fhe became active, laborious, and patient by

the

the foſtering aid of the Prince of Orange, ſhe daily acquired ſtrength and energy, and theſe quiet fiſhermen became the moſt intrepid warriors, through the heroic fortitude, tranquil courage, and unſhaken conſtance in adverſity, of a man worthy of the reſpect of all nations. A religious aſſaſſination, preſcribed by Philip II. deprived the republic of one of its greateſt heroes. Such was the devotion of this ſanguinary monſter!

"This Spaniſh monarch, notwithſtanding the deſtruction of his *invincible* fleet, was on the point of ſubjugating the kingdom of France. By his machinations he eſtabliſhed that diabolical league, and enflamed the minds of the French againſt their lawful ſovereign, againſt a great man, the value of whoſe character they had not yet learned to eſtimate. But HENRY IV triumphed over his intrigues, his deep policy, and his gold, and by his heroic valour, but ſtill more, by his generous magnanimity and exceſſive goodneſs of heart, he reflected honour and dignity to the name of *king*. His memory is bleſſed and revered even in the preſent generation, as much through gratitude as to impreſs his example in the minds of his ſucceſſors.

"That nation, deſtined to manifeſt to the whole world the leaſt imperfect form of government which human foreſight had yet been able to trace, enjoyed greatneſs and ſecurity in the midſt of thoſe ſtorms, by which all Europe was agitated, her inſular ſituation produced her glory and ſecured her power. Royal authority and national liberty were united, without prejudice to either, and James, the weakeſt of monarchs, was dethroned, and replaced by a ſovereign more worthy of reigning over that free people.

"The events which followed this period are too near our own time, and too well known to be repreſented in their

their true point of view; and the severe scrutiny of history can with difficulty either overleap or retrace the century of Richelieu and of Louis XIV.

"With what rapidity the wheel of time rolls on! Those events, those revolutions which excited admiration, which raised such clamours, exercised so many heads, and fatigued them by the contrary assaults of hope and fear, they are all fallen! all overwhelmed in the abyss of Time! with merciless hands he erases those lively and striking colours which engaged the attention and interest of man; he, with his devouring breath, blasts the representation of the most important revolutions, and the memory of empires falls like that of man. Where is now the history of Assyria, from the time of Ninus to that of Sardanapalus? Where are the mementos, which can revive but for an instant the haughty power of Xerxes, his innumerable fleet and armies, his ostentation, and the extent of his dominions, at which, though of so short a duration, he himself was terrified, and wept, when, from the summit of an eminence, he contemplated that prodigious troop of soldiers, and recollected that death (the inevitable avenger of mankind) must shortly preside over that immense multitude!

"Royal greatness then, since it is liable to fade away and be totally extinct, is not the most solid. There is a greatness of the human mind, which imprints a path in the history of ages much more luminous and durable. The progress of the sciences, of the arts, and of legislation, which are the most real benefits conferred on the mortal race of man, secure from oblivion those respectable names, to which are annexed the love and gratitude of nations. The great Homer continues to be read to this day, in his life time, he was poor and unfortunate, but his memory is cherished, his ashes are respected. Ah!

R how

how many names of kings have been effaced before his sublime name! those haughty potentates are extinguished like artificial fires, which shine for a moment, and are buried in darkness, never to re-appear. So uncertain or unimportant is their transitory existence, that the patience of the obstinate antiquary is fatigued in tracing them, and in his fruitless labour excites the contempt and pity of the philosopher.

"The inventors of those arts which are necessary and consolatory, which help us to support existence, and has rendered it dear and precious to us, are therefore the real monarchs of human nature, and their respected names ought for ever to live in the memory of the friends of humanity. These familiar and innumerable arts which constitute the charm of domestic life, are derived (as well as the most useful, though simple notions) from some ancient people, who have left no traces of their existence, whose benefits we enjoy without knowing their source. We inherit those sciences, which have cost them such laborious efforts, yet without recollecting the primitive difficulties attending every exertion of genius. Who was the first discoverer of the elements of written and verbal language, of mechanics, of agriculture, of navigation, of physics, of astronomy, of music, of painting, &c.? The obstacles which he must have conquered confound human understanding. The most familiar of our arts are miraculous efforts of genius, and one single invention, such as the pulley or screw, is a miracle to a thinking mind.

"To what active intelligence are we indebted for those precious and multiplied acquirements, which the vulgar mind exercises without having ever thought of the inventor? Are they the labours of one nation, or many? in what manner have men transmitted and shared them between them? is it from memory? from custom? or is it chance which sent them among us? In short, are not those sciences the rich heritage of a people supposed to be antecedent to every recorded history, and entombed in the impenetrable obscurity of time immemorial, an heritage greatly disjointed indeed, but the fragments of which are still so precious?

"How many other useful and agreeable arts have been lost, or never renewed upon earth but at immense intervals? How many discoveries have been buried for want of a genius analogous to that of the inventor to re-produce them a second time in the world? If some ancient inhabitant of the earth, the predecessor of the Egyptians or Chaldees, (those nations which we suppose to have lived in that period which we blindly believe to be the most antique for want of penetrating to the more remote ages) could return among us, he would sigh to see our extreme ignorance, and our arts and sciences would no doubt appear to him as the unformed fragments of the acquisitions of his time.

"Science, as it has been justly suspected, is indivisible, and has no isolated or separate branches, as our ignorance and insufficiency has supposed. This philosophical idea ought to be thoroughly examined, for already have various shades of affinity been discovered between objects which appeared most opposite, and the wonderful strokes of genius which we sometimes see are points of unity tending to the assemblage of the whole.

"That genius, capable of inventing, has perhaps never existed but in the infant days of the world, when human nature might possess more energy, and a creative power and penetration which she has now lost. However, we ought always to suppose ourselves capable of going beyond that which we discover, in order to give boldness and strength to our ideas, and be enabled to soar up into the

R 2 region

region of poffible things, for then we fhould experience that enlargement which gives audacity and ambition to our conceptions, the point at which the human underftanding may naturally afpire is far more exalted than man has hitherto conceived

" But if we muft caft a philofophic eye on the pageantry prefented in hiftory, fo proud to relate the boafted events of each century, what fhame it reflects upon nations and upon mankind!

" Inftead of that beneficial union which might have exifted between nations, humanity was debafed and outraged by an uninterrupted chain of hoftilities, the bloody ftandard of war was feen waving on every part of the globe, murder became the ftudy, the glory, the occupation of thofe princes, who have fafcinated the minds of their fubjects, and perfuaded them that it was glorious to kill each other, in order to feize upon each others poffeffions, inftead of cultivating that land which they were fprinkling with human blood. In fhort, in this retrofpective view, nature groans to fee that all nations, even the moft remote, have had no other plan in view but their mutual deftruction.

" Thofe great empires have all been cemented with blood, and on whatever point of the globe they fixed their exiftence, it was by the deftruction of the human fpecies. In the moft diftant ages, men have been attached to war. The memory of the great Sefoftris recalls the idea of a conqueror, who fent an army out of Egypt of more than feven hundred thoufand men, with which he ravaged the whole coaft of the Mediteranean, and extended his conquefts to the fartheft part of Colchis thus opened the fcene of the world. Devaftation has fucceffively vifited every part of this unhappy world, iron, inftead of being ufed by the cultivator to draw from the bowels of the earth the

real

teal riches destined for the happiness of man, is sharpened into a deadly weapon, and given into the hands of the ferocious soldier, to strike the heart of his fellow-creature, and clothe himself in his spoils, and this cruel pursuit is styled *glory* and *grandeur*. This troop of murderers, obedient ministers of the ambition of princes, who, by an inexplicable power, direct the progress of several millions of beings, who are themselves ignorant of the cause which sets them in motion, march to the extermination of their own species, and cheerfully wait the signal of those by whom they are governed.

" History can take no notice of Semiramis but to mark the bloody æra in which this queen advanced, at the head of three millions of men, to contend against the Indians, who engaged in the contest with an army still more considerable

" The establishment and the destruction of the monarchies of the Babylonians, of the Assyrians, of the Medes and Persians, have cost the effusion of rivers of human blood, and the military expeditions of the senseless Xerxes have depopulated all Asia. The transitory passage of Alexander on the scene of life has cost so many victims, that it is not possible to establish the exact calculation of them His death, as fatal as his life, was the signal of more bloodshed, and armed his successors, who, during two hundred years, contended for his dismembered kingdoms What carnage and desolation accompanied their respective pretensions!

" It is scarcely possible to conceive how so small a spot as Greece could produce so many millions, who suffered themselves to be slaughtered for such miserable conquests. The Roman power was environed by an ocean of blood what a variety of rival nations, who attack, defend, overthrow, and are overthrown?

" The

"The irruption of the Gauls in Italy, and the Punic wars, which commenced foon after, Mithridates, fucceffively victorious and unfortunate, the barbarous Sylla, the ferocious Marius, and that Julius Cæfar! How many victims they have coft to human nature! My hand fhudders in tracing the melancholy picture of thefe calamities Even the Jews, notwithftanding the infignificant figure they make in hiftory, are diftinguifhed by the cruelties, of which they were fucceffively both the agents and the victims.

"But all the wounds given to human kind difappear before that enormous ftab given at the epoch of the irruption of the Goths, of the Vandals, of the Huns, and of the Oftrogoths, into Gaul, Italy, Spain, and Africa. Mankind feemed on the brink of its entire deftruction, for, while on one fide, this dreadful inundation rolled with impetuofity from north to fouth, another torrent of barbarians poured in from an oppofite quarter, and its rapid courfe extended, on one fide, to the fartheft borders of Perfia, and, on the other, beyond the banks of the Loire Ah! if fome beneficent being had not protected the human fpecies, they muft have fallen under the ruined cities of the earth, which were all reduced to mournful deferts.

"At the time when fuperftition and avarice difperfed mankind abroad to make the conqueft of Spanifh America, and to flaughter thofe newly difcovered nations, is it poffible to calculate the immenfe number of men, who were facrificed to fanaticifm and cupidity?

"Thofe difputes among Europeans for the poffeffion of new regions, that conftant alteration in the form of government, thofe long and terrible wars, which the progrefs in the arts had rendered more bloody and fatal. Alas! the misfortunes of human nature are beyond the power of calculation!.......... wherever I turn

my

my eyes, I see the effusion of human blood in torrents it flows over the parched and sandy deserts of Africa, and amidst the snowy mountains of the Frigid Zone, while the delightful verdure of Asia is every where defaced by its traces and if the wars, the contagious diseases, the devouring famines, and all the scourges which have accompanied and followed the disputes of sovereigns, were assembled together, it would be seen that one half of mankind have caused the death of the other half!

"And while the inhabitants of the world were slaughtering each other with ferocious cruelty, the dawn of that day arose, ever terrible, ever memorable in the annals of the universe, which separated Sicily from the fertile soil of Italy by a most tremendous earthquake, when the roaring waves of the angry element poured with implacable fury into this self created gulf, and dashed against the coasts of this new island

"The Straits of *Gades*, in like manner, were opened in a day of wrath by a concussion of the elements The earth suddenly cleaved her bosom, and the world was divided into two parts, destined ever to be separate The ungovernable ocean poured in with all its weight upon the humble Mediterranean this shock, caused by two seas, confounded and astonished to find their angry waves mingled together, must have resounded over the whole world, and affrighted the timid human race

"It was, no doubt, in consequence of such another concussion of the globe, that the Island of Atlantides[*]
dis-

---

[*] The date given by Plato to the existence of the Atlantides is not to be forgotten The eastern nations had years of various durations, some even so inconsiderable as a diurnal revolution, a simple day and night Those of three and four months, however, seem to have been universally prevalent Plato thus places the
defeat

disappeared from the face of the earth. That fortunate abode, favoured with the softest influence of the heavens, that spacious and superb asylum of peace and happiness, where the inhabitants received for the reward of their virtues a perfect abundance, which excited perpetual hymns of gratitude in their hearts: alas! it was plunged into the vast abyss of the seas, without leaving the smallest trace behind, nor would it dwell at this age in the annals of time but for the traditions of men, whose minds were impressed with the remembrance of that delightful country.

"How many times mankind have been precipitated into barbarism by those sudden revolutions, which, in overthrowing whole cities, and destroying empires, have extinguished the bright torch of the sciences! Such a state may be compared to that of an insect, who, by a sudden gust of wind is shaken from a shrub, whence he was gathering the sweets, stunned by the fall, in vain he attempts to ascend towards the stem, in which he succeeds not till after incredible exertions and labour. Thus the least physical shock breaks the thread of our acquisitions,

defeat of the Atlantides by the Athenians 9000 years before Solon; Solon lived 620 years before Christ. These taken together and calculated as years of three months, the date when this island disappeared does not in any very extravagant degree differ from that of the Deluge. It accords, likewise with the synchronisms, not only of the Septuagint, but of all the nations that we have historical or astronomical calculations to deduce from. But one circumstance is peculiarly striking, the chief of these people, of whom the Greeks afterwards made a mountain, and on whose back they placed the heavens, this man is said to have been the first who exposed himself in a vessel on the ocean. Critics also contend that Atlas was an astronomer, and that he first instructed the Egyptians in the knowledge of the sphere and the planetary system.

FROM SULLIVAN'S VIEW OF NATURE.

and replunges that genius in obscurity which the day before was resplendent with brightness. That day which consumed the library of Ptolemy destroyed all the treasures of human genius. We know not even, at least we cannot ascertain, the primitive origin of the human species, Europe itself may one day be totally obliterated from the memory of future ages, the art of printing will perhaps scarcely save the labours of genius. The one half of the universe may, perhaps, one day be for ever separated from the other, by a new concussion of the elements our printed books may perish with our manuscripts, or perhaps become totally unknown. The existence of a primitive people who have enlightened other nations, is very certain, but in what region shall we place them? the wisest are reduced to conjectures."

CHAP. XLII.

Thence rolls the mighty pow'r his broad survey,
And scales the nation's awful doom
He sees proud grandeur's meteor ray,
He yields to joy the festive day,—
Then sweeps the length'ning shade, and marks them for the tomb.

"WHAT is the actual situation of Europe? In my time, or thereabout, commerce procured the discovery of a new world, and the discovery changed the whole face of things. Then followed a system of equilibrium, which tended to balance one power by the other, to set a curb on ambition, to limit all conquests, and to secure to each state their peculiar independence. But
this

this syſtem, by eſtabliſhing an equality of forces, ſerved only to render the wars more laſting and cruel

"What is become of Ruſſia, whoſe growing power was the aſtoniſhment of my century, though, in the commencement of that century, ſhe had ſcarcely any political exiſtence?"—"This empire, which, from its immenſe extent, united to every ſea, by which it could communicate with every part of both worlds, has been divided in two It was impoſſible for one head to wear a crown ſo ponderous,"—"And Poland ?"—"Is ſubject to an hereditary monarch, having been made ſenſible of the danger of that deplorable exceſs of liberty it formerly enjoyed, and, ſince that period, Poland, with the aid of a ſound and vigorous adminiſtration, is become a flouriſhing kingdom"—"And the Ottoman empire?"—"Has been ſubdued, through the want of a ſultan capable of being both warrior and legiſlator, poſſeſſing that firm deciſion of mind neceſſary to enforce the laws of a neceſſary diſcipline This empire required the genius of conquerors to re-animate and awaken it from the lethargic ſtupor into which it had fallen it is now regenerated and enjoys celebrity and glory"—"And Germany?"—"The ſtates-general of Germany have always conſidered the Germanic body as a republic of ſovereigns, at which an elective and amoveable chief preſided, therefore the Germanic liberty ſtill enjoys all its vigour This vaſt body, penetrated with the pureſt political notions, is never in league againſt any other power, and maintains all the advantages of its political ſyſtem."—"And the United Provinces?"—"The concuſſions of the globe, the trouble and expenſe which her eager commerce occaſioned, joined to her unbounded opulence, cauſed her one day to embark for Aſia, where ſhe poſſeſſed immenſe eſtabliſhments, the produce of which was ineſtimable, Holland, therefore, no longer exiſts in Europe,

Europe, but in the East Indies."—" And Great Britain?"—" Her admirable constitution, sometimes shaken, but never annihilated, still constitutes her force and splendor. Though she has sometimes dearly bought that liberty in which she glories, she still figures upon the globe among the first nations of the earth, as she was the first nation who learned to conciliate the laws of human legislation with the dignity due to man. She no longer aims at rivalship with her neighbouring kingdom."—" And France?" " She possesses Egypt and Greece, both flourishing colonies."—' And Spain?"—" The Spaniards have at length learned to value the vast extent of their possessions, they have given their attention to the culture of their lands, which their predecessors had neglected, and you may suppose that the tribunal of inquisition exists no longer."—" And Portugal?"—" This state is incorporated with England, of whom she receives her laws and constitution, and Portugal is much the gainer thereby, for it is commerce which unites nations, and renders them for ever inseparable."—" And the republic of the Swifs?"—" Aristocracy, which struggled to gain the ascendency, has been repressed. This nation no longer sells her subjects for mercenaries to the ambition of princes, by what name, indeed, can we call that nation so loyal in appearance, who had no other object in view but to sell itself to the highest bidder, who, under the pompous display of liberty, hastened to clothe itself with the livery of independence? What manner of beings were these men, who, unprovoked, would go and assassinate in cold blood any particular people, after being paid to massacre them? and would either fight for or against, according to the highest recompense they expected.

" How shall those states be called who liberally abandoned their auxiliary troops? How long have the laws of nature and the rights of man allowed a traffic so disgraceful?

"No Switzerland now retains all the men born within her bosom. Population is no longer a disadvantage to her, because her children have learnt the art of agriculture, and if they go over to their neighbours, it is not to sell their lives."—"And Italy?"—"All those small sovereignties, which existed under their respective political state, whose interests were diametrically opposite to each other, are now united in one body. The head of the church has employed all his power in a pastoral vigilance over his flock: he attentively examines the general affairs of political states and of princes, he blames or approves, and this decision is always founded upon the basis of profound wisdom, which, by its moral influence, intimidates or persuades. As the common father of Christians, the peace of Europe is the sole object of his solicitations. The limits of the political balance of power have been fixed in an equilibrium nearly equal, by the simple, though advantageous, connections between each nation. The calm tranquillity of every state affords the means of perfecting their administration, or repairing their losses. The dismembering of a kingdom, or of a republic, is the immediate consequence of all rash or senseless projects, as our political state is able to foresee all the alterations which an extravagant monarch might occasion in the general system, the violent shock we cause to revolve upon himself, and make him responsible for the rupture of the equilibrium.

"All those military bodies, which so clearly proved the degradation of the human species, are now annihilated, by this great measure we have found the means of uniting the various parts of Europe, of strengthening those who wavered from the general union, of establishing a constant subor-

subordination between them all, and particularly of disengaging the universal legislation of states from the rust of barbarism which prevailed.

"In order to operate this great work, the scission of three considerable states was required, which Providence soon brought about we improved the opportunity, and formed a counterpoise. This division of the overgrown states proved a new line of support in the general system, which served to cement an immortal project, worthy of the enlightened man. The most generous efforts were made in favour of the European balance, the power of every monarch was traced out with precision; the sceptre was established in the hand of princes the evils of anarchy, and those of ungovernable and mistrustful liberty, were equally repressed. In fine, the distribution of the general advantages was established upon that plan most calculated for the general good, and the political system, recovering its simplicity, no longer deviated from its fundamental principles, or dictated, for the interest of a moment, those combined powers, which frequently separated that which ought to have been united, and united that which should remain separate.

"Every nation found their advantage in a revolution, whose principal effect was to re-invigorate empires, by depriving them of that encrease of power, which naturally tended to alter the equilibrium and ruin its system: by this means every part of the grand legislation was re-united, and every private movement had a more regular and energetic influence upon the general scale.

"Besides, as knowledge increased, the republican form of government became more and more general. In America, or in Europe, those monstrous bodies called *military powers* no longer existed. This revolution among the states, which happened about three hundred years ago,

has

has contributed to strengthen the bonds of peace; and the political laws are so constant, and established on a basis so regular, that no private mistake of ministers can vary their influence, for soon or late the laws will return to their natural efficacy. Man being a sociable animal, it was impossible that, after so long a series of error and calamity, he should not at last fix upon the great and sublime laws of perfect society.

CHAP. XLIII.

But sav'ry!—Virtue dreads it as her grave,
Patience itself is meanness in a slave.

"IN all ages Europe has had very little knowledge of the interior parts of the continent of Africa, and of every country to the north or south of the Line, or even of those parts which were anciently so well known, *i. e* the two Mauritanias and Numidia. To the Roman pride this loss may be attributed, for, after having subjugated Africa, they ordered every book to be consigned to the flames, and erased every ancient title and inscription, that the Roman name might absorb every other memento of past ages.

" After these imperious masters the Caliphs next took possession of Africa, and made a strict search for all their books of history or science, of which they destroyed as many as they could find, fearing that, if these writings were perused, they would impede the belief of their new tenets Such was the reasoning of ambition and fanaticism, those two antique scourges which have pursued mankind in every corner of the earth.

" We

"We are now acquainted with every part of Africa. In your time Egypt was under the dominion of the Grand Turk, at present it is under that of the King of France, that is the French

"This nation was the first who cultivated the sciences, while every other part of the world were shaded in ignorance This fertile and interesting country had long been soliciting inhabitants worthy of possessing it, and is at length restored to its ancient glory, for it is the government which forms the people The ferocious Cambyses, and his successors, ravaged all Egypt, during a space of two hundred years, and extinguished the sacred fire which for ages had enlightened the radiant circle of human knowledge. It was reserved for a nation who befriended the arts to restore the commerce of the world to Egypt, and *we* have kindled the bright luminary among them It was evident that nature had established that foundation for the re-union of Europe with Asia. Having, from its situation, a free communication with all the seas of the east or west, it favours the intercourse of our ships with all nations they depart from the Arabian Gulf to the Indies, and sail into every Mediterranean port, Nature having done every thing for this privileged people, it was to the interest of the whole world to exterminate that race of barbarians from it, who opposed the reminiscence of a country formed to unite all the different nations of the earth. Our monarch possesses the famed Pyramids, those antique wonders of the world. We have discovered a ray of light through the deep obscurity which enveloped the former ages this ray, hitherto entombed under the veil of hieroglyphics, has invested science and history with a new glory. This beautiful part of the world, which was become the prey of plunderers and banditti is now regenerated, since the expulfion of defpotifm and ignorance, and *we* have effected this grand operation

"At this time Paris, Athens, Grand Cairo, are all under the generous and powerful protection of Louis XXXIV whom we all cherifh as a moft prudent and wife monarch.

"Alexandria is emerged from its ruins through our laborious exertions, for our ambition is to poffefs thofe antique monuments, whofe folid mafs has withftood the deftructive power of ages, the fall of empires, the ravages of time Defpotifm, the enemy of good order and of the laws, whofe progrefs is accompanied with deftruction, its attendant, all thefe objects eloquently fpeak the language of philofophy to our hearts, and we applaud ourfelves for having reftored thefe countries to the arts and fciences.

"You muft acknowledge that thefe inexhauftible treafures, in the fineft climate of the world, form a much more precious eftablifhment than all the colonies of America. Thofe immortal works, thofe canals and aqueducts, executed by princes who made their happinefs confift in the profperity of their people, and in the glory of their empire, are now reftored by our hands.

"We have effected the long meditated project of forming canals from the Nile to the Arabian Gulf, without any caufe to fear the overflowing of the gulf by that communication. By this means Egypt is open to every nation in the world, and is become the great mart of commerce between Europe, India, and Africa. Thanks to our mechanic arts, we have operated all thofe wonderful changes, or rather, we have revived and effected the fublime projects of former ages.

"The lawful deftruction of the barbarian fway was concerted, in the nineteenth century, by the maritime powers. Thefe wars were of a fhort duration, and thofe countries, subdued by the happiest and the most just conquest, became the domain of the conquerors, who punished the barbarians for their tyranny, and exterminated their whole race, as they were a disgrace to human nature.

"We have the greatest veneration for those countries, rendered famous by the residence and travels of Orpheus, Homer, Herodotus, and Plato, and as these superb monuments have been respected by the devouring hand of time, we possess the only history which retraces the first periods of the world, and the primitive dignity of man.

"All *Delta*, or Lower Egypt, is now filled up by the slime, conveyed from time to time by the current of the Nile. We make frequent visits to the island of Madagascar, the largest on the globe. We already possessed the *Island* of *Bourbon* and that of *Mauritius*, but their value was greatly diminished by being destitute of ports. We have now imitated your astonishing improvements at Cherbourg, for we must do you the justice to say, that those prodigious cones, or sea-breakers, capable of vanquishing the fury of the ocean, were the finest monuments of the indefatigable industry of your time.

"The *Island* of *Teneriff*, from whence the Hollanders reckoned their first meridian, the *Island* of *Ferro*, and many other islands, which enjoy a wonderful abundance of every thing which can render life desirable, where the air is salubrious, and which nature has placed at different distances, for the conveniency of navigators of every nation, are infinitely more beneficial than those American colonies, so disputed, so chargeable to the nation, and which had caused so much bloodshed, and yet produced very little besides sugar.

"We are no longer guilty of exciting perpetual wars between the various people of the coasts of Africa. We no longer fow the fpirit of difcord between them, to engage them in the moft treacherous outrages againft human nature, which armed them againft their fellow-creatures, to furrender them, bound hand and foot, for our flaves nor do we tranfport them to the diftance of fifteen hundred miles, in veffels infected with difeafe, to fell them to the inhuman planter, whofe lacerating lafh was ever lifted againft them. The fugar-canes of their own paternal eftates are far preferable to thofe which occafioned a traffic fo difgraceful to humanity After having devaftated America, in order to effect the produce of fugar therein, you were ftill obliged to derive both the canes and negroes from Africa. Alas! was it neceffary to be at fo much expenfe and fatigue, and to practife fuch cruelties, for the fake of an article fo uneffential to our fubfiftence? The fugar-cane was much degenerated in your American iflands. We are returned to the African coaft, where it grows without cultivation, there we have formed fome peaceable eftablifhments, and as nature herfelf defrays all the charges of the production, fugar is ten times cheaper than when you procured it by the inhuman traffic of your own fpecies. The barrennefs of thefe immenfe countries has difappeared, fince the outrages committed to human nature have ceafed, and that men, under the protection of the laws, have recovered their liberty and their intelligence

"Our merchandife is conveyed upon the Nile and upon the Senegal, up to the various cities fituated upon thofe rivers, and from Alexandria and Grand Cairo we derive all the treafures of every part of the world, while our imaginations are exalted by the fight of thofe admirable pyramids, of the roaring cataracts of the Nile, and of all thofe magnificent palaces, half buried beneath their own ftupendous ruins The granite and porphyry,

2 with

with which this soil abounds, and every other natural curiosity, profusely scattered over the earth, all prove the riches and magnificence of this quarter of the globe, and no part of Europe can produce any monument or public edifice, in any degree comparable to those precious remains of Egypt.

"In fact Egypt is no longer a state dependent on the Ottoman empire. The anarchy which constantly prevailed in the government opened a door to the first invader. This country, dismembered from an empire both ignorant and barbarous, fell to our share, and the Ottomans recalled their captain pachas without a murmur.

"This immense kingdom derives every benefit from our government, a wise and well-directed police has radically removed the seeds of that dreadful scourge which annually spread death and desolation over all Egypt, by which means population suffers no diminution, and the inhabitants are enriched by our immense trade upon the Red Sea, from which we derive innumerable advantages. Our operations were not opposed by any neighbouring power, and our happiness, which from our peculiar situation on the globe, and our own enjoyments, both moral and physical, was arrived at an eminent degree of superiority, became still greater by our abilities to contribute to the felicity of other nations, by modulating and perfecting legislation and the art of government.

"The greatest part of Africa was successively regenerated from the most debased state of despotism, by the discoveries and acquisitions, from time to time conveyed to them by the apostles of reason and the arts, and that abundance which in your time prevailed at the Cape of Good Hope is now diffused over all the neighbouring states; for stupidity is not the character inherent in the people of Africa. The climate, the soil, the waters, are still the same, but the laws have changed, and this change has had the most beneficial influence upon the inhabitants.

"Thus Africa, which in your time was in a manner separated from all the known world, is now flourishing under a new form of government. The inhabitants, no longer groaning under the oppressions of bashas, equally insolent, barbarous, and ignorant, appear cheerful, and are surrounded with domestic enjoyments. The face of the country is totally changed, we have transplanted our northern trees, which seem to acquire additional beauty and strength, in that soil, amidst palms, and other trees natural to the country. We have even overcome the disadvantages of the ardent heat by forests of lofty trees, and the diversified shades which industry has ingeniously created over rich pasturages, where our European cattle are seen grazing upon verdant plains, like those of our own country.

"We have totally abandoned America, which for so many centuries had caused your misfortunes, and began our's, and had given you much more trouble than profit, for though you derived no advantages from her, still she owed her happiness to your succours. The grand epoch of her liberty was in the hands of the French. We made her *free*, and she ought never to forget the name of our ancient king, Louis XVI.

"We have directed our attention to the moral and political disorders of Africa, and we reciprocally enjoy the fruits of our labours. Therefore we have completed that which no other people had ever attempted. Emulous to revive a country favoured with all the riches of the creation, and where, at every footstep, we trace some remains of the prodigies of nature, we have been able to elucidate the variety of mysteries contained under

the

the hieroglyphics, by which we have acquired a great many valuable secrets. In short, our arts, our knowledge and labours, after having regenerated the wild African, have corrected his climate, by enriching his barren soil with our elegant vegetables, and have diffused happiness, abundance, and comfort, through every province

CHAP. XLIV.

*Nature imprints upon whate'er we see,
That has a heart and life in it,* BE FREE!

"WAS not the taking of Constantinople a noble exploit?"—"Russia, suddenly emerging from insignificance, found it impossible to have an equal sway over Asia and Europe. Peter the Great had fixed all his views upon the latter, in order to procure the most solid glory and durable grandeur to his empire. The happy situation of Petersburg constituted the strength and opulence of the Russian empire. Hence the preponderance in the balance of Europe; but this growing power was suddenly divided into two parts, and Asia presented the prospect of rich spoils and easy triumphs.

"However, their commerce with the East Indies suffered great alterations, and after many unavoidable and unexpected struggles, Asiatic Turkey became a great republic. Those immense political bodies, which had threatened all Europe, at length devoured their prey, and that formidable deluge of soldiers, after such continual oscillatory movements, at length arrived at that permanent state to which all their efforts seemed directed. Constantinople now belongs to the Russians, and it is a circumstance from which all Europe derives satisfaction and advantage.

"In your time the plan was held in contemplation of renouncing all military establishments in the East Indies, and maintaining factories in the different cities for carrying on the commerce of India, which was to be done by means of caravans, travelling through Persia and Turkey. Every nation undoubtedly had a right to contribute to the advantages of trading with those rich countries. The English acted as every nation ought to do on such an occasion, they wished to engross all India and its commerce to themselves, but this we took care to prevent.

"We acquired possession of those ports which would enable us to protect both the coasts of Coromandel and Malabar; but we soon discovered that, if we wished to effect a solid establishment in the Indies, the first measure to be taken was to effectually calm the alarms of the Indians by a peaceful conduct, and not to employ a military force for making conquests or territorial acquisitions, which would immediately inflame their minds against us. And how imprudent such a proceeding, knowing the impossibility of contending against all the nations of Indians, who are as well disciplined as our own troops! However, the method of carrying on an extensive commerce with India and Persia by caravans, through Persia and Turkey, was attended with many difficulties, and almost impracticable; therefore all the nations of Europe have, with one accord, entered upon a plan, which convinced the Indians that they relinquished every *idea of conquest* and *this system of peace*, well established in their minds, has conciliated their affection, and secured their friendship.

"The Spaniards, the Portuguese, the English, and the Dutch, have consented, as well as ourselves, to evacuate all their establishments, and to withdraw all their military forces

forces. Such a body of troops could only serve to create suspicion and aversion in the natives, and engage us in wars, both cruel, unjust, and ruinous.

"Our peaceable factories, by removing every idea of ambitious views, have had more effect, by the respective advantage of commerce on both sides, than those factories you formerly possessed, surrounded with military forces, which successively occasioned a thousand bloody revolutions. In order to stop the effusion of human blood, we should remove all military establishments. When the Indians have seen that we banished all offensive weapons, they become accustomed to us, and were our friends; but if they found us constantly armed, they naturally would acquire our discipline, and have risen against us, in order to drive us from their country. Our real strength, therefore, consists in being disarmed; our profits may be less considerable, but they are more secure and more lawful, and we have preferred a limited but permanent advantage, to those moments of glory and splendor which were soon extinguished in blood and carnage. How could we, without remorse, diffuse among these simple nations all the artifices of a cruel policy, and arm those Rajahs and Nabobs against each other, who, in espousing our quarrel, filled all Persia with death and confusion, and shook the very throne of the Moguls? Alas! it is but too true that the Europeans, in your time, only subsisted by violating the natural and political rights of these nations, in the most horrible and perfidious manner. To those prodigious and almost romantic conquests we have preferred the ascendency we possess over the minds of the natives, whereby we have acquired a commerce both victorious and peaceable. The Indians invite, protect, and cherish us; and this generous resolution on their part has been a more powerful protection than all our armies.

"In fact, what glory could we derive from subduing the Indians? Bacchus, Sesostris, Semiramis, Alexander, the Parthians, the Tartars, the Arabians, and after these, new tribes of Tartars, were successively the masters of those rich countries but the rapid decline of these conquerors proved that it was possible to conquer, but not to maintain their conquests, though the Indians opposed no other defence but the avenging arm of time But our upright and pacific proceedings have accustomed the Indians to look on us as their benefactors, and our establishments among them are cemented by the most solid friendship on both sides, and therein we make our glory to consist."

CHAP XLV.

LIBERTY OF THE PRESS.

OF all the properties which appertain to man, the prerogative of thought is undoubtedly the most essential and unquestionable. It is that which eminently distinguishes him from other beings, who share in common with him all the other benefits of creation How then could despotism ever conceive the project of depriving man of this faculty, which constitutes his greatness and felicity? How despoil him of this noble attribute? Is it not the birthright with which nature has invested him? therefore, to rob him of a quality inherent with his existence, is the very height of outrage. There is no blessing incident to man which the laws of nations ought to preserve with more care, as it is the dearest and greatest he can enjoy · therefore, to lay any restraint on his

his power of thinking, is to degrade him, and to place him on a level with vegetating animals.

"How great is the power of thought! and whence arises that astonishing influence with which it modifies the moral universe, and even the physical world, by which it regulates or overthrows the systems of all nations, and extends its activity over distant ages? It is from its union with human reason, that faculty to which every other must submit. Men, whose understandings are enlightened, are endowed with the power of appeasing the spirit of faction, of submitting all individuals to the laws, and of ensuring the peace of governments, which will always exist inasmuch as human reason prevails. It is ignorance which leads the people to rebellion: a citizen must be acquainted with the laws of his country, ere he can be supposed to love them; and when these laws are made known to him, they insensibly acquire more weight, for while the people are enabled to reflect on the reciprocal ties of society, they will know how to resist the dangerous impressions which might be given.

"In England the effect of this power is evident: the universal knowledge which prevails ensures the tranquillity of its civil and ecclesiastical state: her politicians seem to understand wherein her happiness consists. That nation, which had long been a prey to faction, at length, by being enlightened, became tranquil. A happy liberty of thought having assigned to each body of the state its lawful limits, all false reasoning naturally falls of itself, because sound principles are more cultivated than in any other country. The factions, after having agitated themselves, and all around them, are at length placed where they should be. The real strength of this republic is derived from *that powerful spring*, which, by presenting the advantages of the constitution in their true point of view,

engages

engages the inhabitants to contribute to its happiness. If you take from this people their understanding and intellectual advantages, they will soon fall from their prosperous state."

" But tell me, how did you become free?"—" With great facility. That sentiment natural to man, when once propagated, soon causes every member of the state to ferment, their sensibility is then gathered in a mass, they all feel themselves aggrieved, and, from the resentment of all, a plan of public revenge arises, which is carried as far as it can go.

" When the sovereign appears to despise the nation, the public indignation communicates to every member of the community, with the force and rapidity of electrical fire, for then all ranks are equally vilified and debased.

" It was in consequence of this species of contempt and insensibility which sovereigns have testified for their own weakness, that the Swiss, Holland, and the colonies of Anglo-America, were excited to rebellion. In all great revolutions, the sentiments of the man who feels himself oppressed, are like elastic bodies, which acquire more strength, the more they are compressed by an accumulation of weight. Nothing is thought of in those times but to unite in a body, and to entrust the management of public affairs to him who offers to be *their leader* and *avenger*. If this leader has the art of stimulating the people, and inspiring in their minds the generous resolution of encountering death or liberty, they will assuredly conquer. The leader of a revolted people should not suffer the effervescence of their minds to calm, while they are making the last efforts to recover their liberty, nor their wounds to close, until the completion of that great undertaking. The union of forces and sentiments greatly depend on that kind of communicative pity or sympathy,
which

which never operates more forcibly and efficaciously, than in those times of public calamity, when all men share an equal degree of danger; this is the substance of our history, which is not very ancient.

"Those leaders of the insurgents of their times, Guise, Cromwell, and William Nassau, had so influenced the minds of the people, that they had not even the power of proposing terms of reconciliation. The bare mention of a truce would have excited their minds to suspicions of perfidy, and with difficulty they would have escaped popular rage.

"The Spaniards were more odious to the irritated minds of the Batavians, than Turks and Moors; and the deliverers of Holland could never have calmed the fermented minds, or re unite them to the ancient masters of the Low Countries. the Hollanders would rather have been overwhelmed by the ocean, than have submitted to that rich and haughty nation.

"Though the first encounters are sometimes uncertain, men should not be discouraged. The strength of those sentiments, which animate the minds of men, lead on with the most rapid progress. The Helvetian union, the league of Utrecht, the expulsion of the King of England, the confederacy of the American states, were the operations of an instant. These explosions are the more terrible and rapid by being unpremeditated.

"A series of outrages committed against the constitution of the country, will at length lead the minds to struggle for independence; and the monarch who exasperates the people, may be compared to a rider thrown off his courser. That nation which is hastening towards a republic, necessarily interests all her neighbours in her favour. And even sovereigns themselves prefer the neighbourhood of a republic to that of a monarchy, being less liable to molestation from the free states.

"We

(268)

"We have continued our monarchy, but it is limited by fixed laws, we have retained the monarch as a necessary personage in a well-directed government, particularly where population is extreme, but the authority he enjoys is never detrimental to the nation, he is armed with the power of life and death, but never uses it, unless against the exterior enemies of the state, whom he is obliged to punish. But in the interior of the kingdom, he cannot attempt to infringe upon the liberties of the citizens, any more than the citizen dare violate the respect due to his lawful authority. These respective rights, decided with rigour, prevent any deviation in the subject from his duty and obedience, and in the monarch from the fundamental laws, defended by every tribunal in the kingdom, who would all rise up against him so soon as public or private rights are aggrieved. We have determined that the succession to the crown should be hereditary, and that males should only succeed, this wise and ancient law prevents interior troubles, and preserves the nation from bloody factions. Our monarchy is formed on the true principles of a republic, enjoying all the perfections of that form of government, without the disadvantages of being without a chief, by which a state is exposed to the invasions of foreign princes, and to frequent changes in the character of the nation. If the springs of government lose their elasticity in consequence of the long reign of a weak prince (and some such we sometimes meet with), we have the prospect of some change in the reign of the next heir, who perhaps may have a different character from that of his predecessor, and the nation then receives a new form, when all the losses are repaired. These advantages are not to be enjoyed in a republic without a monarch, for they perceive their decline without the power of offering any remedy, except in a patriotic loqua-

city,

erty, which always proved ineffectual. A monarchy, particularly when it admits a happy mixture of other governments, is liable to none but temporary maladies, from which it easily recovers its courage and principles. Your Henry IV. repaired in a few years all the disorders which the civil wars had caused under the reigns of his predecessors. When a republic is corrupted, the evil goes on increasing, factions and cabals rise up in all quarters, and being divided against itself, without a central point wherein to take refuge, it naturally must fail, particularly when ambition and interest are in league to profit by these disorders. Thus the folly and wickedness of men frustrate the best designs, and impede the practice of the wisest laws.

"If a monarch happens to be a great man, he is the greatest blessing for the nation he governs, he has an opportunity of displaying all his heroic qualities, and is not obliged to struggle against the various passions of the multitude, as it frequently happens in a republic. This form of government, therefore, has many advantages, but its disadvantages are innumerable. However, a republic without a chief will never possess that durable and powerful spring which commands the rising storms of faction or opposition; in our monarchical government, we have lopped off the spreading tendency to despotism, that it might not view with jealousy or mistrust, either the virtues of the good, or the courage and knowledge of the enlightened. Under this aspect, monarchy is the best ordered government, and best calculated to curb the tumultuous passions of men, and prevent their sacrificing the political order to their ambitious or evil designs.

CHAP

CHAP. XLVI.

*You may as well go stand upon the beach,
And bid the main flood bate his usual height,
You may as well use question with the wolf,
Why he hath made the ewe bleat for the lamb
You may as well forbid the mountain pines
To wave their high tops and to make a noise
When they are fretted with the gusts of heaven
You may as well do any thing most hard,
As seek to soften that, (than which what's harder?)
His Jewish heart ——*

"SINCE our revolution, Europe has experienced an interval of alarm, which had never been foreseen in your time, and we may say, that you had never even turned your thoughts towards that subject.

"There exists a nation of foreigners, who, by interest, morals, religion, and obstinacy, are for ever separated from every other nation of the earth. Their number was immense, but their dispersion in different countries prevented that serious attention, with which they ought to have been watched They were much more numerous in the eighteenth century, than they had formerly been in the land of Canaan, having multiplied in every country, in the most surprising manner, and this prodigious breed was dispersed over the whole earth.

"This people, under the influence of a sort of fanaticism peculiar to themselves, inviolably attached to their private customs, from their infancy, the declared enemies of every nation but their own, had been, during a long succession of ages, aggrieved by unceasing injuries, and a prospect of revenge, though distant, was peculiarly gratifying to them. Persecution had only rendered their character

character more inflexible. Reduced to wander through sea and land, they employed artifice and craft in their commerce with different nations, and acquired a large benefice by means of usury. Without the least attachment to any government, they were incorporated with every one, always siding with the strongest, and the money they acquired, compensated for the ignominy with which they were treated, and the vexations they encountered. So prodigiously encreased by their strict union with each other, by their tenets and their customs which separated them from other men, acknowledging every victorious prince, and attached to the car of good fortune, the Jews were indifferently subject to every monarch, and held in their power, in several states and cities, all the riches of the country. In your time they already amounted to three millions in Poland and the adjacent provinces.

" Vile, but useful instruments to some relaxed governments; their possessions were no longer confiscated, as they had formerly been, though with great injustice. They no longer experienced those dreadful cruelties which have disgraced the memory of so many Christian princes. But these Jews constantly bore the remembrance of the ill treatment they had received, of having been, in all ages, first driven away, and afterwards recalled for the sake of their money. Being the devoted martyrs of their ancient religion, never bearing arms, given up to commerce, and being accustomed to marry very young, they experienced an almost supernatural accretion and ascendency, in spite of the contempt of every nation, who at length became so tolerant towards them, that they encouraged the hopes of reviving the Mosaic law, and of announcing it to the universe, by every means which their opulence, and their sober and austere life, enabled them to do.

" The

" The moſt able politicians had not foreſeen the fatal conſequences which might follow the ſudden exploſion of a numerous nation, inflexible in their opinions, whoſe ideas, ſtrongly contraſted with thoſe of other nations, became cruel and fanatic, ſo ſoon as their laws were called in queſtion, or the pompous promiſes, which they retraced to the origin of the world, for, according to theſe, the whole earth was in their poſſeſſion, and every other nation were uſurpers

" The Jews, conſidering themſelves as a people many centuries anterior to the Chriſtians, and created to ſubjugate them, re-united themſelves under a leader, to whom they ſuddenly attributed every thing marvellous, in order to prove his ſupernatural miſſion, and thus, by prepoſſeſſing the imaginations of men, diſpoſed them to the greateſt and moſt extraordinary revolution. This nation formed at that time an immenſe multitude, diſperſed to the number of twelve millions in Europe only, beſides thoſe who were eſtabliſhed in the Weſt Indies, in Africa, in China, and even in the interior parts of America, who all flew to the ſtandard, or ſent thoſe ſuccours which were neceſſary The firſt irruption was violent it then remained with us to repair the want of vigilance of the preceding ages, and we needed great wiſdom, conſtancy, and firmneſs, to diſſolve a fanaticiſm ſo ardent, to appeaſe a fermentation ſo dangerous, and to reduce the Jews to be ſatisfied with their former purſuits of induſtry and commerce. They had in all ages purſued that plan, with a thirſt for gain, and an indifference to every other object, which Jews alone can feel Ever eager and fortunate in mean or intereſted ſpeculations, and eternally acquiring an accumulation of money, their enormous, and almoſt incredible riches, had inſpired in their minds an audacious fanaticiſm, which made them ſuppoſe the whole world at their diſpoſal.

difpofal. One of their ambitious ringleaders affumed the title of *King of the Jews*, which occafioned a political ftorm calculated to create much inquietude. We wifhed to avoid the effufion of blood, but this people were difpofed to renew all the horrors mentioned in their former hiftory, of which they have always been the agent or the victim

"You had fuffered this ferment to remain dormant, while it filently pervaded every commercial country of Europe, and it broke out when leaft expected It was neceffary to ufe the utmoft decifion to reprefs that ferocious fuperftition, which, during a fucceffion of three thoufand years, had contributed to confirm the belief of their claim upon the whole earth. The eager obftinacy of this people then appeared moft daring, accompanied with all their intolerant vices, the extent of which we had never been acquainted with. Their extreme avarice alone was confpicuous in your days But now their rage and fury were moft terrific, and one would have thought, they intended to exterminate the whole race of man from the face of the earth, fave thofe who were attached to the law of Mofes. Your anceftors had treated them very cruelly, although thofe fevere and violent profcriptions were equally condemned both by philofophy and chriftianity but in your time the moral corruption of, and the vices inherent in this people, were totally forgotten, their deteftable doctrine, and their blind and inveterate hatred againft every other nation, had been unnoticed. You were far from fufpecting, that foon or late their ancient character would revive, and that it was dangerous not to watch over this fanatic and cruel nation, who would fhortly take advantage of their own religious tenets, and of our's, that is to fay, of our toleration, and of our mild and humane government, whereby they at length provoked our

T   venge-

vengeance, and have obliged us to revive some ancient laws, which ought never to have been abrogated, considering the constant opposition of this people to the general morals of the nations who tolerate them."

CHAP. XLVII.

*Loix, qui de la nature ont les sceaux respectables,
Loix, que l'arret du ciel rendit irrévocables*

I WAS highly gratified by the books I found in this library, and equally so, by the conversation of several literary men, the substance of which is contained in the preceding chapters. I now listened attentively to the discourse of a professor of natural history, who was explaining a *thesis* on generation. I was curious to be acquainted with the ideas of this people, upon a mystery which amazes and confounds all our reflections and conclusions I therefore attended to what was said

The professor, raising his voice, spoke in the following manner· " The most incomprehensible of mysteries is now elucidated. It is Spallanzani who first disengaged it from the veil of obscurity, let his name be ever revered in your memory (and with his hand he respectfully pointed towards the bust of Spallanzani). he taught us in what manner the powers of digestion performed their functions, and now he teaches us how we came into existence Listen to the astonishing marvels unfolded by his pen

" Every system antecedent to this, is now reduced to nought. Spallanzani has seen every thing in a different point of view No naturalist was ever more attentive,

more

more patient, more correct. He sacrificed his brilliant eloquence to the desire of expressing with simplicity, all the wonders which his profound sagacity had discovered, in consequence of the most laborious observations and researches.

"The mystery of generation appeared beyond the reach of man's understanding, because he had examined it upon the principles of his erroneous imagination, or with imperfect organs. For there scarcely exists a man, who has not formed some system on the cause of his origin, or who has not been struck with wonder, when considering his birth. These various systems have exercised all the powers of men's imaginations, in different ways. Thus, while some in the deep silence of the closet exerted all the faculties of their minds to produce a fine poetic dream on this subject, others, aided by the microscope, were diving into the depth of nature's secrets. But, ah! what avails the eye of man in these deep researches? If it is in the power of optical glasses to change the form or size of objects, how much less is this feeble organ to be consulted! Man had rashly concluded, that, where there was no visible object, there could not exist any. Vain reasoning! the immeasurable depth above him in the immensity of space, which he readily admitted, terrified and astonished him much less than the divisibility of matter. His imagination was capable of containing the vast multitude of the celestial bodies, in the unlimited regions of space, yet staggered at the descent into the no less profound abyss of the infinitude of matter, when, instead of acknowledging the deficiency of his own organs, he preferred to rest satisfied in the false conviction of his limited visual faculties.

"And yet the intelligence of man had in many instances overleaped the boundaries of science. Charles Bonnet

Bonnet, by the depth of his meditations, and the power of his enlightened genius, had created the system of the pre-existence of germs, because it was according to reason, but this idea only existed as an hypothesis, enveloped in impenetrable shade, when Spallanzani appeared, and pierced the obscurity with a ray of light. This naturalist, full of sagacity, of patience, and ardour, considered this subject in every point of view. He has demonstrated that every fœtus, either animal or vegetal, was an organized body in miniature, that it existed in its diminutiveness, before its birth, that is, before the developement of its parts, though invisible to our sight. The eye of man, being, as I said before, infinitely limited by nature, and even frequently illusive in the objects it represents, it was reserved for human intelligence to pierce farther into the labyrinths of science than the eye could perceive, and Haller, and Charles Bonnet, had already, by their extravagant reasoning, ruined the famous system of organized animalcula.

" Human intelligence alone ought to teach us, that a being so perfect as man, so connected in its whole, though prodigiously complicated in its various parts—a being capable of extending his intellectual powers to the utmost limits of the globes, terrestrial and celestial—could not be the produce of two separate powers, or derive his existence merely from a simultaneous injection, or, in short, that a machine so perfect, was not the effect of a double mechanism.

" The metaphysician had discovered that the fœtus pre-existed, and that the fortuitous union of the male and female, did not effect its creation, but the extension of its powers, and the developement of its parts.

" Contemplative reflection had said, How should man, with all his combined faculties, his heart, his arteries, his
veins,

veins, his viscera, his muscles, his nerves, his bones, his senses—how should so admirable a machine be the produce of chance? Can it be supposed that the birth of Newton was in consequence of the accidental union of his parents? No, that important being who was destined to connect a luminous chain of affinities, and manifest the sublime finger of the eternal God imprinted upon every point of the creation, can never be the offspring of blind impulse.

"But Spallanzani clearly saw all that the metaphysician had conceived. He saw the fœtus pre-existing in the womb of females before their impregnation. The man, who contracted all his faculties within the circle of pyrrhonism, was forced at length to examine these incontestable facts, and acknowledge these truths so clearly demonstrated. Therefore we have existed these thousand ages, and we were all sleeping, though invisibly, in the breast of our first mother. The Supreme Being, by a mere act of volition, created at once all the generations of organized beings who were to appear in the world during the existence of that planet they were to inhabit. All those generations which are now on the earth, were all compressed in their diminutiveness, in what we blindly call annihilation, and there are many such worlds contained in the world we behold.—Such is the will of our Eternal Architect.

"The imagination of man may be overpowered by this grand system, but his reason is strengthened by meditating upon it, and at length receives it. Nothing is difficult to the Almighty, who with the same hand has organized every germ in their incredible minuteness, and darted in the immensity of space the sun and planets. A finite being cannot be the cause of his own, or of the existence of another: it would be derogatory to the wisdom and greatness of the Creator to establish such a system.

"We admit, that a child who is only two feet high will become a strong man, and increase to the height of six feet; then why should we disbelieve the former imperceptible existence of the same being, ere he issued from the incommensurable abyss of nature? It is our imagination which deceives us, with the help of our visual organs; for where our sight fails, we conceive annihilation. And must we then reject a truth, because our faculties are not equal to its sublimity? Do we not see within the root of the hyacinth, that very flower, which will in due time unfold its beautiful leaves? Does not the small elm-seed contain within its narrow shell, that immense tree which will vegetate during many ages? The tenuity of light and of sound, the philosophy of atoms, and many other inconceivable objects, sufficiently prove the existence of a variety of strange phenomena beyond the powers of sight.

"Nature, though under a mysterious veil, follows her unerring course; her hidden laws amaze our cecity, but her occult majesty is not less existent. Spallanzani, however, has been able to pierce through this veil, and has presented to our eyes and to our understanding, the true system of generation, in its wonderful greatness and in it's primitive simplicity; he has proved that copulation was not necessary for the production of the foetus, that the seminal liquor always maintains its fecundating power, without the agency of the male. In short, by an unheard-of stroke of genius, Spallanzani first discovered the possibility of impregnating a bitch by artificial means; this was a phenomenon which had never been suspected, by the most fertile genius.

"Thus

"Thus then we existed before our birth in our infinite diminutiveness, and are we in reality much less insignificant in our present state? considering the immensity of space, and the depth of the abyss by which we are surrounded. If our imagination is terrified at this idea, let us be humble, but let us not deny the truth of that which is beyond our comprehension. It is our material eye that leads us to doubt our preceding existence, but let us call reflection to our aid, and form this objection to ourselves. how do we know whether the vitreous humours which compose our visual orb, are not purposely formed to present that particular optic, suitable to our peculiar wants or circumstances, therefore, we ought to credit our understanding in preference to our senses.

"The majesty of Nature is not to be conceived but by an investigation of facts. And Spallanzani has followed Nature in all her phenomena, and has related his discoveries with that simplicity of style, which ought always to accompany the truth."

All the company looked respectfully at the bust of Spallanzani, and separated, exclaiming, "*O Altitudo!*"

CHAP. XLVIII.

Thine, Freedom, thine the blessings pour'd here,
Thine are those charms that dazzle and endear.

I WAS so well pleased with the company, that it was with regret I saw them depart: however, the master of the house, whose library I had already examined, afforded me the opportunity of seeing the interior of the house, by inviting me to supper, with his friend who accompanied me, which invitation I accepted with pleasure, as I wished to see the manners and domestic life of this people, so perfect in every other respect. The houses, which were nearly all alike, were not built as they were in my time, with thin walls, about six inches, which admitted both the intense heat and excessive cold but on the contrary, they were both thick and strong, and calculated to preserve the inhabitants from every inconveniency of the seasons. The apartments were large, lofty, and airy, and that which was appropriated for company, was an immense hall, where several persons might walk conveniently. My kind host introduced me to his wife and children, who received me with cordiality and respect free from affectation. These children testified their good education in their manners and conduct, the boys were neither pert nor pedantic, and the girls conversed without either restraint or boldness. Every thing was neat and simple, and there were no ornaments in this apartment but a few excellent engravings.

We engaged in conversation, which this people always suited to their company, without any affectation of wit or learning, but with cheerfulness and good humour, nor were we obliged to play at cards to supply the want of conversation. This amusement was sometimes admitted, but it was never to gratify the designs of avarice. They had also continued the games of chess and of draughts, but merely for diversion, and a few others, which might be called mathematical recreations, with which even children were familiarized.

Here every one followed his particular inclination. In different parts of the room, some were conversing, some looking over paintings and engravings, while others were

were reading, instead of being formally seated in a circle, where the yawn of weariness was soon communicated to the whole party.

In the course of the evening, we were entertained with the soft and harmonious music of wind instruments, playing in unison with some delightful voices. I was always an admirer of vocal music, than which, in my opinion, none can speak more powerfully to the heart. And yet the enchanting harmonica which was then in the highest perfection, seemed to contend for pre eminence, it afforded the fullest, purest, and most melodious sounds which can flatter the senses, it was most ravishing and celestial music, very unlike the horrid din of our operas, where the man of taste and sensibility sought for the union of sounds, and never could find it. But here I was perfectly enchanted, and with great regret retired from this entertainment, on being told that supper waited. We all adjourned into the eating-room, where I was astonished, on looking at the dial, to find it was only seven o'clock. My friend observing my surprise, said to me, "How different is this manner of life to that which prevailed in your time! You see that we (instead of changing day into night, and night into day) enjoy all the daylight which is granted us, we think the sun is the most beautiful object in the creation, and we always rise to see him glance his first rays upon the horizon therefore, we take our last meal at this hour, that we may retire to rest in moderate time, and not lie down with a full stomach, lest our sleep be interrupted by fantastic dreams but we take care of our health, for on that blessing greatly depends the comfort of life."

When we were all seated, the master of the house asked a blessing, and I was glad to see this holy custom renewed, as we ought never to forget the gratitude we owe to the

Creator

(282)

Creator and Author of all things. I had not much inclination to eat, so much was my mind engaged with all I had seen; however, I was invited, by the cleanliness and comfortable appearance of every thing, to taste of the dish which was next to me. Here I found no artificial seasoning, or refined ingredients, or high spices, or rich juices and heating sauces, which had in the destruction of the human species by burning up their entrails, but every thing had a natural flavour, far more delicious than any thing of that kind. This people were neither voracious nor epicures, who ruined themselves to support their table, and devoured much more than the riches of Nature, with all her prolific powers, could produce, but every luxury was banished, particularly that of the table, which is almost detestable, for, while the rich man takes an unworthy use of his opulence, and monopolizes all the fruits of the earth, the poor must necessarily buy them at a very high price, or, at a great scarcity, under the necessity of denying himself of another article. Cheerfulness and a decent freedom of manners dilated and expanded every heart, whilst they added new beauty to every countenance. Every one helped himself without ado, and the servants, who were seated at the bottom of the table, were always ready to lend every necessary aid. There was every vegetable according to the season, and the custom of forcing nature to yield the fruits of summer, at any other time, was discontinued. The wine also was excellent, but we saw none of those high coloured liquors distilled from spirits of wine, which were so much the fashion in my time, they were as strictly prohibited as arsenic. When the dessert was brought, I was pleased to see every thing in its simple state, without any prodigal extravagance of superfluities merely for shew, as the wholesome food, and moderate use of it, caused every one to rife from table with the fame cheerfulnefs and good humour with which they fat down, and, after having returned thanks, the company difperfed.

CHAP XLIX.

Thus fitting, and furveying thus at eafe
The globe and its concerns, I feem advanc'd
To fome fecure and more than mortal height,
That lib'rates and exempts me from them all

I RETURNED into the hall wherein I had been before, and faw upon the table feveral large fheets of paper, as large again as the Englifh newfpapers. I was eager to fee what they contained, and found they were entitled, PRIVATE AND PUBLIC NEWS. Nothing could equal my aftonifhment at every page I perufed, although I had determined not to be furprifed at any thing I fhould fee after having feen fo much. I will now mention thofe things which made the deepeft impreffion, as faithfully as my memory will allow

" *Pekin, the* ..... *of* ......

" The tragedy of Cinna was performed before the emperor for the fi.ft time The clemency of Auguftus, and the ftriking beauties and noble pride of the Romans, made great impreffion on the minds of all the courtiers, but more particularly on that of the emperor . . "

On reading this paragraph, I obferved to a perfon who fat by me, that there could not be any truth in what I had juft perufed —" Indeed,' anfwered the man, with great compofure, " nothing is more true, for I have

feen

seen the performance of that play myself at Pekin, as well as that of *the Chinese Orphan*. Know that I am a Chinese mandarin, and that I love *literature* as much as *justice* and *integrity*. I have traversed the royal canal, and I arrived here in four months, though I frequently stopped to make observations in several places, being curious to see this famous city of Paris, of which so much has been related. The French language has been universal in Pekin within these two last centuries, and when I return I shall take some of the best French works with me, and translate them, for the benefit of those whose circumstances do not admit of their learning the language."—"How!" said I, struck with astonishment, "have you altered your hieroglyphic language? and have you abrogated that singular law, which forbad any of you to go out of the empire?"—"Yes," said the mandarin, "we were obliged to alter our language, and adopt more simple characters, else we could not become acquainted with your's. It was not more difficult than to learn algebra and mathematics. Our emperor has annulled the ancient law you mention, because he discovered you were not all like those dæmons who formerly kindled the fiery torch of discord among us, under pretence of inculcating a better religion than our's, and because he found that many useful discoveries were made among you, which he was desirous of introducing in his dominions. For instance, the art of engraving upon copper was singularly admired, and we have greatly improved upon it. We have some pieces, on which the histories of sieges and battles are represented, which were sent to our emperor by one of your sovereigns, to whom Voltaire addressed the best of his poems, and since that period the communication of sciences has been established, and they have circulated from one province to the other like bills of exchange.

By

(285)

By the delightful art of printing, light and knowledge have been diffused all over the world, the tyrants of human reason have not been able to stop their invincible progress; nothing was so rapid as that salutary commotion dispersed through the whole moral world by this luminary of science, which has now encompassed every nation. Our mandarins are not, as they were in former times, a set of college pedants, neither are the lower class of people knaves and cowards, for their souls are exalted by education, they are brought up with the most refined notions of honour, and therefore they are never degraded by the lash, the cane, or any such disgraceful chastisements, beneath the dignity of rational man.

"We still maintain the same veneration for *Confucius*, who was nearly cotemporary with *Socrates*, and who, like him, avoided all vain subtilisation on the Principle of all beings, but he was satisfied with believing that all things were known to him, and that he will punish vice, as he will reward virtue and goodness. But our Confucius possessed this advantage over the Greek, that he never endeavoured audaciously to subvert those religious principles which serve as the basis of morality to the common people, who are incapable of acquiring that most noble support of the mind, philosophy, but he patiently waited for that day when truth should silently penetrate through every deep recess of darkness. In short, it was he who first discovered that a monarch ought to be a philosopher, ere he can govern with wisdom. Our emperor still continues to attend to the labours of agriculture, but not as formerly, to fulfil a vain childish ceremony, in which there was more ostentation than . . . ."

I was full of the desire of listening and reading too at the same time, and while I was attending to the el-

course of the mandarin, I continued to cast an eager eye over the page of this singular newspaper. My soul was divided between both, and I continued to read thus.

* * * *

"*Jeddo*, *the* . . . . . *of* . . .

"The descendant of the great Taico, who had erected the impotent idol of Dairi, has caused the inimitable work of Montesquieu, called the Spirit of the Laws, and a treatise on the penal code, to be translated into the *Japanese* language.

"The entrance into Japan is now *free to all strangers*, and every one is at liberty to examine and copy the arts. *Suicide* is no longer a virtue among these people, they are now convinced that it was only the effect of a mad despair, or of a stupid insensibility."

* * * *

"*Persia*, *the* . *of* . .

"The king of Persia dined with *his brothers* some days ago, and they were publicly seen in the gardens of the palace. They are very handsome young men, and are not deprived of *their eyesight* therefore they are enabled to assist the emperor in the avocations and duties of government; and their chief business is to read the dispatches to him. The sacred books of *Zoroaster* and the *Sadder* are still read and held in great reverence, but neither *Omar* nor *Ali* are ever mentioned."

* * * *

"*Mexico*, *the* . . . *of* . . .

"This city is recovering its ancient splendour, under the august dominion of the descendants of the noble house of the famous Montezuma. Our present emperor, when he ascended the throne, ordered the palace of his fathers to be rebuilt as it stood in their time. The Mexicans no longer go naked and barefooted; the large statue of Guatimala extended upon red-hot coals, with these words engraven, ' *And I—am I on a bed of roses?*' has been placed in the centre of the principal square.'—" Pray," said I to the mandarin, " explain this to me; is it forbidden to call this empire by the name of New Spain?" The mandarin thus answered:

" When the avenger of the new world had driven away the tyrants (and the genius of Mahomet and Cæsar united could not have formed a being in the least comparable to this astonishing mortal), he was satisfied with being the legislator of the people he had protected: he sheathed his sword, and gave the sacred code of laws to the nations under his dominion. You can form no idea of such a being; his manly eloquent voice seemed that of a god descended among mortals to dispense blessings and felicity. America was then divided into two empires. The emperor of Northern America reunites Mexico, Canada, the West Indies, Jamaica, and St. Domingo. The emperor of Southern America possesses Peru, Paraguay, Chili, the Magellanic lands, and the country of the Amazons: but each of these kingdoms was under the dominion of its respective monarch, who are all subject to the general laws, in the same form as the government of Germany existed in your time, and flourished, though divided into several sovereignties, which were all united under one chief.

" Thus the descendants of Montezuma, who had long remained obscure and unknown, have now reascended the throne of their faith is. All these monarchs are good and kings, whose only desire is to maintain public liberty. This great man, this famous legislator, this American, for whom Nature seemed to have established all her worth,

has

has diffused the influence of his virtues and greatness of soul. These vast territories are in a state of perfect concord and union, they flourish in the most profound peace, and these blessings are always the infallible, though slow result of reason. The sanguinary and cruel wars of the old world, the inutility of shedding innocent blood, the shame of having caused so much destruction among mankind, in short, the emptiness of all ambitious pursuits, properly displayed, all these considerations have been sufficient to persuade the new continent to erect the God of peace as the divinity of their country, and in these days war would disgrace a nation as much as theft degrades an individual." I still continued to attend to the sensible discourse of my Chinese companion while reading....

* * * *

"PARAGUAY.

"*Extract of a Letter from the City of Assumption, the* ......

"The inhabitants of this city have given a public festival, to celebrate the abolition of that disgraceful traffic of slaves, under which the nation groaned during the despotism of the Jesuits, and within these six last centuries we have rendered continual thanksgiving to Providence for having destroyed these ferocious tigers, and hunted them from their very last resorts, neither is the nation ungrateful, but acknowledges that it has been saved from impending misery, and formed to agriculture and the arts by these same Jesuits. Happy it would have been for us if they had been satisfied with instructing and giving us good moral laws

* * * *

"Pr-

"Pensylvania

"This corner of the earth, where humanity, honesty, and liberty, have resided so many years, is now filled with the finest and most flourishing cities. Virtue has operated more in this spot than courage has had power to effect among other nations, and these generous Quakers, the most virtuous of beings, have served as a mirror to all men, wherein might be contemplated the reflection of every virtue, and universal love towards all mankind. It is well known that since their origin they have always given a thousand instances of generosity and benevolence, that they were the first people who refused to shed human blood, and who have considered war as a foolish and barbarous madness. It is they who have undeceived those nations who were the miserable victims of the debates and quarrels of their kings. The annual register of all their virtues, which give the seal of perfection to their laws, will shortly be published."

* * * *

"Morocco.

"A comet has been discovered which is drawing nearer to the sun. It is the three hundred and fifty-first which has been discovered since the observatory has been erected. The observations which have been taken in the interior of Africa exactly correspond with our's.

"A native of Morocco who had struck a Frenchman, was punished with death, conformably to the orders of the emperor, who wishes that all foreigners may be considered as their own brothers."

* * * *

"Siam,

" *Siam, the* .. . *of* ....

" Our navigation has undergone the moft aftonifhing improvements we have lately launched three three-deckers, which are deftined for remote enterprifes.

" Our king *converſes* freely with all thofe who wifh to fee him no monarch is more affable than he is, particularly when he fhews himfelf at the *pagoda* of the great *Sommona Codom*.

" The white elephant is at the menagerie, and is now no more than an object of curiofity, as he is perfectly managed for military exploits."

* * * *

" *Coaſt of Malabar, the* ..... *of* ....

" The widow of ...., who is young, handfome, and in all the bloom of youth, has fincerely mourned for the death of her hufband, whofe remains were committed to afhes, but fhe did not think it effential to her eternal happinefs to facrifice herfelf upon his funeral pile, but, after wearing mourning more truly in her heart than by her outward garb, fhe accepted the hand of a young man, whom fhe loves as tenderly as her former hufband. This new tie renders her ftill more dear and more refpectable to her countrymen."

* * * *

" *Terra Magellanica, the* ... *of* ..

" The twenty fortunate iflands, whofe inhabitants lived without being known to each other, in all the innocence and happinefs of the golden ages, are now all united, and they form a fraternal fociety of men reciprocally ufeful to each other."

* * * *

(291)

"*The Land of Papous—a Country lying in the Indian Ocean, near the Line, between the Moluccas and New Guinea*

" This fifth quarter of the world gives daily proofs of approaching perfection in civilization and refinement. The farther we travel in the interior parts, the more interesting and extensive are the discoveries which are made, and the fertility of the soil, its numerous population, and perfection in the arts, are all equal subjects of surprise and wonder. The moral benefits this place enjoys, are still greater than the physical. The sun, which sheds its beneficial influence over immense countries, more extensive than Asia and Africa, does not witness one unfortunate being in the whole territory, while our Europe, so small, so despicable, and always disunited, has hardened its soil with human bones, and deluged it with blood."

* - * - *

" *From the Island of Otaheite, the . . of . .*

" When M. de Bougainville, the French circumnavigator, discovered this fortunate island, where the peace and innocence of the golden age reigned, he took possession of it in the name of his master. He then embarked, and brought away with him a young Otaheitean, who, in the year 1770, for some time arrested all the curiosity of Paris. It was not then known that a Frenchman, who was struck with the beauty of the climate, with the candour of the natives, and still more with the misfortunes which awaited that innocent people, had concealed himself, while his friends were embarking to return to their native country, and that, as soon as the ships were at some distance, he presented himself to the inhabitants; he assembled them in an extensive plain, and held the following discourse:

U 2 " It

" It is among you that I wish to remain; not only for
" my own happiness, but for your's · receive me as one
" of your brothers, you shall see that I am truly so, for
" I mean to preserve you from the most disastrous cala-
" mity. Oh! happy people, who live in all the simpli-
" city of nature, you do not know the misfortunes which
" await you! These polite foreigners, whom you have
" received, whom you have loaded with caresses and pre-
" sents, and whom I am now betraying (if it is betray-
" ing them, to prevent the ruin of a virtuous people),
" these men, who are my fellow-citizens, will soon
" return, and with them they will bring all the scourges
" which afflict and distress other nations, they will make
" you acquainted with poisons, with calamities, of which
" you are ignorant. They will load you with fetters,
" and, with their artful sophistry, they will attempt to
" prove that it is for your good. Behold that column
" erected on your shore, to attest that this country is under
" the dominion of a sovereign, whose name and empire
" you have never heard of You are all destined to receive
" new laws, your lands will be ploughed up, your fruit-
" trees will be stripped; your persons will be seized, and
" that charming equality which now reigns among you
" will be destroyed. Even this grass, enamelled with
" flowers, whereon you enjoy that calm repose, which
" your innocence ensures, may one day be sprinkled with
" human blood. At present, Love is the divinity of this
" island, which is consecrated to his worship. Hatred
" and revenge will fill its place. You will be taught the
" art of war, you will be made acquainted with murder,
" with slavery .. .."

At these words the people appeared in the utmost
dismay. The Frenchman thus continued " People,
" whom I love, and who have awakened all the feelings
" of

"of my foul, there exifts a mean of preferving your
"liberty and your happinefs. Let every ftranger who
"fhall ftep on this fortunate fhore, be facrificed to the
"happinefs of your country. It is a cruel fentence, but
"the love of your children, and of your own pofterity,
"ought to make you execute this barbarity. Were I to
"defcribe all the horrors which the Europeans have
"created among nations, who were, like you, inoffenfive
"and innocent, it would make you fhudder. Beware of
"the contagious poifon of their words, even their very
"fmile is the fignal for all the misfortunes which they
"meditate againft you."

"The chiefs of the nation affembled, and unanimoufly
agreed to inveft this Frenchman with all authority, fince
he offered to become the benefactor of the whole nation,
by preferving it from the moft horrible calamities. The
law condemning all ftrangers to death, was received and
executed with the ftricteft patriotic rigour, in the fame
manner as it was formerly practifed in Tauris, which was
a nation equally innocent, but jealous of its liberties,
and defirous of breaking up all communication with a
tyrannical and cruel people, though they might be very
enlightened.

"This law is now abolifhed, becaufe, from reiterated
experience, it is proved that Europe is no longer the
enemy of the other parts of the world, and never attempts
to invade the peace or liberties of remote nations; that
the ambition of Europe is to have many friends, but not
to have flaves, and that her veffels are employed in the
difcovery of nations who enjoy true fimplicity of manners,
rather than in the invafion of cities and provinces, &c."

"   Peterſburg, the .... of .....

"The greateſt of all titles in this country is that of LEGISLATOR A ſovereign who can dictate and eſtabliſh wiſe and ſalutary laws to a nation, is revered as a God. The name of the moſt auguſt CATHERINE II. is ſtill repeated with tranſport, and held in the higheſt veneration. Her conqueſts and her triumphs are no longer mentioned, but her wiſe laws are continually held forth and it will ever be recorded, that ſhe ſought to diſperſe the cloud of ignorance which had ſpread over all her dominions, and that ſhe annihilated the barbarous cuſtoms which ſtill prevailed in her time, and eſtabliſhed a code of laws dictated by humanity—happier and more truly great than the Czar Peter, who was flattered by that ſurname, inaſmuch as, notwithſtanding the difficulties ſhe had to ſurmount, and the example of her cotemporary ſovereigns, ſhe particularly ſtudied the means of making her ſubjects happy, and her empire flouriſh, in which ſhe ſucceeded, notwithſtanding all the public and domeſtic broils, which ſometimes ſeemed to threaten her power but her courage was equal to every thing, and it was that courage which preſerved the diadem which the whole univerſe were pleaſed to ſee her wear If we wiſh to make a due compariſon of this wiſe empreſs with any legiſlator of equal dignity and depth, we muſt look back to the remoteſt ages of antiquity; for no ſovereign of latter times has ever equalled her. *She* broke the fetters of the induſtrious peaſant, *ſhe* exalted him to his wonted dignity as man, and created joy and gratitude in his breaſt, to which he had ever been a ſtranger. The genius of humanity has publiſhed this ſhort ſentence over all the north of Europe *Men, be free, and let it be remembered by all future generation.*

tions, *that to a woman you are indebted for all your present enjoyments.*

"From the last enumeration of the inhabitants of all the Russias, it appears that they amounted to forty-five millions, and in the year 1769 they amounted only to fourteen. But the wisdom of the legislator of the eighteenth century, her humane code of laws, the throne of her successors, which was solidly established, because they were generous and popular, all these causes combined have produced a degree of population equal to the extent of the empire, which is more vast and powerful than that of the Romans, or that of Alexander. The constitution is not military, and the sovereign no longer styles himself Autocrat, and the whole world is too much enlightened to admit of that odious formality

* * * *

"*Warsaw, the .. of . . . .*

"Poland is no longer under the influence of the most absurd anarchy. The outrages formerly committed against the rights of man, born to be free, and the oppressions of the most industrious class of individuals, are no longer known. The august *Catherine, of revered memory*, encompassed this country with her beneficent influence, and it is remembered with gratitude, that she restored personal liberty, and appropriation of property, to the useful peasant

"The king of Poland died this morning at six o'clock, and his son peaceably ascended the throne, and has already received the homage of all the nobles.

* * * *

"Con-

"*Constantinople, the* .... *of* ....

"It was considered a great happiness for all mankind when the Turks were driven from Europe in the eighteenth century. Every real friend of mankind rejoiced at the fall of this fatal empire, where the monster of despotism was careffed and encouraged by a set of infamous bashaws, who, while they prostrated themselves before him with servile humility, exercised the most tyrannic pride towards his subjects, and surpassed their master in their despotic oppressions. The usurpers of the throne of Constantine have disappeared, and the barriers which superstition, and tyranny, his inseparable colleague, had set against the influence of reason and the progress of the arts, from the banks of the Save and of the Danube, to the borders of the ancient Tanais, were totally broken down, as well as the iron hand which supported them. Philosophy reappeared in her sanctuary, and the native country of Themistocles and Miltiades is once more restored to Liberty, whose statue is erected with the same lofty pride as in those happy days, when she flourished with so much splendour. She now extends her influence over all her ancient domain, and has extinguished even the very name of Sardanapalus, and of all such despotic tyrants, who, while they were plunged in the sleep of barbarous ignorance, without any laws but instruments of execution, suffered his vast dominions to remain inactive, and pining in stupid lethargy; but, in these happy days, the vivifying breath of liberty animates them, it is a creating spirit which performs prodigies, unknown to nations labouring under the shackles of slavery.

"The territories of the Grand Signor were at first divided among his neighbours, but in the course of the two succeeding centuries they have formed themselves into a republic, which, by their commerce with other nations, is prosperous and flourishing.

"A ball and masquerade have been given on the spot where the Seraglio formerly stood. The most exquisite wines were served, and all sorts of refreshment, with profusion and delicacy. On the next day was represented the tragedy of Mahomet, by Voltaire, in the playhouse, which was erected on the ruins of the famous mosque of St. Sophia."

* * * *

"ROME.

"The emperor of Italy has received a visit from the bishop of Rome in the Capitol, who assured him of his best wishes and prayers to heaven for the preservation of his life, and for the prosperity of the empire after which the bishop retired on foot with all the humility of a true servant of God.

"All the fine monuments of antiquity, which have been drawn from the Tyber, where they had been buried so many years, have just been placed in different quarters of Rome, where they serve as useful lessons and valuable ornaments

"The bishop of Rome is ever employed in writing the most pathetic and moral exhortations. The catechism which is taught by this pastor, is consistent with reason, and, from the valuable store of his knowledge, he is ever confirming the evidence of those truths, so important to man. He keeps the record of all generous, illustrious, and charitable deeds, and publishes them, to serve for models to others, he is the judge of kings and nations, and, by his love of humanity, his wisdom, justice, and truth, he possesses the affection and respect of all men he conciliates all dissensions, and reconciles the most inveterate enemies.

enemies. His bulls, or rather his pastoral letters, written in all languages, are no longer a tissue of obscure and useless dogmas, or of sentences of eternal excommunication, but they speak of the Supreme Being as a merciful and tender Father, of his universal omniscience, of a future happy life, and of the sublimity of real virtue. The Japanese, the Chinese, the inhabitants of Surinam and of Kamschatka, all read them with pleasure and instruction."

* * * *

"*Naples, the . . . of . . . .*

" The Academy of Belles Lettres have adjudged the prize to . . . . The subject was to determine exactly what sort of persons were the *cardinals* in the eighteenth century, what were the morals and opinions of these singular personages, what they said, and what they did in *the Conclave*, and at what time they returned to that pure state of religion and morals wherein they were in the primitive centuries. The author fully satisfied all the questions of the academy, and received the crown for his labours. He has even given a description of the *scarlet cap*, and this dissertation is both entertaining and learned

" The farce of St Januarius, formerly so serious, has been represented on the theatre. A very witty parody was made upon this absurd superstition, which diverted the whole audience.

" All the treasures of our *Lady of Loretto*, part of which have been employed in clothing and feeding the poor, have been expended in erecting an aqueduct, there being no more poor to be found. The riches of the ancient cathedral of Toledo, which was destroyed in 1868, are

intended

intended for the fame ufe *See the learned diſſertations of .. ., printed in 1999 on this ſubject."*

* * * *

" MADRID

" An edict has lately been publiſhed, that no perſon ſhould in future be called *Dominick*, as that was the name of the barbarous monſter who founded the Inquiſition. Another edict has likewiſe taken place, importing that the name of *Philip II* ſhall for ever be erafed from the liſt of Spaniſh kings

" The active ſpirit of the nation daily gains ſtrength, and adds new and uſeful difcoveries to thoſe of the philoſophers of other nations, and the Academy of Arts and Sciences has juſt given out a new ſyſtem of electricity, founded upon a variety of experiments."

* * * *

" *London, the* .... *of* ..

" This city is three times larger than it was in the eighteenth century. England ſtill maintains the ſame ſyſtem of government as heretofore, and the whole force of the kingdom refides, without danger, in the metropolis, becauſe commerce is the foul which influences the whole body, and becauſe the commerce of a republican nation never produces thoſe fatal effects which are ſeen in monarchies This ſyſtem of government is good, becauſe private individuals have the power of enriching themſelves as well as the monarch from hence ariſes that degree of equality which prevents exceſſive opulence and exceſſive indigence

" The Engliſh are ſtill the firſt people in Europe, they enjoy the glory of having formerly taught their neighbours that kind of conſtitution, moſt worthy of

men

men who were jealous of their rights, of their liberties, and of their happiness. Their political opinions do not admit of their commemorating the death of Charles I and they have erected a new statue to the memory of Oliver Cromwell, but the marble of which it is composed, is so veined with black and white, that it is scarcely possible to say which of the two colours predominates This statue is to be placed in the parliament house, as being the image of the great man who was the real author of their immutable and happy constitution

"The Scotch and Irish have presented a petition to parliament, praying that the names of Scotland and Ireland might be abolished, and that they might all be united and called by one name, as they are all animated by the same spirit of patriotism."

* * * *

"Vienna.

"It is well known that Austria has always had the honour of giving the finest princesses to Europe. There are now seven, who are all of the most exquisite beauty, and are to be disposed of in marriage to those princes who can produce the greatest proofs of the attachment of their subjects."

* * * *

"*The Hague*, ...

"This laborious people, who have metamorphosed the most ungrateful and marshy soil into a fruitful garden, who have reunited ll the treasures of the earth upon the most barren spot, still continue to exercise the most laudable industry, and manif t it to all the world the power of courage, patience, and activity. They no longer are famed for their insatiable thirst of gold. This republic is

become

become powerful, by having in time discovered the snares which were artfully prepared for her ruin, she formerly had found it less difficult to set boundaries to the angry ocean, than to resist the power of gold, but now she defends herself as courageously against avarice and luxury, as she does against the assaults of the ocean."

* * * *

" *Paris, the* . . . . .

" Twelve ships of six hundred tons burden are arrived at this metropolis, and have diffused riches and plenty throughout the city. The new bed which was made some time ago for the Seine, from Rouen to Paris, requires some repairs, the expense of which, amounting to a million and a half, will be paid out of the national treasury.

" The banks of the Seine are no longer the scenes of the most extravagant, the most capricious, and childish luxury, but industry prevails every where, creates new comforts, and an easy affluence, free from ostentation or arrogant pride.

" The Parisians are studious, well informed, and have distinct notions of their political and civil rights. They have reformed all their former opinions, but they never can forget their natural inclination for writing *songs, vaudevilles,* and *bons mots,* though they have not that degree of flimsy puerility they formerly had, for the character of the nation is totally changed.

Thus I turned over from one article to the other, and still I wished to find something curious. I sought for something relative to Versailles, but in vain. The master of the house perceived my inquietude, and asked me what

I was

I was seeking for? "Indeed," said I, "I am looking for the most interesting article, in short, for some news from the court, from Versailles, which formerly used to be the most curious article of the French gazette." He smiled, and said, "I know not what is become of the French gazette, but our's I know is dictated by truth, and no omissions are ever found. The monarch resides in the capital, under the eye of the multitude, and his ear is ever attentive to their wishes. He never conceals himself from us, but remains in the midst of us like a rather in the bosom of his family, and it is by the universal voice of his children, that he is always informed of those things which he ought to know; for the monarch belongs to the people, but the people do not belong to him."

CHAP. L.

Let not Ambition mock their useful toil,
Their homely joys, and destiny obscure,
Nor Grandeur hear with a disdainful smile,
The short and simple annals of the poor.

I WAS very curious to know what change, among all these changes, Versailles might have experienced, where I had seen on one side, the splendour of kings display the highest degree of opulence, and on the other, the impertinence and idleness of placemen and *financiers* emulating the magnificence of princes.

I inquired the high road to Versailles, and set out. I passed through a village, where I saw a crowd of peasants
who,

who, with mournful looks, were entering a temple. Being rather surprised at this circumstance, I ordered the coachman to stop, and followed the people. In the aisle, I saw extended on a bier, the corpse of a deceased old man in a peasant's dress. The pastor of the place ascended a kind of pulpit, and spoke thus to the assembly

"Citizens,

"The man you there behold was, during a life of
"ninety years, the constant benefactor of his fellow-
"creatures. He was the son of a peasant, and from his
"infancy, his hands have helped to raise the ploughshare,
"when he arrived to years of maturity, and that his
"strength was confirmed, he no longer suffered his father
"to labour in the field, but he constantly maintained him
"as long as he lived, and each revolving year has witnessed
"his successes. He has cultivated more than two thou-
"sand acres of land, and planted the vine and all the
"other fruit-trees in the village. He was not indefa-
"tigable through avarice, but through his love of labour,
"for which he knew we are all destined.

"He has had twenty-five children, who are all worthy
"members of society, because they were all formed to
"virtue and labour. All his grand children were brought
"up with him, and you know what unalterable cheerful-
"ness always reigned among them, and with what tender
"affection they all seemed to dwell together. On days
"of festival or rejoicing, he was always one of the first
"to found the rural instruments, and his voice and looks
"were the signal for mirth and joy. His cheerfulness
"was the emanation of a pure and virtuous soul, his wit,
"though keen and ready, never gave offence. He was
"ever kind, and willing to render service, either private

"or

"or public; he loved his country, and would have sacri-
"ficed his life to its happiness and prosperity.

"You have seen him, all of you, and heard him,
"distribute the lessons of his experience to all the young
"farmers. His memory was treasured with the observa-
"tions of eighty years, on the variety of seasons, and the
"manner of deriving some benefit from each He knew
"by heart all that which men usually forget, the plentiful
"and defective harvests, and their causes—all the deaths
"that happened in the village, and the legacies left to
"the poor. He seemed endowed with a prophetic spirit,
"for he usually knew how every circumstance would turn
"out. On the eve of his death, he spoke thus to those
"about him. 'Children, I am now going to the Supreme
"Author of all good, whom I have always adored, and
"in whom I put my whole trust. Let your pear-trees
"be pruned to-morrow, and at the setting sun let my
"remains be conveyed to the bottom of my field'

"You will therefore carry him thither, children, who
"are bound to imitate him, but ere you cover his vene-
"rable hoary head, which inspired respect and affection in
"every beholder, behold in his venerable hands the
"respectable remains of his hard labour"

After this, the orator took one of his hands, which
seemed, by the daily exercise of the spade and ploughshare, to have acquired a callosity impenetrable to brambles
or thorns, or even to the sharp flint. He killed it with
reverence, and every one followed his example.

His children carried him upon three gavels of corn, and
buried him according to his desire, and on his tomb they
placed his hedging bill, his spade, and his ploughshare

I could not forbear exclaiming, "Ah! if those men,
so celebrated by Bossuet, Flechier, and Mascaron, had
had

had but the hundredth part of the virtues of this tiller of the ground, their pompous and futile eloquence might then be forgiven them."

CHAP. LI.

Lo! rising from yon dreary tomb,
What spectres stalk across the gloom!
With haggard eyes and visage pale,
And voice that moans with feeble wail!
O'er yon long resounding plain
Slowly moves the solemn train,
Wailing wild with shrieks of woe
O'er the bones that rest below!
While the dull night's startled ear
Shrinks aghast with thrilling fear!
Or stand with thin robes wasting soon,
And eyes that blast the sick'ning moon!
Yet these, ere time had roll'd their years away,
Ere death's fell arm had mark'd its aim,
Rul'd yon proud tow'rs with ample sway,
Beheld the trembling swains obey,
And wrought the glorious deed that swell'd the trump of fame.

AT length I arrived, and sought, as far as eye could reach, for that famous palace, whence had issued the fate of many nations. But, oh! unspeakable surprise! I could trace no remains but its amazing ruins, all which bespoke its ancient magnificence. I was ruminating as I walked over these stupendous ruins, when I espied a venerable and very old man, sitting in a pensive mood on the base of one of the broken columns: I went up to him, and requested he would tell me what had happened

X   to

to that noble palace, the pride and glory of the seventeenth century? " Alas!" he replied, " you see its present state! it has given way. A man, the proudest of mortals, vainly thought he could surpass nature herself, and heaped one edifice over another, till it was top-heavy. Eager to gratify his capricious desires, to enjoy every extravagant pleasure the most voluptuous could create, he here expended all the wealth of his empire, and caused the ruin of thousands in erecting buildings, in digging canals, and forming cascades, of which there are no traces left. Behold what remains of that immense colossus, raised by a million of hands with the most painful labour. This palace was defective in its foundation—true image of the greatness of its builder! The kings, his successors, have been obliged to fly left they should be buried beneath its ruins ah! what a lesson is contained in them, and how clearly they seem to say, that those who make an improper use of their transitory power, do but expose their real weakness to the ensuing generation . . . ." At these words he shed a torrent of tears, and raised his repentant looks towards heaven — " Why do you weep?" said I · " every individual appears to enjoy the greatest felicity, and these ruins are no evidence of public misery, on the contrary .. . . ." He now interrupted me, and with dignity raised his voice, and said " Know then, venerable old man! that I am that LOUIS XIV. who built this melancholy palace— Divine Justice has rekindled the vital spark of my life, that I may sorrowfully contemplate my deplorable vanity and folly . . . . How frail are the monuments of pride! . . . . — I weep, and shall never cease to weep . . . . . Ah! had I but known . . . . . Alas! how vain . . . . ." I was going to interrogate him on many things I particularly wished to know, when suddenly

denly one of the adders, with which thefe ruins abounded, darted upon me, from beneath a broken pedeftal, and ftung me in the neck, at which I awoke

END OF THE DREAM

CHAP. LII.

POST SCRIPTUM.

I AWAKE from the moft delightful dream, and grieve to find myfelf awake *Quando hæc erunt, diu visa nostra fecundent.*

Alas! and is then public felicity no more than an empty dream? muft our wifhes and exertions ever remain ineffectual? Let us banifh this fatal idea, for it ftrikes death to every heart of fenfibility.

And yet a generous hope, founded upon the univerfal knowledge which prevails, feems to whifper comfort As in thofe uninhabited iflands, where thick forefts are involved in deep eternal gloom, inacceffible to the rays of the fun, it becomes neceffary to fet fire to the furrounding wood, in order to purify the atmofphere from infectious exhalations, fo in like manner, ere we eftablifh good laws, it is neceffary to abolifh the bad ones.

The filly pride of the Spaniard has concluded, through the moft ridiculous prejudice, that it is noble and great to be unemployed, in confequence of which, idlenefs prevails in every ftate While fleeping on a forry mattrefs, his guittar befide him, having nothing but a morfel of bread to fave him from ftarving, poor, naked, and proud, he dreams of his dignified indigence, but never ftrives to improve

improve his condition by induſtry. No doubt, the climate does not admit long and continued labours, but it would be poſſible to regenerate this kingdom, and obliterate the ſtain by which it is covered, by means of a few wholeſome laws diſperſed abroad by an eloquent pen. Nothing leſs can awaken this nation from its lethargy. But ſo long as this people are enſlaved by the vileſt ſuperſtition, their political evils muſt increaſe.

Thus then the evils of the ſtate are known, and the remedy is pointed out, but weakneſs diſappoints the effect Truth, they ſay, ought not to be made public, but truth ought always to be made known for the happineſs and proſperity of the ſtate, and for the peace of the whole world. The philoſopher may deceive himſelf, but he never deceives. He does not ſeduce men by a vain authority, but by the influence of reaſon. When men have acquired ſtrength of mind by the power of philoſophy, they will no longer be the ſport of ambition, and of falſe principles, but they will examine every depoſitary of the public peace with the torch of reaſon, and ſtrictly adhere to the dictates of truth.

F I N I S.